MENTAL STATES AND CONCEPTUAL WORLDS

MENTAL STATES AND CONCEPTUAL WORLDS

JASON BROWN

Foreword by Bruce D. MacQueen

RESOURCE *Publications* • Eugene, Oregon

MENTAL STATES AND CONCEPTUAL WORLDS

Resource Publications
An Imprint of Wipf and Stock Publishers
199 W. 8th Ave., Suite 3
Eugene, OR 97401

www.wipfandstock.com

PAPERBACK ISBN: 978–1-5326–7804–2
HARDCOVER ISBN: 978–1-5326–7805–9
EBOOK ISBN: 978–1-5326–7806–6

Manufactured in the U.S.A.   FEBRUARY 11, 2019

Contents

Foreword

MENTAL STATES AND CONCEPTUAL Worlds is, by my count, the fifteenth book Jason Brown has written on microgenetic theory. It is, then, the culmination of a series that began with a clinical study (*Aphasia, Apraxia and Agnosia*, Brown 1972), and culminates (for now, at least) in the present volume, a far-ranging examination of an impressive set of problems that can usefully be addressed from the perspective of microgenetic theory. It has been a rare privilege for me to assist the author – a personal friend of mine for over 20 years now – in preparing the manuscript for publication. The only thing to which I can compare this task would be to imagine Michelangelo asking a younger painter to touch up the Sistine Chapel.

The term "microgenetic theory" can be very misleading to readers who may be encountering the work of Jason Brown for the first time. Before I proceed, then, it might be useful to begin by stating clearly what microgenetic theory is not: it is not a theory of genetics, nor is it primarily concerned with microscopic phenomena. "Microgenesis" is the generally accepted English translation of a German word that constitutes one of the basic terms in Gestalt psychology: *Aktualgenese*, which means "the genesis of the present moment." The German adjective *aktual*, though it resembles the English adjective "actual" and is derived from the same Latin root, has a rather different meaning: what is *aktual* is what is present here and now. For example, a newspaper coupon for a certain product is said to be *aktual* if the offer has not yet expired or been withdrawn.

Perhaps the best way to approach the concept of "microgenesis" is to regard it as the third in a series of terms:

1. phylogenesis (sometimes "phylogeny"), the process of development of a species over evolutionary processes that last for millions of years;

2. ontogenesis (ontogeny), the process of development of an individual over the lifespan;

3. microgenesis (microgeny), the process of development of a mental state over milliseconds in the central nervous system.

It has long been an axiom of evolutionary theory that ontogenesis replicates phylogenesis: that is, the path of development of a human being from conception to birth follows the pathway laid down by the evolution of *homo sapiens*. Microgenesis, then, is the emergence of the present moment in the mind, as phylogenesis is the emergence of a species over millions of years of evolution, and ontogenesis is the emergence of an individual over years of development. All three processes, according to microgenetic theory, follow the same path through the same stages of transformation, consistent with the same (or at least strongly analogous) laws. What Jason Brown has done is to argue very consistently that every mental state, which is to say, every present moment experienced by the individual mind/brain, retraces in milliseconds the same path, the one laid down by evolution and then retraced by individual development. The process begins with something archaic and largely inchoate, in deeper and older brain structures; this "something" is gradually refined and articulated as it is transformed into conscious mental activity, moving from what is archaic, simple, deep, and central, upward and outward to what is new, complex, and articulated at the outer surface of the brain. It takes only a few dozen milliseconds for this to occur, but the path is an ancient one.

It should be emphasized at this point that the phrase "upward and outward" used in the previous sentence is not really metaphorical: it describes rather literally a wave of activation passing from brainstem (where the spinal cord reaches up into the head), up through thalamic and limbic structures, up and out to the cortex, the gray matter at the outer surface of the brain. The brainstem is the starting point, and is macroscopically very similar to the brains of fish and reptiles, for whom this is the whole brain. The "up and out" movement takes us to the limbic system (the "emotional brain") and basal ganglia, and the thalamus, which are structures shared by all mammals, and from the thalamus to the cortex, the outer layer of the brain, where the most significant differences occur between the human brain and that of our nearest relatives, the larger apes.

As the product of phyogenesis is a species, and the product of ontogenesis is an individual, so the product of microgenesis is a mental state, which both defines and is the product of the present moment. This can be a percept, a concept, even an action, insofar as human action requires a mind/brain that is able to conceive an intention to act and activate the neural pathways involved in setting the body into motion. All of these mental states, which in conventional neuropsychology are treated as independent processes linked only by feedback channels, are manifestations of processes that begin at the same place and follow the same stages of transformation, but diverge into different modes of actuation as they develop. Consciousness is not, then, a finished product that emerges from an assembly line, nor a river that flows from point A to point B, but a fountain: the stream of water begins as a single column of water propelled upwards, and then differentiates into separate streams as it rises, until the individual drops reach their apogee and fall back into the substrate, where they can be subsumed into the material for a subsequent realization. The appearance of continuity results from the rapid succession of traversals, so that before one state has reached its culmination, the following state has already begun, following so closely behind it that we feel no transition at all. Paradoxically, then, an essentially processual understanding of the mental state is predicated upon an epochal understanding of time, perception, action, and thought.

This theory has much in common, then, with evolutionary theory on the one hand, and process thought on the other, but it is based on a theory of the symptom, which emerged in the author's clinical practice with brain-damaged patients. This explains why the roots of Jason Brown's work remain in brain science; even his most recent philosophical work is difficult to understand, in fact, without some notion of the symptom, and specifically, of clinical symptoms: that is, symptoms that are described qualitatively, by observation, rather than being defined quantitatively, by comparison of a patient's parameters to statistically defined norms. No explication of microgenetic theory would be complete without at least a brief consideration of Jason Brown's understanding of symptoms (for a more complete exposition, see Brown & Pachalska, 2003).

It is a common assumption that a symptom of brain damage or dysfunction must be a behavior or experience that is abnormal, which implies that it is something new, a pathological state caused by the damage or dysfunction. Jason Brown insists that damage to particular parts of the brain is not the cause of new behavior, because damage by its nature does not contribute anything new to the process; rather, the damage disconnects or retards some segment of the process, revealing the substructure of both perception and action, which is usually concealed (but not suppressed) by the superstructure of cognitive processing. The struggles of an aphasic patient to recall and utter the right word to express a thought or a feeling result from the exteriorization and slowing of the process that occurs in normal speech, a process that is normally invisible (that is, below the threshold of conscious choice) because it is fully subsumed in the utterance, when the process reaches its conclusion in the form of an articulated utterance. Instead of undergoing the final levels of cognitive processing, the utterance emerges in an unfinished or inchoate state. The symptom is not, then, simply an error, a zero where a one was expected, but something rather like the foundation of a house with the walls unfinished, or walls without a roof.

This whole movement from brainstem through limbic structures to cortex also informs the microgenetic theory of perception, which is the starting point for the first chapter of *Mental States and Conceptual Worlds*. Conventional views of how perception works in the brain are based on the accretion of details to identify the object as a whole. Input from the eyes, so the standard theory goes, makes its way through the optical chiasmus to the occipital cortex, where specific processors analyze the visual parameters of the object, and the resulting "sketch" is then compared to images stored in long-term memory to enable the identification of the object. This seems logical enough, rather like a police artist working with the victim of a crime, sketching the nose, eyes, hair, etc., and then altering them as needed until the victim recognizes the perpetrator. It is also the way a computer "perceives" objects in the world outside of itself: that is, the computer's sensors gather up bits of data and assemble those bits into objects identified according to a programmed algorithm.

The microgenetic theory of perception challenges this familiar model of perception at its very foundation. The process of perception actually begins with wholes, perhaps Gestalts, that are processed from category to member, whole to part, shape to detail; the processors of specific visual details located in the occipital cortex are in fact the end-point, not the starting point, for the process of object formation. It is now known that 75% or more of the neural input coming in from the retina is directed to the thalamus, and from there to subcortical structures (including the limbic system), while the rest is directed to the occipital cortex. The visual object is recognized by the brainstem and midbrain as an object belonging to a rather small set of primitive categories (food, threat, etc.); at the limbic level, the object is imbued with affect; in the temporal and parietal cortex, memory is engaged; and finally, the cortex analyzes the object to identify it more specifically. Philosophers should recognize in all this the Aristotelian model of definition *per genus et differentiam*: the brainstem provides the genus, then the successive layers of processing add differences.

The details and implications of the microgenetic approach to perception is the starting point for *Mental States and Conceptual Worlds,* just as Copernicus's critique of the Ptolemaic geocentric universe was the starting point for *De Revolutionibus*. In subsequent chapters, then, we follow this theory from perception and memory into a series of topics, with each discussion developing from the previous one in the manner of evolution: that is, the ideas emerge out of a central unity, but branch out in different directions, seemingly independent of each other but all rooted in the same place. The last chapter, on will and agency, is only one of many possible endpoints, some of which can only be glimpsed now. All this to say, then, that the implications of this understanding of how the brain/mind works are considerable, not to say profound. Previous philosophical theories of mind, for perhaps obvious reasons, focused most of their attention on thought; previous psychological theories, on feeling; previous neurological theories, on reflex. What Jason Brown has done is to develop a "theory of everything" for how human beings think and feel – and act. Perception and action are not separate processes, in which perception provides images upon which the individual may choose to act, but rather two branches of the same tree. This, in my view, has the potential to become nothing less than a Copernican revolution.

In 1543, when Copernicus' famous work on the heliocentric model of the universe was published, nothing even remotely similar to the New York Times Bestseller List existed. Even if there had been such a list, however, it is difficult to believe that *On the Revolutions of the Heavenly Bodies* would have been on it (Koestler 1959; cf. Gingerich 2004). The same can be said of any number of truly revolutionary works across the sciences: the number of people who have actually read the books that are generally recognized as having initiated a scientific revolution (Kuhn 1962) in any of the natural sciences is surely very small. The reasons for this are perhaps obvious: the subject matter is usually abstruse, comprehensible only to a fairly narrow circle of specialists, and the authors of such works typically take no particular pains to make that subject matter accessible to a larger public. Any expectation that a scientific book of genuinely revolutionary stature would find millions of readers would be unreasonable. On the other hand, if such a book reaches too few readers, it can hardly be expected to resonate beyond a handful of true believers, in which case nothing deserving to be called a revolution is likely to occur.

What then, is the "critical mass" of readers? In the case of Copernicus, for example, Koestler argued in 1959 that only a very few astronomers actually read the book, which would suggest that the term "Copernican revolution" is unjustified; he went so far as to call *De Revolutionibus* "the book nobody read." In 2004, Gingerich argued that Koestler had grossly underestimated the number of copies of Copernicus' book in circulation over the century that followed its publication. The point at issue, then, is precisely that of "critical mass": both authors, Koestler and Gingerich, assume that the answer to the question of readership – how many people, of how much importance and influence, actually read the book? – is important enough to merit a book-length study.

There is a painful dilemma here for anyone who, like Jason Brown, has an important idea that they have decided to promulgate. Such authors seem to face a choice between two unpalatable options: either (1) to give up the idea of making their ideas available to a larger public, and address themselves instead to a mere handful of highly specialized readers (who, in many cases, may be the most resistant to the arguments, since they typically have the most to lose from a significant paradigm shift); or (2) to make their ideas more accessible to a wider public and avoid technical arguments, even at the expense of the kind of precision that is necessary to initiate a real paradigm shift, rather than a momentary sensation. If a book is dismissed by the authorities in the field as "popular science," it has little chance of actually changing anything within its own field.

In either case, the great idea dies without issue.

How is it even possible, then, for a single book, or the work of a single author, to change in a fundamental way the way we look at the world? Copernicus despaired of ever gaining an audience; in 1859, the year of publication of Darwin's *Origin of Species*, the president of the Linnean Society remarked at the annual meeting that no revolutionary discoveries had been made that year. It is never entirely clear why a particular work, or body of work, begins to resonate in that particular way, or what critical mass of readers is necessary for something like a paradigm shift to occur.

Microgenetic theory has, in my view, the potential to change our way of thinking about thinking itself. This affects both the philosophy of mind and neuropsychology, in very fundamental ways – provided, of course, that the theory reaches that "critical mass" of engaged readers. These two fields of study, however, despite their obvious overlapping interests, have so far shown depressingly little inclination to learn from each other, quite possibly exactly because of those overlapping interests. It would be difficult, in fact, to find a clearer example of C. P. Snow's "two cultures" in conflict with each other, because of profound differences, in terms not only of methodology, but also (and especially) of epistemology and teleology.

Contemporary neuropsychology tends to see the brain in two dimensions. The ongoing efforts to map the neural circuitry of the brain that began with the work of Paul Broca (1865) and Karl Wernicke (1874) are motivated by an underlying assumption that brain functions are performed by discrete processors located at particular places in the brain. There are "cortical" functions, performed by clusters of neurons in the cortex, the outer layer of gray matter, and "subcortical" functions, performed in grey matter structures located deeper in the brain, separated from the cortex by white matter. Today, this model of structure and function is all too familiar from computer technology: packets of data are delivered along electrical circuits to a series of processors, sometimes in parallel, sometimes in series, each of which performs a very particular transformation of the data it receives before sending the product to the next processor. All of these products are finally assembled into output; in the case of the brain, viewed as a kind of organic computer, the "output" of all these converging functions is a perception, a cognition, or an action.

A closer look at how the brain is actually constructed and how it performs, and especially what happens when it is injured or affected by some pathology, should give any judicious observer many reasons to question whether this whole model of brain function is really accurate. Still, the "IT" model has taken on the status of a fundamental theory (in Popper's sense), and as such limits the scope of most ordinary neuropsychological research to discrete brain functions. Memory and perception are the current favorites, as the most cursory review of conference programs and journal contents will reveal. Language, where the history of neuropsychology actually began with the pioneering work of Broca and Wernicke, has all but vanished from neuropsychology. The only two concepts of consciousness that seem to apply in neuropsychological research are the neurological model (anyone who is not unconscious is conscious) and the psychological model (consciousness is the sum of all cognitive processes). Philosophers may be aware that neither of these models really explains what consciousness is, or what the mind is, of the self, but few philosophers can contend with the scientific certainty of modern neuroscience, with all the apparatus and prestige of empirical science behind it.

Jason Brown's microgenetic theory is a theory of mind and consciousness that emerged from his clinical work with brain-injured patients, but it is not a reductionist theory, not committed to a purely materialistic account of mental processing, not in the slightest molecular (which for many neuropsychologists may render it outmoded and uninteresting). On the other hand, it is not a dualist theory that posits the "mind" as a disembodied entity ontologically separate from its putative physical home, the brain. That will explain, among other things, how often the phrase "brain/mind" occurs in all of Brown's more recent work. In fact, microgenetic theory, by focusing on process rather than structure and function, provides a way for neuroscientists and the philosophers to actually come together and learn from each other, rather than alternating between ignorance or uncritical emulation and antagonism. This is where the importance of Jason Brown's work on microgenetic theory lies, and the present volume is in many ways the capstone of that project.

Unlike other contemporary theories of brain/mind, microgenetic theory takes up and accounts for creativity and mental processing on the highest level, as well as esthetic experience, rather than focusing on discrete mental processes that can be measured by empirical tests. At the same time, it begins at the base, the core of the central nervous system, and follows the development of the mental state up through the brain to the cortex, and out into the world. The highest expressions of human genius are not disembodied ideas, pure abstractions which, if they exist at all or matter at all, are entirely metaphysical entities, nor are the drives and instincts that set us in motion in our daily lives merely animal behaviors to be left behind as we become steadily more human. There is a continuity in microgenesis: what is sublime is the end product of a process that begins in the most elemental needs and drives, and cannot be fully understood without reference to its origin. Neither, however, can the sublime be explained by reducing it to its starting point. It is pointless to think of the mind without any consideration of the neural processes that pass through the brain out into the world, but it is equally pointless to confine our interest to neurochemistry with no regard for the whole range of things that the brain/mind actually does.

Much of our contemporary science seems to be moving in two opposite directions. On the one hand, this is the era of "big data," as computers bring ever increasing computational power to bear on a mountain of data pertaining to a steadily expanding array of problems. On the other, the frontiers of medicine and psychology seem to be found on the molecular level: not the mind, not the brain, not even the neuron, but the molecules, explain why things happen. The temptation in all this is to assume that vexing, perennial human problems could be solved if only we could reduce phenomena to the lowest, smallest level of organization, at which point they could be fully understood, and thus managed; or, conversely, if we can bury the infuriating vagaries of individual difference in numbers large enough that the outliers no longer seem to matter.

What both these directions, "macro" and "micro," big data and molecular biology, seem to have in common is a movement away (in two different directions) from the individual self and its effort to find a place for itself in the world. We seem to have given up the idea that we can find whatever it is we are perpetually seeking within ourselves, and now we are looking for the answers somewhere else, far out in the cosmos or deep within the tiny particles of matter that compose our bodies. The problems that have always consumed us, as individuals and as societies, can thus be solved by computer-driven statistics, or by electron microscopes, which is to say, by turning away from the level of the self. Anyone who finds this idea appealing is welcome to pursue it; for my part, though, I find myself wanting to paraphrase Shakespeare: "The fault, dear Brutus, is not in our stars, but in ourselves, that we are underlings."

In this respect, microgenetic theory constitutes a return to what must surely be the starting point of all reflective thought, which is to say: how can I understand what I think and what I feel, in relation to the world outside of myself? However popular it has become to attack Descartes, the question he attempted to answer with the Cogito remains unanswered in our times, and what is more, largely unaddressed.

Since my own first encounter with Jason Brown's work, over twenty years ago, even before I fully understood how microgenetic theory works, I have always felt quite sure that something profoundly important is at stake here. I can only hope, then, that a "critical mass" of you who read this book will agree.

BRUCE D. MACQUEEN

REFERENCES

Broca, P. (1861). Remarques sur le siège de la faculté du langage articulé, suivies d'une observation d'aphémie (perte de la parole). *Bulletin de la Société Anatomique de Paris*, 6, 330–357.

Brown, J. & Pachalska, M. (2003). The nature of the symptom and its relevance for neuropsychology. *Acta Neuropsychologica*, 1(1), 1–11. Available on-line at: https://actaneuropsychologica.com/resources/html/article/details?id=18709

Gingerich, O. (2004). *The Book Nobody Read: Chasing the Revolutions of Nicolaus Copernicus*. New York: Walker.

Koestler, A. (1959). *The Sleepwalkers: A Vision of Man's Changing Vision of the Universe*. London: Hutchison.

Kuhn, T. S. (1962). *The Structure of Scientific Revolutions*. Chicago: University of Chicago Press

Wernicke, K. (1874). *Der aphasische Symptomencomplex. Eine psychologische Studie auf anatomischer Basis*. Breslau: Crohn & Weigert.

Preface

THIS BOOK IS A summation of the main features and implications of a theory of mind and brain that began with studies of language disorders in patients with focal brain damage and the analysis of symptoms in general neuropsychology, and evolved over time into a model of the mind/brain state and its relevance to most of the central problems in speculative psychology and philosophy of mind. I began with a new interpretation of the aphasia syndromes in relation to brain process, applied to the dynamic structure of perception and action, in which phases in word – and act-production mapped to evolutionary patterns in forebrain growth. The ideas generated by these studies later expanded to an account of perceptual disorders and a theory of normal perception that involved a radical revision of classical theory. In effect, by turning the standard account of object formation upside-down, I was able to align the process of object development with the formation of acts, including speech acts, such that all cognitive systems could be framed in terms of a unitary model of brain and mental process, which (borrowing a rather obscure term from Gestalt psychology) I called "microgenetic theory."

Frankly, it has been an uphill battle to gain a hearing for this kind of organic, process-based theory, given the computational and modular trends in experimental cognition and empirical philosophy. The revised account of perception met with resistance or neglect; not only was my theory incompatible with the hegemonic influence of physiological research (which tended to find what it was looking for), but it challenged what seemed to be the common sense view as to how we perceive the world and the nature of the real world around us, and posed challenges to comfortable orthodox answers to the ultimate questions regarding perceptual reality and the illusory quality of mental phenomena. The internal coherence of the microgenetic account of act and object development and its relation to word production and perception, as well as to memory, feeling and other aspects of cognition, was not convincing to brain scientists, given the dominance of localization studies in neurology, then and now, and the modular—even mosaicist—approach that dominates cognitive psychology.

To paraphrase Bergson, the time given to disputation is lost time. So I continued to follow the theory wherever it led, regardless of the indifference of colleagues, and only now and then pointing to a divergence from conventional models. The scope of the theory was such that it constituted a *Bauplan* or general model for the organization of mentality and the nervous system and led, organically, to a theory—the only theory—of the mind/brain state, then to the nature of process, change, subjective time and a theory of the present. Since the account was based on symptoms interpreted in relation to evolutionary concepts, it was essential to work out a theory of symptom formation, which gave rise to a more comprehensive view of the link between microgenesis and phylo-ontogeny. My more recent work has focused on the importance of the whole/part or category/member transition as critical to the understanding of brain and mental process.

The theory underwent a slow growth over the years, as I explored its application to these different topics, and it has now reached a point of maturity and generality where a concerted effort to confirm or refute its foundational principles can be undertaken. In this effort, the attentive reader will no doubt see my debt to thinkers past, to Arnold Pick, Paul Yakovlev and Paul Schilder in neuropsychology, Friedrich Sanides in anatomy, writers on parcellation and sculpting in morphogenesis, and Henri Bergson, William James and Whitehead in philosophy, but for the most part I have assimilated a notion here, a symptom there, not a bricolage of observations but the outgrowth of a single idea with ramifications in many domains of thought.

A word on the structure of this book seems necessary. It opens with a recent update of a theory of perception first advanced over 30 years ago, a theory that has finally found some support in current neuroscience research. This paper, a heavily-referenced review of the theory of perception and its relation to memory and the mental state, provides a foundation for the more speculative essays that follow. Since the approach to perception, though controversial, is the linchpin of the theory, I would encourage any serious reader to work through the account of object formation, and perhaps resort to some of my earlier work on this topic, as a basis for the chapters that follow, which are discursive essays on a variety of topics informed by the theory. The aim in this book is to expand the central arguments of microgenetic theory in order to widen its scope and elaborate new approaches to many long-standing problems. If more questions than answers are raised, my hope that is that at least some readers will take up the task of continuing work on the theory, and will seek additional support in neuroscientific research.

Parts of a few chapters have previously been published, though all of them have been edited for publication here.

- Chapter 1 was published in *Journal of Consciousness Studies*, 24:51–70, 2017
- Chapter 5 is in Texeira, M. (Ed) *Proceedings of the annual Whitehead conference*, Azores, 2019
- Chapter 9 is in: *Orpheus' Glance: Selected Papers on Process Philosophy*, Fontareches meetings 2002–2017. Pp.15–32, Edited by P. Stenner and M. Weber. Les Editions Chromatika, Belgium, 2018
- Chapter 12 is in *Mind and Matter*, 195–212, 2018

1

The microgenetic theory of perception, memory and the mental state

SUMMARY

FOR OVER A CENTURY, the theory of perception that has dominated thinking and research in neuropsychology, with implications for the understanding of all other cognitive domains, assumes a process of progressive assembly in the occipital cortex of the brain, leading to the construction of a visual object and secondary spatial updating and recognition. In recent years, however, difficulties with this theory have emerged in neurophysiological research, though a compelling alternative has not been forcefully argued. The purpose of this essay is to review the main features of the microgenetic account of perception, which inverts standard theory 180 degrees, and aligns the perceptual process with patterns of evolutionary growth. This theory was developed on the grounds of clinical study, and perhaps for this reason has not received sufficient attention in mainstream cognitivism and neuroscience, though it provides an account not only of perception, but of stages in memory, imagery, the present moment and the mind/brain state.

INTRODUCTION

Any philosophy of mind, and indeed any coherent conception of reality, must be based on a theory of perception. This is, of course, a philosophical problem with a very long and convoluted history, with the number of

theories more or less equal to the number of theorizers. For all their sometimes tortuous complexities, however, all these theories must begin at one
of two possible places: either from the object (the thing perceived) or from
the subject (the mind of the perceiver).

Many theories, perhaps most modern theories, begin with the assumption (often tacit) that the object of perception is a real, material thing in a
real, material world (hence the term *material realism*), and that the whole
task of the perceptual apparatus (sense organs, brain, mind) is to produce *in
here*, in the mind, an accurate image of a real object that exists *out there*, in
the world. With this assumption as a starting point, we would naturally assume that the world is more or less what we perceive it to be, while such perceptual perturbations as illusions or afterimages can be explained away, as
isolated artifacts, byproducts or dysfunctions of mechanisms that otherwise
allow us to perceive the world *as it really is*. The inescapable fact that human perception is limited to middle-sized objects, and to relatively narrow
portions of the sound and light spectra, does not challenge the underlying
confidence that a perceptual object is real, and is what it seems to be, unless
and until proven otherwise.

To be sure, scientific research typically searches for tools to extend the
range of perception (through microscopes and telescopes, for example, to
mention only the oldest and most obvious techniques) to detect the constituents of objects and the processes that sustain them. The results obtained
in this way would seem to suggest, upon reflection, that there is a deeper
reality ingredient in the perceptual world, or in the interstices of what we
perceive, as when Galileo discovered the craters of the moon, or van Leeu-
wenhoek found the microorganisms inhabiting a drop of water. Overall,
however, ordinary science assumes that the world is delivered to us by the
senses in all its realness and vibrancy, while the tools of scientific research
serve primarily to bring reality that is beyond our perceptual range to a
convenient distance and scale. It is a world that may indeed be differently
perceived by bats, fish, or insects, but even so, it is still the same world: it
exists quite independently of the mind or eye that perceives it.

One critical implication of this form of material realism, and the empirical or analytic philosophy to which it leads, is that real entities exist as
atomic, stochastic substances or logical solids that undergo causal change:
that is, the realness of the object is assumed to be an inherent feature of
the object in itself, and whatever changes occur to it are caused by factors
that are themselves real, regardless of whether or not anyone perceives
them. This kind of realism, preferred by empirical science, extends the objectivity of the world to include the mind of the observer, which is either
eliminated from consideration as something whose real existence cannot

be empirically demonstrated, or is reduced to the brain, conceived as yet another physical entity, composed of smaller units or modules that combine to form percepts, acts and thoughts. As Schopenhauer argued, this kind of material realism fails to make a place for the subject himself, that is, for the mind in which the perceptual image arises. Thanks to its assumed heuristic value and obvious analogies to computational networks (in which the mind of the user is seldom if ever included in the model of the process), this kind of material realism has had a significant impact on research in cognition, and has become the primary model of reality for both analytic philosophy and empirical science.

The alternative approach takes its starting point, not from the object, but from the subject: that is, from the mind of the perceiver. This approach has a pedigree that traces from Heraclitus, Pythagoras and Plato, through Berkeley to Kant and the German idealists, as well as Asian philosophy. Its central argument is that the world of perception, though for the most part indistinguishable from the objective reality to which it refers, is *in itself* nothing other than an image that is generated within the mind. Accordingly, there is something illusory, or at best phenomenal, in all perception, and indeed all mental experience, while physical reality, the *in-itself* of reality, Kant's *die Dinge an sich*, consists in a material world that is real, but beyond the reach of our direct cognition and ultimately unknowable. The world we can actually know is a subjective entity whose genesis occurs within the mind of the observer, with no clear distinction to be made between mind-internal and mind-external, which is to say, between the perceiving subject and the perceived object. From this starting point it is possible to generate many varieties of *subjectivism*, in which the mind is continuous with the images of the world it generates. Subjectivism usually describes change in terms of the dialectic of potential and actual, which gives it a coherence in its account of the subject-object relationship that is strikingly absent in the piecemeal models of modular or atomic realism; still, perhaps because it may end in solipsism, subjectivism has not been widely accepted by contemporary thinkers. Indeed, the lack of a subjectivist model of perception has left the field of cognition in the nearly exclusive possession of some form of scientific materialism.

This book constitutes the fruit of my own efforts to rectify this situation, based on a processual theory of mind and perception (microgenesis) that began to take shape in my mind over 30 years ago, in the course of my medical practice, working with neurological patients with focal brain injuries. I have been refining the theory ever since, pursuing its ramifications and implications far beyond the clinical framework in which it first took shape. Much of this theory, which has since found further support in current neuroscience research, is detailed here in the first chapter, along with its implications for our understanding of memory and the mind/brain state. This chapter, though much of it may seem counterintuitive and difficult to follow at first to readers habituated to scientific materialism, provides a theoretical foundation for the speculative essays that follow, the purpose of which is to apply the central arguments of the microgenetic model to many long-standing problems in philosophy and its often rebellious daughter, psychology.

STANDARD THEORY AND MICROGENESIS

The two fundamental ways of thinking about the mind described above have rarely been clearly distinguished, though they influence both psychological investigation and philosophical thought. This divergence of perspective has manifested itself in different fields of inquiry: for example, Freud vs. Sullivan in psychiatry, innatism vs. objectivism, or the varied forms of first-person internalism vs. third-person externalism, or idealism vs. naïve realism in philosophy of mind. Generally, however, most interpretations are a mix or confound of the two perspectives. From one approach, it is intra-psychic events that generate mind and externality; from the other, interaction with the environment, social and physical, is not only an important supplement, but an essential constituent of mental process. The psyche, according to the latter perspective, acts in and responds to a world that is independent of mind, while the world fills the mind with experience. Thus mind is generated and enriched by experience, and is embedded in the world, the *Umwelt*, which becomes ingredient in mental process. This version of externalism has to reconcile dependence on experience with the inescapable fact that knowledge and perception are mental processes realized entirely within the brain. Alternatively, for intra-psychic theory, mind is shaped and altered by experience, but experience is not acquired by the inflow of sense data into the mind from the world; rather, sense data influence the content and character of endogenous process, which is the basic source of mind. Outer conditions serve to constrain and shape a process that originates and develops within the mind.

Essential to this distinction is the contrast between associative or constructivist models and holistic or specification models, analogous to building up an object by addition of elements vs. revealing it by the elimination of whatever is extraneous or irrelevant. Are wholes assembled from parts, or do particulars arise from the modification of wholes? Generally, science takes the former position, since the epistemology of science is based on a continuous analysis that represents the trend of scientific thought and perception: namely, the dissolution of the complex to its constituents, the study of smaller bits and their reconstruction into the (putative) originating whole. The more fundamental question is this: does multiplicity flow from unity, or the reverse? In the field of perception, this translates to the question of whether the diversity of the world is assembled in the mind and projected outside, or the mind elaborates diversity in the particulars that arise from unified wholes.

The problem of finding specificity in multiplicity, or selectivity in diversity, or the synthesis of mental phenomena from constituents, is not unique to the transition from external to internal or the reverse. In the largely intrinsic events that underlie emotion, especially the subtler affect-ideas such as pride, envy, humiliation and the like, there is presumably some interaction between idea and feeling. Here, two internal events, the concept of the emotion and its affective tonality, are combined into a single act of conceptual feeling, much as recognition and feeling are conceived as additions to object-construction. Yet how the idea attracts the feeling or the feeling lures and invests the idea is an insoluble problem from an interaction or associative standpoint, as I have elsewhere argued (Brown, 2016). The only plausible solution is to conceive of idea and feeling—substance and process, being and becoming—as aspects of a single construct that partitions to discrete emotions. Could something like this characterize the process of perception?

It may appeal to common sense to interpret this interaction as an exchange between mind and world, a sort of conversation of psyche and environment, with an interposition of the mind and the conscious self between two physical realms: the brain that elaborates psyche, and the external reality that confronts it. This approach, however, avoids any examination of the microstructure of interaction. If the physical and social environment is in opposition to mind, how are ongoing stimuli integrated with prior experience? That is, why is each moment of experience, which depends on constantly shifting sensory input to the brain, not distinct from all other moments? If the world with which mind interacts becomes part of mind (as it evidently does, in that we learn and remember what we experience), then how does the assimilation of world to mind occur? How is each novel moment of physical sensibility integrated with the experiential history of the individual? Interaction is often mentioned, but never elucidated, while its correlate in the term *"experience"*—a catch-all for the incorporation of incoming stimuli—has no definite boundaries; it does not resolve localization and multiplicity with synthesis and pattern, nor distinguish experience that is conscious or unconscious, incidental or focal, or with respect to the inner and outer environment, as well as the effects on experience of mind itself, as in thought. In interaction, mind appears to be a combination of inner and outer, an interior psyche and the "out there" of reality.

The central issue in this controversy has to do with the nature of (object) perception. Are objects, and object concepts, built up over regions in the neocortex of the brain from the sensory data that impact the primary perceptual zones, or are innate, intrinsic concepts—categorical primes—parsed to the point where sensory input applies the final featural detail that transforms a concept or proto-image to an object detached from the mind/brain? In some of my earlier writings (Brown, 1983; 1989) I have consistently argued in favor of the latter view: namely, that sense data provide the featural detail at the final phase to sculpt or partition endogenous categories. External objects are the final individuation of categories that, through cortical input, lead to externalization and apparent mind-independence.

This approach to perception is clearly unorthodox, even counter-intuitive, especially since the single-unit studies of Hubel and Wiesel (1968) seemed to support the constructivist idea, and suggested a progression in visual cortex from the detection of lines and edges to the assembly of three-dimensional shapes, implying a serial constructive process passing from the visual cortex to the temporal lobe for object identification. However, in the nearly 50 years since this seminal work, the putative transition from feature detection to object recognition, object concepts and categories has found little support in experimental studies, while the alternate and more inclusive account of microgenesis has not received serious attention.

From a psychological perspective, microgenesis exhibits greater explanatory power in the approach to many of the most puzzling aspects of standard theory and perceptual experience. For example, the transition from two-dimensional pre-objects arising through the major input of the optic nerve to the pre-tectal area forms a preliminary construct that passes to limbic-temporal regions, with a relative suspension of sensory input. In the limbic-temporal regions, the pre-object comes into relation with experiential memory, recognition, and the egocentric or volumetric space of dream and hallucination. From this point, the pre-object passes to a three-dimensional Euclidean space centered in parietal lobe formations. We see this phase in the periphery of the arm's reach, the space of infants and the congenitally blind, and the manipulo-spatial field of patients with parietal lesions. Finally, the object gestalt passes to the primary visual areas, where it is sculpted by adaptation and detaches to the fully external space of perception. The reverse sequence occurs in the perceptual disorganization associated with pathology.

Since it postulates an emerging endogenous construct that develops outward to object perception, microgenetic theory accounts for the findings of sub-surface perception prior to, or in the absence of, the activity of the primary visual cortex. These underpinnings of perception include blindsight, masking (Marcel, 1983; Breitmeyer & Ogmen, 2006) and priming (van den Bussche et al., 2009; also Doyen et al., 2014), the extraction of meaning prior to recognition (Smith, 2001), the relation of objects to images, hallucinations and other transitional forms and the relation of memory to perception. This account, based on a process of object formation *prior to* conscious perception, can explain a variety of pathological disorders, e.g. palinopsia, blindsight, patterns of loss and recovery with cortical blindness, visual neglect, ground-figure and contextual relations, and so on.

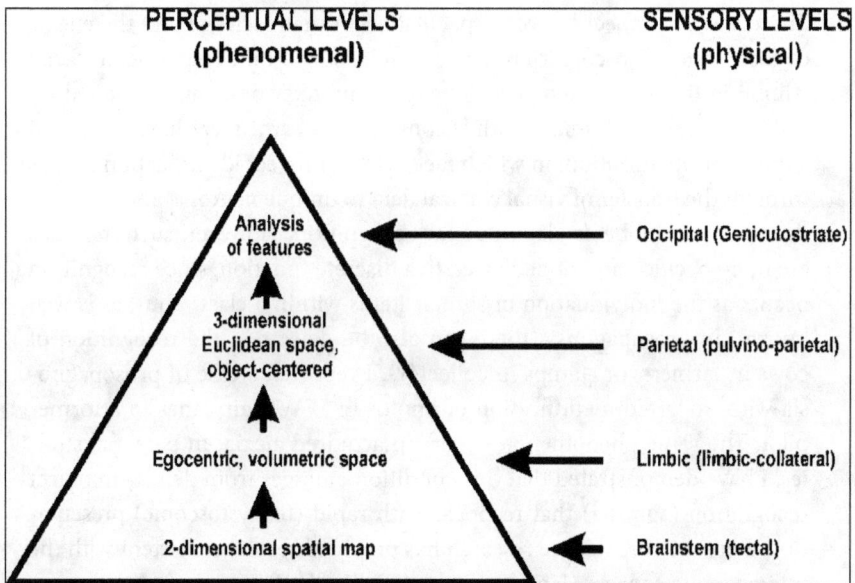

PERCEPTUAL LEVELS
(phenomenal)

SENSORY LEVELS
(physical)

Analysis of features ← Occipital (Geniculostriate)

3-dimensional Euclidean space, object-centered ← Parietal (pulvino-parietal)

Egocentric, volumetric space ← Limbic (limbic-collateral)

2-dimensional spatial map ← Brainstem (tectal)

Fig. 1.The progressive micro-temporal development of a perception is a purely internal process, constrained by successive layers of sensory input (see text).

Most importantly, this theory is consistent with patterns in the evolution of the forebrain (Sanides, 1969), since growth trends in phylogeny predict or lay down "force lines" in morphogenesis (Pribram, 1991), which in turn determine the pattern of cognitive process. Microgenesis has also contributed to the interpretation of problems in philosophical psychology that were previously resistant to explanation, such as subjective time, serial order, the self and mental state, anticipation, creativity and the temporal lag in perception. Unlike classical theory, microgenesis accounts for the persistence (recurrence) of perceptual moments over time, which allows for object identity, the perception of language and music, intentionality and consciousness. In contrast, standard theory, which is largely based on neocortical activity with relative inattention to sub-cortical structures and forebrain evolution, offers no compelling account of perceptual awareness, since it understands consciousness as meaning and object recognition, but shows no apparent interest in any sort of process that would entail or imply creative activity in the act of perception.

CLINICAL STUDY AND PHYSIOLOGICAL RESEARCH

There is a disconnect between speculation in neuroscience and the effects of focal lesions on cognition. For example, single-unit responses to facial stimuli in the inferior temporal lobe of the monkey brain and impaired facial recognition in humans with lesions in those same areas have suggested a modular organization, in which face, letter or object identification occurs through the transfer of visual cortical data to unique neurons, and responses in temporal lobe or elsewhere for recognition. However, such modules are non-specific and not dedicated to a discrete function, since recognition occurs as the individuation of similar items within a class. Thus, as is well known, in prosopagnosia there can also be defects in the recognition of cows in farmers, or stamps in collectors. I reported a case of prosopagnosia with impaired identification of photos of WWII airplanes in a former pilot. The same phenomenon occurs in acquired alexia. In personal studies, I have demonstrated that this condition emerges from defects in object recognition (agnosia) that reappear with rapid (tachystoscopic) presentation. Recent neuroscience research has provided results consistent with the microgenetic concept (Hoel et al., 2016; Schindler & Bartels, 2016).

The role in object recognition assigned to the (inferior) temporal lobe, which is claimed to be the destination of initial stages of feature detection through a hypothetical binding process, has not been demonstrated in experimental or clinical studies. Instead, as found in numerous studies of temporal lobe lesions in monkey, as in humans, the pathology affects visual categories: specifically, the ability to select objects, faces or words out of a competing array. The idea of "a transformation of visual-feature encoding in early visual content" into categories (Freedman and Assad, 2016) has meager research support, while the contrary view, that objects are selected out of categories, not combined into them, is consistent with a great deal of clinical data and evolutionary theory. One example from aphasia study is that word perception and production occur as a specification within a lexical-semantic category, with word-recognition evoked by, or issuing through, a category of meaning relations. Moreover, in defects of object recognition (agnosia) initial in-processing is intact, while errors tend to reflect not defective visual input, but category relations, e.g. plate for spoon, or one face for another. Studies that focus on single neuron activity, not cell populations, cannot record activity in widespread populations—distributed networks, wave or field effects—that are more likely to be the underlying substrates through which categories unfold.

The view proposed here is that early stages in visual processing do not combine into object representations, but rather carve out final objects from pre-object categories that develop over successive fields of space representation. Categories are innate templates that are specified to diversity. In other words, changes induced by the impact of incoming sense data on cells in the visual cortex are not constructed into objects, but rather shape and direct an emergent process of object formation, in which memory, or thought-like representations, constrained by the sense-data, realize a model of the world to which the data conform. Current predictive coding theories of cognition have begun to accept this position (e.g. Bar, 2004; Heeger, 2017; O'Callaghan et al., 2017). For example, cells that respond to lines or angles parse endogenous images to facilitate externalization and detachment in a way that seems hallucinatory, but in fact gives a more or less veridically sculpted cognitive model of the world. In this way, a mental image maps to entities in the external world, but this mapping occurs in an "inside-out" direction, not the reverse. This implies that feature detection is not the initial, but rather the final phase in object-formation, providing terminal sculpting to the derivation of object-concepts or categories that individuate over ancestral stages. Whereas cortical in-processing presumes successive stages of object assembly, with subsequent projection of objects into, with, or as part of external space, microgenetic process leads outward from brain stem to cortex, from the past of memory to the present of perception, from intra-psychic to extra-personal, from mind to world and from unconscious simultaneity to conscious temporal order.

As regards the continuity of external data with the physiology of the brain, the neural signals that arise from visual input, for example, come into contact with those that arise spontaneously in the visual cortex. We may ask, then, how the neural firings that result from incoming data, such as those depositing information about shape, size or motion, can transmit patterns in perception to the neurons presumed to mediate those properties. The role of sense data is not to carry over information directly to cortical neurons that wait for this data, but to modulate their pre-existing membrane potentials and firing rate. Data arrive for the most part piecemeal, perhaps sequestered in retina but unassembled, and are categorized in the geniculate area, and then proceed to the visual cortex, where isolated impressions are presumably collated from simple to complex to hyper-complex cells, into three-dimensional objects, then matched to memory for recognition. As noted, cells in temporal cortex that respond to faces have been found in the inferior temporal cortex of the monkey brain, in an area presumably related to object recognition (Gur, 2015).

The usual assumption is that a convergence of receptive fields in the lateral geniculate region transmits specific properties such as shape or motion to pre-destined targets in visual cortex. The concept of feature detection implies that data encoded in axons that arrive in the striate cortex signal the properties of external entities, and that cells dedicated to size or shape constitute the endpoint of sub-cortical connections and the initial stage of cortical in-processing. These feature-specific cells, isolated in the manifold of sensory input, are conditioned to respond to property-specific signals. Conceivably, such signals locate the relevant cells or connections that are antecedent to the configured populations of brain cells which mediate the pattern formation essential for perception.

If brain cells are conceived as detectors, which receive, attract or sort through a multitude of sense data, with specificity in the connectivity of input, what happens to the data once the initial effect is over? Since incoming data are mediated by brain cells, like their endogenous targets, then we are dealing with a system of fixed cells and pathways stimulated by specific attributes. Once geniculate axons impact neurons in the visual cortex, which detect the signal or lure the axonal discharge, the data become elements in brain activity by inducing change in the resting potential of striate neurons. Sense data in retina are informants, affecting and contiguous with the brain cells that elaborate perception.

So far so good, but the problem is less the initial stage of cortical reception than the ensuing stages, through which the object is presumed to be constructed. If object-construction occurs prior to recognition, how do we know what to look at before we have seen it? What guides the detection of lines and angles, first to two-dimensional, then three-dimensional shapes? Does the constructive process that occurs after the cortical registration of elementary data then receive additional sense-data that determine object size and shape? Cortical in-processing postulates object-construction in (visual) cortex, with relay to limbic and other regions for recognition, meaning, object-concepts, and spatial updating. In current theory, a neuron that conveys simple or complex data entrained in the object construction corresponds to the data in the object. The strategy of transferring the properties of perceptual objects to cells that encode these properties inserts attributes of the external object back into the brain as their source. The construction of the object merely utilizes the features of the object as elements in its construction.

This resolves the difficulty of what integrates the data to combine to a configuration that represents an object, not only for size and shape, but for color, motion and especially recognition, which, in the externalist model, is consequent to input. One has to know, to some degree, what the object is before it can be consciously perceived, so that recognition, in the form of a memory image, prefigures and guides the configuration that is assumed to result from the ingression of sense data. This implies that imagery is not the residue of object perception, but that objects are the realization of images in memory sculpted to a model of external reality. The preliminary recognition in forming endogenous images provides the experiential knowledge, minimally the category, to which the object belongs, while cortical input carves out the final object configuration.

THE MICROGENETIC THEORY OF PERCEPTION

Microgenesis refers to the rapid and uni-directional derivation of an act of cognition along pathways that retrace phases in the evolution of forebrain. We know that perception and purposeful action are not immediate (there is temporal lag, readiness potential), but the stages between the inception of an act and the final outcome have largely eluded experimental study. However, focal brain lesions constitute a natural experiment, the symptoms of which are not anecdotes or guesses, but rule-bound and regular responses that, when exposed by the destruction of subsequent, higher cortical structures, reveal earlier phases in the cognitive process. If we accept that symptoms are neotenous phases in a normal process (Brown, 2014) relating to the evolutionary level in the brain, and that serial development recaptures the main lines of evolutionary growth, we can reconstruct the normal sequence that underlies surface cognition, that is, the endpoint or final phase in cognition.

Perception is the linchpin of microgenetic theory, as it posits a "core-to-surface" transit in which developing acts, objects, thoughts and feelings form a unified whole that fractionates into what appear to be separate or modular functions. The direction of percept formation is here assumed to be aligned with evolutionary and morphogenetic growth, in contrast to models that dissociate processing from growth trends in phylogeny and ontogeny. The transition over growth planes constitutes an individuation of categories initially based in instinctual drive to form a preliminary two-dimensional construct, which fractionates to categories of word—or object concepts or meaning relations, then to the final specification of object shape. The perception devolves through a series of whole/part or category/member specifications, as the final particulars actualize out of background potential; i.e. not assembled to experiential wholes, but derived from them (see Bachmann, 2000).

This development begins with drive categories in upper brainstem and hypothalamus, which receive substantial input from the optic nerve. The structures involved in instinctual drive constitute a primitive space-field of axial motility in concert with pre-objects. We know that affective display occurs with upper brainstem stimulation and lesions (Brown, 1967; cf. Nauta's "limbic-midbrain"). Limbic-temporal regions modulate instinctual drive or unconscious need to the affective tonality of conscious desire. Sense data carve out a preliminary two-dimensional construct, while the relative suspension of sensory input to limbic-temporal regions allows the endogenous configuration to traverse phases of experiential memory, feeling and meaning.

Percept-genetic studies (e.g. Smith, 2001) suggest that affect and meaning are prior to object awareness. Even before the individual is conscious of the object, a memory image forms, with provisional recognition. Blindsight studies confirm pre-object recognition. Similar effects occur in masking and priming studies (Whalen et al., 2004; Ohman et al., 2007)). I have observed more pronounced semantic priming in total aphasics who show no apparent comprehension of word presentations. The limbic construct is part of a viscous, fore-shortened, ego-centric and volumetric space of dream and hallucination, intra-psychic but partly extra-personal. At this stage, the pre-object can be termed a "drive-representation" (though not in the sense of Freud's metapsychology), with features of the dream-work pointing to an earlier syncretic mode of thought: condensation, fusion and metaphoric displacements. Hallucinations with upper brainstem or temporal lobe pathology tend to be multi-modal.

From this point, the pre-object and the primitive space-field pass through parietal regions, which do have some sensory input, e.g. from the pulvinar, to form a three-dimensional space of object relations. Lesions produce illusions, spatial alterations of objects that only appear when the eyes are open, unlike hallucinations, which are independent and occur with the eyes closed. Illusions are closer to a later phase in object development, while hallucinations are closer to an earlier phase in the endogenous image. As the construct passes from a memory-like to a perception-like image, space develops from dream to waking perception. The construct is extrapersonal but not fully extra-psychic; i.e. the image is in an outer space but not fully independent, as it appears when extra-psychic. Parietal lesions give defects in a "manipulo-spatial" field of the arm's reach on drawing and object-construction tasks. Hallucinatory images dissolve when one reaches for them. The construct, initially multi-modal or synesthetic (Cytowic, 1989), fractionates to the separate modalities, as well as from the parallel action development. The final object, sculpted by visual input to a specific object and object field that appears to be mind-independent, actualizes in (as) an external articulated space field. Sensory processing channels the endogenous category in such a way that it partitions into an image that adapts and conforms to an external world. The parsing of the category to the final object carries the image outward from memory to perception.

This account, which also entails a radically different theory of memory (see below), provides a new way of thinking about image, object, the mental state and nature of subjective time, problems that have baffled classical theory. A memory image can approximate a veridical object in hallucination or lucid dream; an object may dissolve to a memory image, as in eidetic imagery or psychopathology. From the microgenetic perspective, objects differentiate out of remembered experience by sculpting in visual cortex. The currently fashionable views based on predictive coding have only begun to accept this theoretical position. Sensation is not the primitive foundational ingredient, the raw material of perception, but rather something that constrains endogenous process. Recognition, affect and valuation are incorporated as the object specifies, with feeling carried into the object as value. These are not, as in classical theory, additions to the object construction at later stages of brain activity, but partitions of foundational endogenous categories (see Fig. 2).

MEMORY AND PERCEPTION

The transition from intra—to extra-psychic space carries the memory image outward to perception. Contemporary work on memory tends to follow standard perception theory, in that the memories deposited by perceptions are thought to be secondarily evoked for recognition. The "copy" theory of memory—bits of information that are stored and can then be looked up—conforms to perception theory and computer models. In contrast, for microgenesis the object is a memory image that arises in a background category—as a figure in relation to a ground—and externalizes under the constraints of sensation. An act of cognition, or perception, begins with categorical primitives in drive, which pass to sensory-free limbic-temporal phases for assimilation to experiential or long term memory, then to short term and iconic memory through occipital-parietal layers, and final detachment as an object, not the reverse (Fig. 2). The connectivity within and across hemispheres, from base to surface and from anterior to posterior regions of the visual cortex, is reciprocal, and no less consistent with the microgenetic direction (from core inside to branching outside) than with standard theory (from bits outside to categories inside). The transition from core to perception that constitutes an act of cognition and the mind/brain state is an endogenous series, partly intra-psychic (a "default mode network" in modern terms), partly experienced as intentionally extra-psychic, but in fact wholly subjective. Essentially, it is an objectification of subjectivity—iterated each moment as a spectral theater in which life is played out.

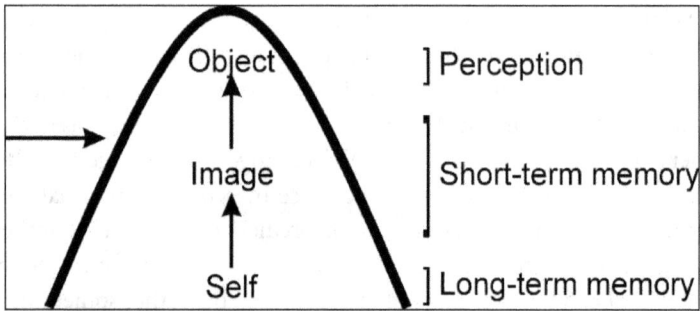

Fig. 2: *The transition in perception from core to object occurs over stages in memory that recur as incompletely revived phases in subsequent mind/brain states (see text).*

On this view, forgetting constitutes incomplete revival of perceptions, not decay of memory traces. There is no persistence in the literal sense. Synaptic growth favors widely-distributed configural patterns, but the trace is not localized. It is the entire sequence or the successive whole-part specification of a series of developing configurations that is re-created when the memory—or pre-object—is revived. Each state undergoes progressive attenuation in successive revivals as novel perceptions individuate, with the decline in revival uncovering traversed phases in the original perception. Thus the incomplete revival of the mental state first recovers the evanescent phase of iconic (eidetic) memory. The image recaptures much featural detail and is perceived in an almost veridical manner, as a penultimate phase in externalization. The image rapidly fades, to be replaced by the next perception. Further attenuation of the initial state allows the recurrent image to reach the stage of short term memory, in which many "physical" features of the original object are still accessible. The perception, greatly attenuated, is then revived until it reaches the phase of long term memory, which engages personal meaning and feeling. In other words, the progression from long term memory to perception in the original object development is exposed, in reverse, in its forgetting, which is not the decay of a memory trace or a logical solid, but an incomplete revival of the original percept. The antecedent mental state provides a template for the arising of the occurrent one, as it is effaced in its replacement by repeated volleys of novel objects (Fig. 3).

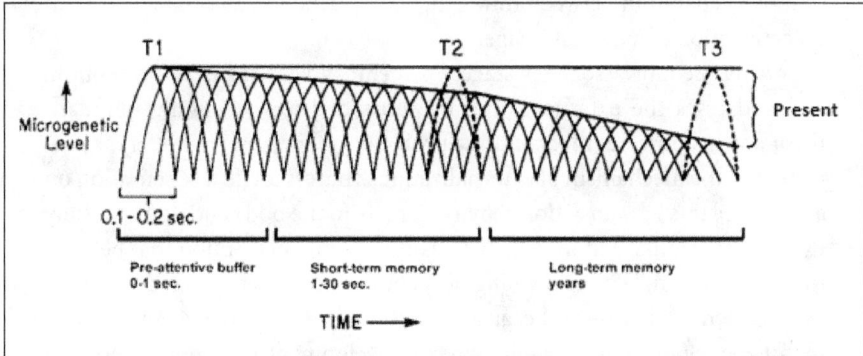

Fig. 3: *The mind/brain state, or act of perception (T-1), which arises from core to object, is successively revived in ensuing perceptions, but incompletely. The incomplete revival exposes different stages in memory (iconic, short-term, long-term) that were traversed in the original perception. At some point (T-3), the revival does not reach beyond the "floor" of long-term memory. The disparity between the object at this point (T-3) and the attenuated revival of T-1, within the mind/brain state of T-3, is the specious present (cf. Fig. 4 below, with accompanying text).*

According to this interpretation, there is no decay of memory, no persistence or abiding of the object, but a constant forward-looking and prediction (subjective aim), with every act of cognition a brief recurrence that progressively subsides. Instead of decay, which supposes a persistent or stored trace that somehow disintegrates, phases in the object-formation are uncovered by incomplete recurrence, accompanied by data update. In the microgenetic account, storage refers to synaptic modification in widely distributed configurations, primarily at early phases in the mental state, while successful retrieval depends on the ability to revive an image to a phase of actuality. A mental pre-object that does not become a veridical perception is a thought or memory image. The earliest phases in the original perception remain unconscious or inaccessible, but nevertheless they shape the object.

Phases in a perceptual moment antecedent to the occurrent object do not consist in a combination of features extracted by neocortical detectors, but constitute a progressive series of memory phases that achieve veridicality as an imaginary model that adapts to external conditions by the sculpting effects of sensation on the emerging configuration. Sensation eliminates what is irrelevant (unfit, maladaptive or redundant), thus "selecting" the final image from the antecedent category, trimming generality to precision, and forcing the detachment of the image as a seemingly independent object in the world. The abrupt parsing of the final category, the pre-object gestalt or configuration that adapts the image to the outer world, gives the conviction of a separation between mind and world, when in fact the world is an objectification of a mental image.

This account associates stages in memory with those in perception, and addresses the externalization of perceptual images, unlike standard theory, which finesses most of these problems, relying on post-afferent projection as the mechanism of externalization. The lesser effect of sensation on action explains why an action remains largely in the body and does not fully externalize. Unlike action, which remains a bodily perception that belongs to the actor, along with the feeling of agency, perceptions detach and appear independent. Partly this is because the action development generates a feeling of agency or activity, while percept development is accompanied by a feeling of passivity, though there are intermediate stages in act and percept. For example, earlier phases of imagery can show voluntary "manipulation," while comparable phases in action may not give a feeling of agency. From this point of view, one can say that memory is the intra-psychic segment of perception, while perception is the becoming-veridical of a memory image in confrontation with the massive input of sense data to visual cortex at the final phase of object development.

The separation of self/mind and object/world, the transition over evolutionary strata, from ancient to recent and in the direction of forebrain growth, the passage from memory to perception, mind to world or past to present—all this appears sudden and decisive, as the image adapts to an experiential world. However, many well-documented pathological or fringe phenomena and observations, such as eidetic, palinoptic, hallucinatory or after-images, or the relation of illusory to hallucinatory phenomena, or insufficient sensory data (as in dream, sensory deprivation or fantasy), or instances where the endogenous process overcomes sensation with excessive force, provide evidence for a continuous transition from image to object. This is also apparent in psychotic states, for example in de-realization, when objects become thought-like or thoughts objectify.

On this view, dream foreshadows waking perception, as an endogenous image that lacks the adaptive constraints of sensation. Dream is the undersurface of perception, displaying features of preliminary phases in object formation, such as meaning, fluid images, transformations, whole-part relations in substitution and displacement, intra-psychic space, and so on. The images that precipitate in dream are not antecedents of objects; rather, the substrate or phase of the dream image partitions to waking objects. What actualizes in dream is a truncated percept development, with an evanescent self that apprehends a flood of images that, on waking, point to transitional phases, not the actual images that occur when those phases are endpoints. Specifically, the unconscious of dream is not exactly the unconscious buried in waking perception, for the suspension of sensation allows the free play of memory imagery which, in wakefulness, is constrained by adaptive pressures. The creative individual, in trance, concentration, meditation, etc., suspends the external, in order to access subliminal content that is ordinarily transformed to a subsequent phase.

This account of memory as incomplete perceptual revival sheds light on so-called working memory, the maintenance of perceptual experience in memory or thought as a more sustained recurrence. The content recurs to a phase of verbal or visual imagery, expanding memory content to active thought. What happens is not stability of memory or free association of traces to related contents, though metaphoric extension is a primary means of conceptual growth, but a revival of untapped potential in an object development or its successors. The persistence and plasticity of memory is a result of a diminished sensation that accompanies inward focus. A retreat to the interior of the mind entails a slower fading, i.e. an accentuated revival, which is implemented by constancy or reduction of sensory input and a diminished effect of the competing perceptions that efface prior actualizations.

This explains the re-shaping of memory content in the generation of thought as a prolongation of revived imagery. The generation or revival of mental content, as reproductive memory transforms to productive thought, is a deviation from exactness. The focus on the recurrence of memory rather than its sculpting and completion to perception highlights a phase of visual and verbal imagery prior to externalization. For microgenesis, this intermediate phase of introspection is an enhancement of antecedents in the mental state, with recurrence thwarting forgetting, as the individual withdraws from world to mind and sense data are reduced. Introspection is not a supplement to the cognitive repertoire, but an enhancement of pre-object phases that are ordinarily traversed and transformed. This is consistent with the evolutionary principle that new form arises from preliminary stages of greater potentiality, not from endpoints of specialization to which new potentials are added: evolutionary change consists in branching, rather than accretion. Within the mental state, this refers to categorical possibilities that precede the definitiveness of perceptual actuality.

CONSCIOUSNESS AND THE MIND/BRAIN STATE

Wittgenstein said that thought begins with instinct. For microgenesis, the instinctual core generates the mental state. In the human mind, an early derivation of this core is the self-concept (an all-embracing category), through which the contents of the mental state are derived. The core stands behind the acts and objects into which it develops. The self that is an early derivation of the core apprehends the objects into which it distributes. The relation of self to the object world is consciousness; the relation of self to pre-terminal imagery in the presence of reduced sensibility is introspection, or self-awareness and mental content.

The mind/brain state consists of a rapid, iterated trajectory from onset to termination that begins in drive-based categories, passes to desire in relation to object—and lexical-concepts, to an endpoint in perception or action. The integral mind/brain state is an epochal realization of the entire sequence with the overlapping succession (Fig. 3) necessary to create the bubble of mental process in which experience occurs. James (1890) argued that overlap is necessary for continuous identity. Microgenetic theory expands this idea to a model of (1) memory as a template for perception, (2) the relation of memory and perception to the present moment and (3) the survival of character and personality at the core (Fig. 4).

The sequence is epochal and relatively uniform, though variable as to content. The basic process is a specification of wholes to parts, or categories to members, with the partition repeated from one phase to the next. This means that a single process or law of transformation governs the state, not multiple processes acting at different points or regions. Wholes, like categories, are not mechanical sums or compilations, and parts or members are themselves categories, not static, indivisible constituents. Each state arises and is replaced by the next (Figs. 3 and 4). The process of transition that leads to an object has a feeling tone accompanying the derivation, which can be conceived as a becoming-into-being (Atmanspacher & Filk, 2011). The subjective aim of becoming is driven by feeling; the objective outcome is a realization of being. The inseparability of feeling and concept, drive and category, affect and object, incorporates a becoming-into-being into every mental state.

Wittgenstein famously called it a "conjurer's trick" to speak of mental states and leave their nature undecided. The microgenetic account is the sole theory of the mind/brain state, not as a piece of isolated content, e.g. a proposition, qualia, but, in normal wakefulness, a complete traversal from unconscious depth to conscious surface, with gradual perishing or fading of the final objectification, as each mental state is replaced by its successor.

Thus, in successive states T-1 and T-2 (Fig. 4), the arising of T-2 begins before the completion of T-1. In most standard processing models, stages follow each other in causal succession, though there are exceptions (e.g. McClelland, Turvey). If we can agree with Whitehead that an entity requires one complete cycle to become what it is, i.e. to exist, or that nature cannot be freeze-dried, or that entities do not exist at an instant but have some minimal duration, the normal waking mental state does not achieve existence unless there is a complete actualization, or one that reaches an endpoint, that is, until its segments have been traversed and can be revived in the ensuing state. This allows initial phases in T-1 to recur in T-2 prior to the completion and actuality (existence) of the T-1 or the T-2 state. The rapid replacement in the state of superficial layers that mediate imagery and perception, and the relative preservation of earlier ones associated with the self, character, core values, beliefs and experiential memory, is explained by the revival in T-2 of early segments in T-1 prior to the existence, thus the perishing, of the T-1 state. This explains how, over the succession of waking states, early phases show continuity but never actualize in consciousness, while later phases recur partially in revived images with a brief existence before they are replaced. The continuance of the replacement and the slow growth at the depth also explain the "persistence" of personality across periods of sleep or anesthesia. This is illustrated in Fig. 4 below (Brown 2010).

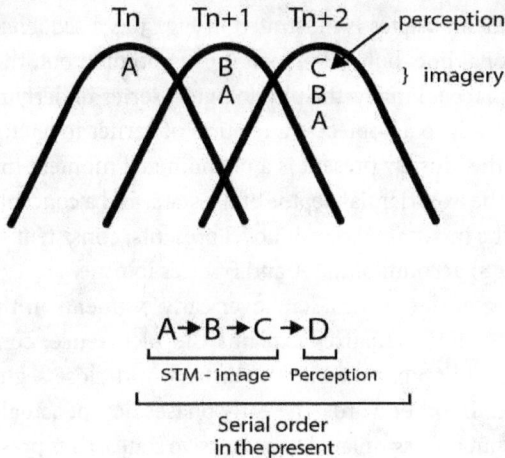

Fig. 4: Overlapping mental states. The state A is revived in the next state, B, then in the ensuing state C. Each state is less completely revived, giving a succession from earlier to later. Revivals within each state fall within segments that mediate mental imagery. Succession within a state is a simultaneity that actualizes to

the simultaneity of conscious time-order in the duration of the now. This figure also
illustrates how state B overlaps state A before A actualizes. This implies that early
phases in A are revived in B prior to the completion and existence of A. This accounts
for the perishing of perceptions at the endpoint and the preservation of character and
personality at the onset.

An account of successive mind/brain states and their partial recurrence leads to a theory of the present moment as a disparity between the "ceiling" of the occurrent perception—the perceptual endpoint—and the "floor" of a prior state not revived beyond long term memory. For instance, in Fig. 3, the disparity between the perceptual endpoint at T-3 and the lapse of T-1 to long-term memory exemplifies this. The temporal disparity is felt longitudinally as the duration of the (specious, illusory) present, analogous to the spatial effect of binocular disparity necessary to depth perception. Depth is, indeed, the ghost of transition. The perceptual surface is fixed in wakeful awareness, but the floor can vary with the degree of memory recruitment. In meditative practice, the duration may expand. In dream, the lack of realization of a veridical endpoint foreshortens the state and contracts the present to a brief duration. In dream, as in the waking mental state prior to conscious realization, there is no past or future, only before and after. The waking unconscious is not timeless; it is simultaneous. The realization of a series of mind/brain states creates a present, a past and a future, with a shift from unconscious simultaneity to conscious time-order. The revival of mental states is illustrated in Fig. 3 as a sequence over time, a two-dimensional line, but as Bergson (1923) pointed out, the "now" is a point that is replaced. Finally, the physiological series underlying the phase transition that leads to an object is a relation of earlier to later, i.e. physical passage, while the illusory present is a phenomenal moment in time, when a past arises in the experiential depths of the state, and a conceptual future is inferred from the incessant surge of novel presents, consistent with McTaggart's (1934/1968) account of the A and B series in time.

The arising of the present state over early segments in the prior one before the prior state actualizes explains the recurrence, continuity and slow growth of early phases, while the distal world-close segments perish on actualization. In other words, the early phases do not actually exist, and cannot perish, but are assimilated to successive states, thus preserving early cognition, while later stages achieve actuality and perish. We cannot catch a perception, Hume wrote, because there is continuous replacement, incomplete revival and changing sensation. Early phases in a state never actually exist since they are replaced by—assimilated to—early phases in an ensuing one; however, their influence on consequent phases maintains stability in transition. The claim that the self does not exist is true, insofar as the self is an early segment that does not achieve actuality, i.e. existence, yet it is also true that the self exists in the continuity and relative constancy of behavior and personal identity over states through which the self is felt and inferred. The paradoxical absence of existence in the face of an influence or effect is well known in other phenomena. A rainbow does not exist but it can induce spells of rapture. We might say that hallucinations do not exist, but they can direct behavior in susceptible individuals. We might say that a plan of action does not exist before it is realized, but afterwards we retrospectively infer a plan by which the actions were guided. The notion of a plan guiding action is related to categorical antecedents that serially discharge an action sequence, yet arise at a depth ordinarily inaccessible to every day thought. Thus a process that exists perishes, while one that does not exist survives. The actuality that implies existence entails death, while the potentiality that gives existence does not itself exist.

2

From Image to Object[1]

SUMMARY

THE MICRO-TRANSITION TO A mental object described in the previous chapter traverses phases of potential imagery, the developmental features of which, such as feeling, experiential memory and meaning, are embedded in the final object. Attenuation at pre-object phases in the context of an ambient but complete object development allows mental imagery to actualize as thought or fantasy, or in certain individuals as pathological imagery or hallucination. The pervasive imagery of dream occurs with a suspension of the sensation that transforms a pre-terminal gestalt to an actual object in a real world. Observations on the common substrates for image and object formation, for transitional phenomena in the process of object development and the recovery of psychic antecedents in cases of de-objectification, point to the subjectivity buried in the final object. In dream we are unaware of waking perception, so awake we may infer a yet-higher stage of mental experience. The mapping of mental representations to nature, unlike dream, depends on the engagement of mind with the immediate world modeled in perception.

1. See Brown, J. W. (1984) *Hallucinations, imagery and the microstructure of perception.* In: Vinken, P., Bruyn, G. and Klawans, H. (Eds.) *Handbook of Clinical Neurology,* Volume 45, p. 351–372, Elsevier, Amsterdam; Ey, H. (1973) *Traité de Hallucinations.* 2 Vols. Masson et Cie, Paris

INTRODUCTION

The relation of the image as a psychic phenomenon to the object as an ostensibly material thing in the world is a central problem in psychology, as well as in the philosophy of mind. Regardless of the type of imagery—thought, eidetic, dream etc.—the image is experienced in the mind, the object in the world, and it is difficult to see a connection between the two, other than, as in the standard account, the notion that imagery is a storehouse of experience that is initially deposited by incoming perceptions. The unavoidable failure of the mental image to correspond exactly to the external object gives a persistent belief in two distinct worlds: the inner world of the mind and subjective experience, and the outer world of objective things and events, which exist or occur regardless of what we know or think about them. The sense of a clean division between the world of objects and that of the imagination, and the assumption that the nascent mind is a *tabula rasa* apart from the animal inheritance, leads to a conception of the outer world as the source of percepts that enter the brain from without, leave traces in memory, and pass through the brain to return to a locus in the world.

Viewed from this perspective, the object world is the origin of memory and personal experience, while the inner world is a ghostly companion to the material outer one. In waking, the boundary is clear and definite, particularly in the relation of self, feeling, thought and dream to perception. The impression that perceptions enter the brain from outside is so strong that the opposite possibility raised here, that of a continuum from image to object, or from mind to world, is rarely considered as the primary direction of mental process. Historically, images have been viewed as memories deposited by object perceptions, first in a pristine state, a faithful representation unaffected by interpretation, which is then transmuted, contextualized and infiltrated by feeling with varying degrees of conscious access. The topic, though now an obscure corner of psychology, goes to the very heart of the debate on realism and idealism in philosophical speculation.

Normally, we are not aware of the process of object formation, nor the role of imagery in perception, though the "mental apparatus" for imagery is identical to that for perception: that is, the percept is an externalized image that develops over the same distributed systems in the brain as the image, which is a submerged pre-object. Thus auditory hallucination replaces auditory perception; so-called lacunae in perception occur during hallucinatory bouts. Visual hallucination replaces perception in the portion of the field usurped by the image. Visual field defects give rise to, or uncover, visual hallucinations. Cases of visual hallucination studied with caloric stimulation (hot or cold water in the ear) have vertigo in the image, just as occurs in an object. The image behaves and develops over the same pathways as a perception.

Moreover, when perception is replaced by hallucination, especially in more than one modality, the image is taken as real. When the image is the final phase in perception, as in dream, the imaginary world seems real, since the object world no longer exists for the dreamer as a basis of comparison. In order for the world to exist, it must be perceived, which is to say, that the object world has to be continuously revived to exist for the person, which again points to its subjective origin.

The most accurate and parsimonious theory of object formation is that a perception is an external image that develops out of an archaic core combining properties of the immediate object with endogenous memories, feelings and meanings. This multi-layered complex objectifies through the impact of sensation on an emerging endogenous gestalt. The suspension of sensation in pathology, sleep or sensory deprivation uncovers earlier or later phases in image-formation. It is important to note that the image, though its attributes are ingredient in the perception, is not itself transformed to an object; rather, the transition is over the substrate that would give rise to an image if the object-development was attenuated. That is, an image is a sign of varying degrees of incompleteness in object development, with an absence of sensation or a local retardation in the passage to an object.

Through this transition, a continuous sheet of mind actualizes in an object. While perceptions are vividly present in the world, and appear as presentations to the mind, which is presumed to deconstruct, recombine and project them back to the world as perceptual objects, the direction from intra-psychic to extra-psychic is less obvious, indeed, imperceptible, except in pathology or altered states. This approach to perception is counter-intuitive, but it can be documented by thoughtful consideration of alterations in the perceptual process. Among these alterations are: (1) evidence for a progression from image to object, not the reverse, (2) the ostensible gap from mind to world, (3) the reality of the image, (4) the continuity of substrate, and (5) phenomena that are transitional between mind and world.

FROM IMAGE TO OBJECT

The distinction of mental image and external object and the gap from mind to world is an appropriate place to begin. The mental image can be an isolated phenomenon, as in the hallucination of a face, or one can have a complex scenic hallucination that includes considerable detail and is often more vivid than in life. Yet even dream, however creative, is impoverished in comparison to the diversity of objects in nature. Some images have a volitional quality; others are felt as passive in relation to the self. Some images are meaning-laden and symbolic; others express the physical features of objects. Some dreams are wild inventions; others are lucid and realistic. These differences all point to the depth of the dominant phase in the development of the image.

The distinction between illusion and hallucination is pertinent in this regard. At least in the clinical literature, illusions are distortions of perception, while hallucinations are alternate perceptions. This is the case for illusions such as vertigo, acceleration/deceleration effects, enlargement, diminution or change in the form of the image. As with other types of imagery, hallucination appears to arise from earlier, often multi-modal phases, while illusion is modality-specific and closer to the object. Hallucination persists with the eyes closed; illusion disappears. Also, like after-images, but unlike hallucinations, illusions enlarge with increasing distance from the projection surface. The occurrence of images that are close to dream and fantasy and those that realize some featural details of the external object, such as eidetic, palinoptic or memory images, the loose correlation with levels in actualization, the relation of hallucination as an intrinsic phenomenon and illusion as a deformation of perception—all these imply a process through which endogenous form externalizes over phases from experiential content to veridical perception. The relation of hallucination to illusion as a progressive approximation to external objects reminds us, in the continuum of the transition and the subjective aim from image to object, that real objects, *die Dinge an sich* in Kant's phrase, only come into existence for us when they are mental phenomena.

The old idea that mind and world differ with respect to extension should be measured against the evidence that external space develops over stages in forebrain evolution, from a 2–2½D representation in the tectal region of brainstem, through the egocentric or volumetric space of dream and hallucination, to a 3D object-centered space within the arm's reach mediated by parietal formations, and, finally, through primary cortices to the limitless expanse of external space. These stages of object and space formation are implicit and non-conscious in waking perception, but can be demonstrated in clinical and research study. Moreover, though the space of dream is foreshortened, unstable and viscous, it can be interpreted as a precursor of object space, not a deformed residual. At the least, all this shows us that, independent of sensation, the mind can create a space of object relations and depth. Even the space of the eyes closed, the so-called visual gray, has been described as having some depth. It is also worth noting that alterations in perception and transitions in the course of recovery tend to be generalized and coherent, not piecemeal or fragmentary, as a theory of modularity or feature-detection would predict.

The point here is that a progression occurs from inner to outer over layers of space formation leading to—and essential for—the perception of external space. Indeed, some features of preliminary mental space forecast those of accounts of external space in modern physics, such as the curvature of the space of dream and hallucination. The palpable quality of the space of dream, or the melting of hallucinatory images into space, resonates with ancient and medieval theories of "ether" or some fabric to outer space, that is, the theory that space is not an empty container or vacuum. Subjective space has a tangible object-like texture that is a precursor of, and extends outward to, the non-empty space between objects. In this context, it is of interest to note that time and space dissociate with brain damage, time in relation to memory, space in relation to objects, though the psychological relation of time to space is more apparent in younger than older children (Piaget). It was this observation that, as I recall, led Einstein to suggest that his theoretical work was stimulated by a childish imagination.

The progression from (the potential for) a free, fluid and meaning-laden image to an outer field of diverse and relatively stable objects is a progression from generality to precision, from possibility to fact. The agency, meaning and feeling in many forms of imagery extends to the impression of purpose, value and meaning in nature, just as the creation of a world by mind prefigures a belief in the creation of the world by god. These shifts from the indistinct and uncertain to the definite and substantive, from meaning to materiality, from agency to object-causation, are a challenge to explain, but no more so than the progression in a mental state from instinct to reason or drive to mental propositions.

THE DIVISION OF MIND AND WORLD

The confrontation of image formation with sensation or the analysis by sensation of an endogenous gestalt at the terminal phase in object formation, or the clash of an experiential and memorial infra-structure with the sensation that channels the substrate to an object, carries attributes of imagery—experiential memory, meaning, symbolic representation, feeling, the creative imagination—into the final object as implicit or embedded features. Conventional theory presumes that psychic attributes are associated features or interpretations or elaborations of perceptions, but these attributes accompany the pre-object outward and are invested in the object itself. For example, the worth or value of a person or pet, their love and loyalty, or the value and beauty of a possession, are felt as intrinsic, not as attributions of the mind to the object.

This implies that when an individual evaluates an object, or responds to its intellectual or aesthetic values, these values are not clothing placed on a naked object, but are ingredient in the perception revealed through an uncovering and/or elaboration of early phases in the original object-development. An object grows out of the beliefs, values and personal experience of the observer, which are an integral component of the final perception, not something added on. These phases, implicit and rapidly traversed, are recovered when we contemplate an object or consider its meaning or relation to thought or experience. This phenomenon represents a retreat to the underpinnings of the object development. We see this, for example, in the "decay" of an eidetic image of pictorial accuracy to a vague memory image. The notion that non-physical attributes are attached to mind-independent objects, such as feeling, worth, interest and so on, is rendered essential by the inferred external status of objects, which derives from and reinforces the account of in-processing and construction or assembly, as opposed to the sculpting of irrelevance and its return in deliberation.

The fact that an object can evoke an array of ancillary content suggests that the object arouses the data or that it is applied or associated to the object. The theory proposed here is that the knowledge base, which is incorporated in the perception as potential or incipient content, is engaged primarily at initial phases of object-generation, and then recovered in successive revivals. Specifically, when we gaze at the world and reflect on the perception, the mental state recurs to a diminishing extent. This allows pre-perceptual phases in the original percept to be retrieved. The revival of pre-object phases and the elaboration of antecedents in the course of forgetting is the basis for the imaginative growth or metaphoric extension of an object or concept, namely, an exploration of the depths of an object through incomplete revivals that uncover the experiential memories and meanings that are entrained prior to full objectification.

THE REALITY OF THE IMAGE

The sharp division of mind from world depends on the solidity, reality and persistence of external objects compared to the insubstantiality and evanescence of mental phenomena. The perceptual world seems real enough, while the mental world seems imaginary. An internal image lacks the "reality" of an external one; the former is clearly in the mind, the latter just as clearly in the world. However, the feeling of realness in an image or object over the boundary from mind to world is only one part of the division be-tween psyche and external reality. A dream seems real, so does an eidetic or holographic image, though they are not object-like in their realness. The point is that mental images may seem real but do not have the quality of external objects. The transition from the contracted mind-dependent space of dream to the independent space of object relations is one source of stabil-ity. Another is objectification and persistence in the replication of mental states and the creation of a present that provides the stability of recurrence.

In contrast, except for dream and hallucinosis, which have a restricted present and diminished recurrence, with constant change in content that fills the object field, most images tend to occur as isolates in waking cogni-tion and are not usually reinforced by other senses. Nor does the conscious image participate in the duration of the present, which requires a fully ex-ternalized object. The present, as a disparity of the perceptual or imaginal surface and the floor of forgetting, is not generated by pre-perceptual im-agery, but encloses it within its limits. Psychic content in the present is im-agery in a revived perception. Continuing perceptual experience makes the underlying image seem real. A melody or sentence seems real and immedi-ate when it occurs as a revived content in a perceptual series, but in isolation the content is apprehended as a memory image or hallucination. Ongoing perception dominates submerged imagery. This is why when we listen to conversation or music we cannot hear unrelated sentences or melodies at the same time. Unless the perception is unattended, as in reflection, the image substrates that go into object perception cannot generate memories other than those that sustain the perception, since the substrates of imag-ery are given over to perceptual becoming. To actually hear a sentence or melody other than that in ongoing perception is to attend to the memorial content of another perceptual now. The evocation of a memory vitiates the intensity of the current focus of perception.

The reality of dream, hallucination, and some other forms of imagery implies proximity of the image to the object, but it also shows that the feel-ing of realness is not the criterion of objectivity. We can know an experience is unreal and still perceive it as realistic. Thus, studies with "virtual reality" show a 3D image-world as an approximation of perception and support the concept that perceptual realization passes through—and is essentially an objectified stage of—imagery. The proximity of a mental image to the image of the world should convince us that mental images of varying degrees of realness are precursors to the perception of a world image.

Specifically, the revival of immediate memory that helps to create the present, that is, the unfolding of the simultaneous stacking of prior per-ceptions or memory images, differs from conscious memory. The former is perceived as part of the perception, the latter as a memory image. When external perception is the subjective aim, those memories that are part of ongoing perception, such as music or conversation, are perceived as extrinsic events, not as memories. Focusing on a memory produces a separate mental state, in which the external event is no longer in the foreground of attention. That is, the memory image has a quality of realness and objectivity due to its entrainment in the duration of the present; the latter, memorial and intra-psychic, is detached from duration-formation, which depends on the disparity of perception with forgetting. The revival of perceptual imagery to a veridical stage in the duration of the present (conversation, music) supports its reality, while imaginal substrates buried in the perception inform the object development but do not become conscious foci of attention. To fixate on a thought or memory in a conscious present relegates perception to an ambient ground. This allows an image to actualize in consciousness as mental content—in another mental state—that is made possible by the continuity of perceptual completion.

The perception of reality does not reveal its imaginal basis, but is experienced as an objective film of sorts, one that replicates and to some extent occludes the physical reality it models. The imaginal or illusory nature of perception is inferred from its elaboration by the brain as a surrogate reality, not from its image-like quality. Some forms of imagery are clearly psychic in relation to perceptual objectivity, that is, in comparison to an external object, while the idea that perception is an image is an inference from its relation to an imperceptible reality that, unless god is a trickster, is the ultimate ground of being. The progression over grades of image development is from early phases in the physical brain state that generate a subjective image, to perception as an objectified image, to the revival of conscious images (memory, thought) antecedent to perception, to the idea of perception as an imaginary outcome in relation to a physical world that is modeled as an image of reality. Thus, the physical brain creates a mental representation of process in the world, and this reflexively constrains the mental state to itself. If what is ultimately real turns out to be physical constraints on the brain state that produce successive approximations to reality, mind arises between two unknowables—brain and nature—inferred from inside an image.

CONTINUITY OF SUBSTRATE

If the perception is an objectified image, an image and a pre-object should share the same neural systems. While some accounts of mental imagery, especially conscious thought images, suggest a distinct localization in relation to language areas, clinical case study leads to a different conclusion. I recall a seminar on this topic with George Miller, when a visiting lecturer argued for the propositional basis of imagery. George, in frustration, finally asked, what is the propositional basis of a phantom limb? In fact, phantom limb phenomena are related to sensorimotor cortex. Patients with amputation and phantom limbs who suffer a stroke in the opposite motor cortex will lose the phantom, indicating a common localization of perception and imagery.

A brief review of image types shows this to be the case, in that studies of pathological imagery document a common substrate with perception. For example, peduncular hallucinations, which occur in the crepuscule, probably involve—thus the name—formations in upper brainstem that are involved in dream and the wake/sleep cycle. This is also likely the case for hypnagogic hallucinations, which are part of the narcoleptic tetrad, again most likely relating to sleep systems in brainstem.

With temporal lobe lesions, there can be olfactory, auditory or visual hallucinations, depending on the extent to which pathology affects the relevant perceptual cortex. In schizophrenia, auditory hallucination usually begins with a memory image or an illusion or perceptual distortion, such as perceiving the rustle of leaves as whispering, then developing to an externalized image taken as real. This shows the continuity from memory to (false) perception and from perturbed imagery (illusion) to endogenous hallucination. Surgical destruction of auditory cortex has been reported to decrease auditory hallucination, and hallucination can be evoked by temporal lobe stimulation, or as an aura in temporal lobe epilepsy. Visual hallucinations are more common with occipital lesions, whether in tumor, stroke or the transient anoxia of migraine or the effects of hallucinogens (Klüver). In palinopsia with an occipital lesion, there is abnormal persistence of perceptions, similar to that in eidetic or after-imagery.

Dream imagery has been associated with brainstem and orbito-frontal regions, though the complexity of dream and the verbal and perceptual quality of the images indicate a more widespread involvement, most likely engaging temporal lobes and the visual and auditory cortices. I have studied two cases of cortical blindness with damage to neocortical visual areas with only verbal dreams. For example, one patient dreamt she was in a dark closet hearing voices. This implies that visual dream images involve neocortical regions associated with visual perception. There are many reports of musical (Wagner) and literary (Coleridge, Stevenson) composition in dream-like states, which I too have experienced. In one dream, there was punning based on rhyme (docket/pocket), which is specific to left hemisphere and the posterior temporal regions. This implies that neocortical zones relating to phonology are active in dream; specifically, auditory dream images involve auditory cortex responsible for auditory (and speech) perception.

The importance of memory and affect in dream points to limbic-temporal regions, especially with regard to emotions and experiential memory, just as occurs in waking perception. The dream entrains the perceptual cortex as well, accounting for the perception-like quality and realness of auditory verbal and visual images. The dream unfolds like a perception, differing in the absence of the sensory apparatus that sculpts and externalizes the imagery, which instead actualizes with a limited degree of perceptual completion. The occurrence of images in lieu of perceptions results in an attenuated present without past or future and a non-agent self that is swept along by dream events. Dream happens on the knife-edge of change. Without a direction to the future, agency is not possible. Without a past, there is incoherence in most dream narratives.

Occasionally, external stimuli intrude on a dream. An alarm clock may be heard as church bells, indicating the effect of sensation on dream imagery. There are even descriptions, which I have reported with Arthur Arkin, of sleep-talkers who converse with other sleeping individuals. The point is that dreams have many of the features of perception, minus sensation at successive levels, which would constrain the imagery toward a veridical perception. Lacking these constraints, the imagery undergoes an elaboration of meaning and symbolic relations that follow endogenous laws.

Finally, the common experience of full recall of a dream immediately on waking with rapid forgetting supports a relation to iconic memory. Waking perception establishes a present in which the dream events can be serially recalled, but these events fade in the presence of ensuing mental states. Unlike waking experience, dream events do not appear to become memories or part of the experiential past except for occasional dreams that leave a strong impression, presumably because dream contents are already memories, implicit or potentially conscious. The memory, not the distortion, is preserved.

TRANSITIONAL PHENOMENA

The sharp break from image to object obscures the passage of an endogenous construct, largely a memory-based pre-object that takes on a subjective aim at levels of early sensory input and is transported outward by sensation at the perceptual cortex, with phenomena in the objectification of imaginal substrates supporting the outward direction of the object-development. One of these is derealization in psychosis, when the existence and realness of individuals and objects are questioned, with a feeling of a psychic origin. Objects become thought-like and thoughts objectify. The individual believes that thoughts can be broadcast to and from others. The withdrawal from externality, or the de-objectification of the image, is accompanied by an accentuation of precursor phases, revealing the imaginary underpinnings of perception in its incomplete externalization.

We see this transition in auditory verbal imagery, which begins with the agent feeling of inner speech and takes on, in drowsiness, a passive quality, so that the individual feels he is no longer producing but hearing his own thoughts. Even in full wakefulness, many people hear their own voice, thinking, admonishing, instructing and so on. As the individual falls asleep, the voice may shift from active volitional thought to passive listening to detachment and hallucination. This is a normal, perhaps common, experience, as verbal thought passes from voluntary to involuntary, from pre-speech to perception. I have written on the process of inner speech (verbal imagery) taking a path from the preverbitum to motor speech or a path to perceptual externalization as the verbal image objectifies.

When this occurs, there is diversification of the voice as it separates from the thinker. In normal individuals, one can hear the voice of a spouse or parent. In pathological cases, there are multiple voices of different genders. As volition in motor speech shifts outward, the voice assumes the agency that is lost in the thinker, at times resulting in command hallucinations. From these and other observations we learn that the psychotic—a waking dreamer to Freud—is experiencing an unpeeling of the final phase of externalization, either because of a weakening of (the effects of) sensory constraints or their overcoming by a strengthening of pre-object phases. In the half-wake, half-dream experience of psychosis, the individual lives in the transition from image to object.

A similar effect occurs with music. I can be humming or singing a melody, an aria or piece of pure music, which passes to an auditory image that is invariably more detailed and comprehensive than the vocalization. The music heard in the head is not only more complete and accurate, it is disrupted by further vocal attempts. When an aria is heard, it can be only the music or the voice of a specific opera singer. These observations indicate a fluid transformation of the image—visual or verbal—from voluntary to involuntary and from inner to outer. Other transitional phenomena include snow blindness and sensory deprivation, when the waking individual loses perceptual objects and develops hallucinations and features of oneiric thought. Perhaps the experience of a mirage in the desert is like this, with an endless, objectless landscape of sand and dunes. Lucid dreams also seem positioned between dream and perception. In phantom limb, the feeling (tactile or nociceptive) of a persistent limb overcomes visual certainty.

THE IMAGE OF THE WORLD

In the transition over imaginal substrates, the essential nature of perception is preserved. The pre-object infused by drive with affective feeling develops out of the knowledge base, constrained by sensation in brainstem to a preliminary construct and subjective aim, together with revived memory contents of fading objects to actualize as an external world articulated by sensation to a multiplicity of distinct objects (images). Though the subjective quality of the image is lost in the objectivity of perception, the roots of the object in mind and mental imagery are exposed in a variety of altered states and transitional phenomena.

In dream, the imaginary is the limit of experience, like the air over a fish in water. In perception, the world is the totality of the direct experience, though a higher level of image production has been postulated, a noosphere, which is more a belief or act of faith than an outcome of reason or a result of experience. The world beyond perception is the reality toward which it aims, though the immediate correlate of the world is the brain state through which it is generated. The film of an illusory world does not obscure or lie over reality, but refers to a brain state, particularly the terminal phase of object-creation, which gives an alternate or parallel image that partitions and adapts through sensation received from external entities, impacting the brain to mimic them. In this way, a psychic world is elaborated that allows the observer to navigate the actual world of nature.

The situation resembles stepping into a film, as in the Woody Allen movie, and feeling quite at home—except that the observer is generating the film, and the adaptation to the image is independent of the world as it actually is, in nature. The image of the world is in the brain; the world that corresponds to that image is around us. How does a replica of the world in the brain somehow map to a reality that is independent of brain activity? That is, how does an individual adapt to entities in nature from a picture of the world generated in the brain?

The mind of the observer perceives a world that is detached from its representation inside the head, like a dream that corresponds to the world "out there". Yet the perceived world of waking consciousness is an imaginary replication that except for external stimuli, is distinct from the reality it represents. Moreover, it is well to keep in mind that the only direct information we have from reality consists not in the object itself, but in the sensations that model an emerging image; and even this is inferred from the presumed effects of the object on the brain and the receptors that parse this information, all with the goal of creating a model of the world that is so accurate, as judged by experience and survival, that only philosophical speculation supported by occasional cracks in the mirror of objectivity induce us, occasionally, to question the reality of direct perception.

Many philosophers would argue that even the weak form of solipsism inherent in this account is an irrefutable, if untenable, point of view, but the belief in a real world is motivated not only by the need to preserve sanity and satisfy common sense, and abide by the incredulity of an absolute idealism faced with the astonishing creativity of nature, but also because individuals are not killed by imaginary cars, eaten by phenomenal tigers, or stricken by illusory illnesses. Yet there is truth to be found here, in that each person, and every organism, from the lowliest to the most advanced, elaborates a personal Umwelt that contains a multitude of other organisms and objects. The organism is aware of, or responds to, an environment, whether olfactory, sonar, tactile, visual etc. that anticipates human mind, which also creates a capsule of a personal yet shared environment. Consciousness and the present—a self that is aware of objects and mental events—give an impression of a conscious theater, with the individual as a private audience and a world that is distinct from the organism.

When we turn our head or move our eyes from side to side, or in spontaneous oscillations of the eyes, or in the involuntary eye movements of nystagmus, the world remains stable. This is attributed to mechanisms that cancel the eye movements. This is not the case when we tap our eyes and the world shifts in the opposing direction. Are there comparable mechanisms that suppress the image for the object, and/or shift the imagery of representation to the physical world with which it is correlated? Since a strict mind/world boundary is necessary to survive and to cope, there may be mechanisms that abruptly sever the thread of image development the instant it is analyzed and externalized by sensation. This would be like stepping from the film in one's head to the reality that the film models. However, we are situated in the actual world, so the mental image we form of the world will naturally coincide with the entities that give rise to it.

3

Microgenesis and Psychoanalysis[1]

SUMMARY

PSYCHOANALYSIS (PSA) AND MICROGENESIS (MG) are both theories of the intra-psychic structure of the mind, based on the interpretation of clinical errors or symptoms: neurosis in PSA, organic brain pathology in MG. Some of the main principles of each theory are compared and contrasted; specifically, the nature of the unconscious (Ucs), the drives and the concept of repression. The focus in MG is on restricted categories, such as word or object-development, while that of PSA is on more complex behaviors. Both theories are retrospective in their explanations of psychic phenomena: the effects of early childhood on adult neurosis are central for PSA, while MG focuses on the antecedents of the final outcomes of a mental state. For PSA, the past is present as a childhood fantasy or trauma. In MG, errors are the key to micro-temporal process as realization of the self. PSA entails association and interaction, where MG emphasizes continuities and recurrence. Perception is the linchpin of MG as repression is the foundation of PSA. While the theory of repression is vulnerable to many criticisms, it can be assimilated to the concept of elimination of maladaptive form in phyletic, ontogenetic and microgenetic process.

1. Brown, J. (1998) Psychoanalysis and process theory, in: Bilder, R. and LeFever, F. (Eds) *Neuroscience of the Mind: Centennial of Freud's Project.*, Annals of the New York Academy of Science 4:91–106. See recent review of MG in Pachalska, M., MacQueen, B. and Cielbak, K. (2018) The creative potential of microgenetic theory. *Acta Neuropsychologica* 16:125–155.

GENERAL REMARKS

This chapter compares two theories of mind: psychoanalysis (PSA) and microgenesis (MG). The aim of this discussion is to demonstrate the contributions made to mind/brain theory by both accounts, their differences and limitations, and areas for future study. Both theories have much in common, beginning with their origin in clinical observation; in PSA, neurotic symptoms are central, while MG focuses on the effects of brain damage on behavior. Both theories also share the view that symptoms are not additions to behavior, but the uncovering of deeper strata that reveal the substructure of normal process. MG and PSA are both theories of the unconscious (Ucs) that are strictly intra-psychic. In both, there is an emphasis on drive and its derivation to affects, and also, at least in early Freud, a progression from the Ucs through preconscious (Pcs) to consciousness (Csness). There are, however, many important differences as well; indeed, in many respects the theories are orthogonal. Moreover, unlike MG, PSA provides a modality of treatment to ameliorate the symptoms.

First, however, I will discuss some foundational principles of each theory. My aim here is not to critique PSA, but rather to give an overview of the main features of the theory, so as to compare the foundational concepts with those of MG and let the reader decide as to their soundness and compatibility.

PSA

Though it has weathered many critiques from the early days of Freud's work to the present, PSA has managed to survive as perhaps the only comprehensive theory of mind elaborated over the past century. There have been many attempts to discredit the theory, mostly on extraneous details, contradictory assumptions, even events in the life of its author, but the foundations of PSA continue to inspire extreme reactions, whether devotion and belief or incredulity and rejection. However, I would argue that many of the seminal insights of PSA, even those of questionable validity, have not been seriously refuted. There have also been attempts to shore up the legitimacy of the theory by relating it to academic psychology (Rappaport, Schilder) and, more recently, to neuroscience (Solms). Yet the lack of an alternative theory of the structure of mind in contemporary psychology, and general unfamiliarity with the fundamental concepts of PSA, along with the prevailing view that these concerns are of little relevance to clinical practice, have assured that

PSA will remain the dominant theory of the Ucs until a fuller understanding of mental process is achieved.

Some of the most common complaints against PSA include the following:

- the diversity of maturational outcome from similar or comparable early traumas;

- the dubious therapeutic value of insight compared to suggestibility;

- the multiple—even opposing—symptoms postulated from the same construct (for example resistance and its opposite in perversion, or masochism as ego-directed sadism);

- lack of independent verification and reliance on the analysand to confirm the insights of the analyst.

Since the explanatory constructs of PSA are based on putative universal principles applied to a wide diversity of particular cases, they tend to be formulaic, examples of which include:

- childhood sexual trauma or fantasy;

- allocation and attachment (cathexis) of libidinal energy;

- de-cathexis arising in different mental compartments;

- *ad hoc* postulates, such as anti-cathexis for persistent repression;

- the relation of libido to ideas (drive representations), perceptual images and memories;

- transitional events in the passage from Ucs to Cs;

- validation of dream analysis;

- the nature of resistance or repression in selective amnesia and its relation to ordinary forgetting and recall;

- various multi-purpose devices (such as transference) that are routine in psychoanalytical accounts of neurotic symptoms and their treatment.

In spite of these and other limitations, PSA is an extraordinary body of work, with critics left to chip away at an edifice that, in its expansiveness and intricacy, has withstood numerous assaults.

Freud's theory began with studies of hysteria and conversion symptoms, when he worked with Charcot and Breuer. Charcot studied *la grande hystérie* in relation to organic factors; Breuer's approach was from the standpoint of hypnosis. Freud departed from these approaches, focusing instead on what might be called *la petite hystérie*, that is, partial hysterical or conversion symptoms with a sexual origin, independent of brain structure or function. Breuer's hypnotic cathartic method was replaced by free association, though catharsis, or the salutary discharge of Ucs content into Csness, remained a primary ingredient and the basis of recovery.

PSA offers a theory of neurotic defects or personality disorders, not the nature of the psychological functions upon which the interaction with mental faculties depends. That is, there is no clear account of memory, perception or language apart from descriptions of the effects of cathexis or its opposite on verbal, visual or memory-based imagery. Without a dynamic theory of the brain, efforts to correlate PSA concepts with brain regions or chemistry have had little impact on the theory as a whole, since the modularity of current neuropsychological research shaves away complexity to reduce variables.

The selectivity with which the notion of cathexis or de-cathexis is applied to sexual drive does not allow PSA to address the problem that only a fraction of Ucs potential or experiential memory is revived to Csness. If sexual traumas are repressed, what accounts for general and selective forgetting or recall of non-sexual material? Further, intense affect or libidinal investment in a memory can bring it vividly to Csness, or, on PSA theory, accentuate repression or censorship that keeps it confined to the Ucs.

MG

MG also developed from the study of symptoms, not neurotic disorders or personality defects, but the clinical symptoms of focal brain damage. In this respect, the symptom was never severed from the correlated brain area. Still, MG is a dynamic psychology that maps to a processual concept of brain activity, as opposed to the structural diagrams preferred by standard neuropsychology. As discussed in the previous chapter, this was initially achieved by correlating the actualization of mental contents with stages in the evolutionary growth of the forebrain, such that micro-temporal transitions in cognition corresponded to macro-temporal growth trends in phylogeny. The derivation of an act of cognition in micro-temporal process retraces the direction of forebrain growth in evolution. The resolution of microgenetic and phylogenetic patterns with morphogenetic growth (ontogeny) came later in a further analysis of the symptom. By contrast, though Freud was influenced by the brain studies of Hughlings Jackson, evolutionary concepts play a minor role in PSA.

Freud began with aphasic symptoms, which led to the idea of slips of the tongue, word-substitutions, word-forgetting and parapraxes (the

"Freudian slip"). Of interest here is that Freud was highly critical of Wernicke's assignment of specific brain functions to specific brain regions, and rightly so, but he managed only to substitute a theory of psychological association. In neurosis, according to Freud, neurotic symptoms point to the conflict between the ego and unwanted sexual impulses. MG also began with aphasic errors, but related them to submerged phases in normal language production. The relations in meaning between target words and errors (for example, saying "chair" or "throne" for "table") reflect the categorical background from which preliminary contents are elicited. This is the case at the word or object level. When errors occur over larger topics or contents, say at the inter-sentence level, as in cases of confabulation in Korsakoff amnesia or megalomania in tertiary syphilis, the meaning relations are less clear, the plausibility is uncertain, and the validity of the confabulatory discourse requires contextual clarification. Such cases show the relation of thought to memory, or belief to delusion, and are transitional to psychosis and dream content.

The nature of the error is critical. For PSA, an error or symptom points to a deeper (earlier or more archaic) source, generally the repression of a thought that is unacceptable to the individual or inconsistent with the main lines of his or her behavior. The thought is actively prevented from reaching Csness, but can influence behavior in its Ucs locus. Recovery is the discharge of Ucs content into Csness: that is, a kind of unblocking of the repressed idea. In MG, an error in language, perception etc. represents a focal retardation (neoteny) in micro-temporal process that is encountered again and again in each traversal. The fundamental operation in MG is a category/member transformation, which, when the normal transition is retarded, depending on the phase that is affected, accounts for how items related in meaning or other attributes emerge from deeper (wider) or more superficial (narrow) categories. The premature specification of antecedent categories gives the variation in symptom expression. The earlier the source of the error, the greater the role of feeling and the more inclusive the content. The prominence of sexual drive is a result of derailment early in the actualization in proximity to drive-based affect.

More generally, MG provides an account of many phenomena not discussed in PSA, including:

- a theory of the mind/brain state;
- the micro-transition from instinctual drive through successive mental segments to veridical perceptions;
- the relation of image to object or memory to perception;

- the formation of the self-concept in relation to the outer world as a phase in actualization and not, as with the ego, a separate faculty;
- the relation of psychotic symptoms to organic pathology;
- the transition from inner to outer and the reverse;
- the process of self-realization;
- the nature of the symptom, not as a regression but a neotenous retardation in relation to evolutionary and developmental process (which may or may not apply to symptom formation in neurosis);
- a theory of dream-forgetting,
- the basis of change and recurrence in relation to persistence and stability.

THE THEORIES COMPARED

After this very general outline of PSA and MG, we can now consider specific cognitive phenomena in relation to both theories.

1. Dream and the Ucs

In PSA, the Ucs is assumed to consist of interactive agencies, whose nature and activity are inferred from the study of neurosis; in MG, the Ucs is described in relation to a momentary and recurrent process of realization in language, memory, perception and action, the course of which is inferred from their disruption in focal brain damage. In both theories, there is a transition from Ucs to Csness in every act of cognition.

In PSA, there is no change in content in the transition of a perceptual or memory trace from Ucs to Csness, though various mental phenomena represent a difference in the point at which withdrawal of cathexis takes place (Pcs in transference neurosis, Ucs in schizophrenia). The difference seems to depend on the compartment from which cathexis is withdrawn. An image deposited in perception is identical to a memory image, which is cathected by libidinal drive energy to a drive representation or Ucs idea. This construct can remain Ucs or transition to a representation in Csness; that is, the perceptual image is deposited as a memory image unaltered from perceptual experience (the perception is the trace), and the trace may then undergo libidinal cathexis to an idea. On this view, contents in the Ucs are identical to those in Csness, except for the degree of accessibility according to the investment of sexual drive energy. Later, Freud developed a flashlight theory, in which Csness alights on particular contents in the Ucs and brings them to Csness. The point is that there is no transformation of content in the transition from Ucs to Csness, nor, on the later theory, a shift in locus, only an illumination by Csness of Ucs content. Freud did not explain how a Cs spotlight could locate the idea, since it is Ucs.

According to PSA, then, the mind consists of Cs and Ucs compartments, in which memory content enters Csness through the activation of libidinal drive energy, or remains submerged (repressed) if cathexis is withdrawn (de-cathexis). The assumption that most experience is tinged with sexual feeling expands the reach of libidinal energy to contents not ordinarily thought to be sexual. The evidence for this is derived from multiple sources, but is most emphatic in dream (below). The concept of cathexis as the basis of repression and recall developed on the synaptic theory of nerve cell interaction and a humeral or chemical transmission of libido to memory trace.

For MG, as we have seen, there is continuous transformation over phases in the progression to Csness. Perceptual images are not deposited as memory images; rather, the image is an incompletely revived perception. The original track of the object development constitutes the "trace" of the memory, which is ordinarily revived from one mental state to the next to a diminishing extent. The passage of a pre-object from early experiential (long-term) memory to recent (short-term) memory to perception, and the uncovering of this sequence over progressive revivals, reverses the sequence of standard theory. This differs from PSA, where perception is a passive event and recall, or its failure, depends on the energetics of arousal. Among the most problematic issues in PSA are these:

- the concept of selective repression, postulated without a theory of memory to support it;

- the basis of normal recall and forgetting independent of libidinal innervation;

- the extent to which cathexis and de-cathexis play a role in what is or is not recalled;

- the need for non-libidinal cathexis to account for the recall of self-preservative learning;

- the origin of libidinal energy in sexual drive and non-libidinal energy in the ego;

- the unclear necessity for the concept of repression to explain why contents do not surface, when in fact forgetting is a constant occurrence;

- more generally, how the inability to recall early sexual trauma or fantasy that leads to neurosis in adults relates to other forms of memory and forgetting.

For MG, early memories are not repressed because of their sexual content or symbolic value, but because they become the very fabric of the mind: these are the experiences that lay down the core beliefs and values of character, personality and the self-concept. An additional factor in the inability to recall early experience is state specificity. Around age 5, the latency period, the mentality of the child shifts to a more rational mode of cognition (Schactel), such that the dominant focus of early cognition cannot develop to a Cs level. That is, amnesia for early childhood is not due to shame attached to sexuality at a genital phase of development, but is a natural outcome of cognitive maturation with the adult unable to access most memories of early childhood, not just the sexual experiences.

According to MG, a perceptual object or word arises out of layers of drive, passes through object and/or lexical concepts and zeroes in on the fine phonological or featural detail. The formation of objects is an endogenous process with initial sensory constraints on upper brainstem shaping the pre-object, and massive constraints at visual cortex on an emerging gestalt that is specified and externalized into (as) the external world. Consistent with some philosophies (Bergson, Merleau-Ponty), the MG concept of perception is that of an intrinsic productive process, a continuous sheet of mentation from the instinctual core to perceptible reality, and not, as in PSA or conventional psychology, the passive reception of external stimuli that are stored and secondarily activated in relation to sexual drive.

The structure of the Ucs in MG is described in relation to antecedents in the derivation of the main sectors of cognition: perception, language and so on. The transformation from one segment to the next is inferred from clinical symptoms, which allow the alignment of errors as formative phases to reveal the path of object development. Early phases in perception are characterized by phenomena similar to those described in PSA in the dream work, though the process in MG differs from the cathartic theory of PSA. For MG, dream consists of pre-object contents that lack the final sculpting provided by external sensation. Except in dream, introspection, reverie, creative thought or pathology, the image does not ordinarily appear, since its substrate mediates a phase transitional to the object. Absent sensation, the development of the object terminates in mental imagery. A mental image is an incomplete object with distortion, according to the depth, origin, affective charge and degree of incompleteness. The contents of dream, whether close to reality or other-worldly, whether day-fragments or early memories, point to sub-surface modes of perceptual thought. These modes of preliminary cognition resemble some features of dream work, but they decant to varieties of whole/part relations, such as metaphor, paralogic and the elicitation of items from categories related by experience, meaning, function, shape, etc.

The shared properties of disparate objects or categories (von Domarus) determine the nature of the dream image, not necessarily as a clue to dysfunction in the sexual sphere, but as normal events preliminary in object formation. Creative thought in dream and wakefulness displays the same "mechanisms" as those attributed to the distortion of sexual drive. The coming-together of two lines of thought in creative ideation (Koestler) entails a connection of two topics or lines of thought based on a shared predicate. This is an example of category overlap that provides novelty in wakefulness and derailment in dream, regardless of its sexual nature. Imagination, creative thought, psychoses, etc., owe to categorical overlap and fusion based on shared properties. Thus, a syllogism such as, "Mary is a virgin/I am a virgin/I am the Virgin Mary", which is an example of psychotic thought, accounts for the identification of disparate individuals based on a partial resemblance. In effect, the property becomes a category that enfolds its subjects. The substitutions that occur in dream—the distortions, fusions and displacements—trace to a single process of whole/part or category/member relations, as an identification of otherwise unrelated categories by a shared predicate. A partial relation of one or more attributes, as in the example above, becomes the defining feature, thanks to which subjects are conceived as identical. Thus in dream, a knife can be a phallic symbol based on the shared properties of shape and penetration. An aphasic who names a guitar as bullfight or the color red as tomato makes the same error, but within a restricted lexical category.

For Freud, the snakes on Medusa's head and the hardness or turning to stone when they are perceived have a phallic significance. An instance in the category of reptiles (snakes) is identified with the male organ based on one or more shared properties. The same operation applies to the sea (depth, wetness) as a female symbol, or climbing stairs (exertion, fatigue) as a metaphor for sexual activity. Hysterical paralysis of a limb is interpreted in the same way: that is, phallic substitution as a self-protective symptom. However, this process also applies to a church bell substituted for an alarm clock in dream, or the overlap of non-sexual attributes: for example, Wagner's dream of the music for the Prelude to *Das Rheingold* in relation to the current, obscurity and ascent from the slow-moving deep waters of the

Ucs to the publicity, turbulence and speech or song at the Cs surface. We also see this relation in animistic thought, in the identification of a person with a tiger based on the common attributes of strength or ferocity, or, in Aboriginal populations, the correlation of an experience with a concurrent event to create a totemic object, for example, the quickening in pregnancy with the song of a bird or a crab carried to sea in the tide.

The point is that the non-sexual is not suppressed or distorted by anti-cathexis from the ego, but undergoes a metaphorical shift by way of the same process that applies to sexual content. When I was an army doctor I saw young men with hysterical or conversion symptoms, such as limb paralysis or blindness, due to intense combat. It was also not unusual to see displacement of instinctual reactions (Lorenz) such as falling asleep in battle. It is difficult to resolve such observations with the notion in PSA that hysterical symptoms (conversion reactions) are an expression of repressed sexual desires.

For PSA, the content of dream imagery is a compromise of wish fulfill-ment (drive-based need) and the censorship or defense (repression) that prevents Cs access. Interpretation of metaphorical substitutions in dream allows the discovery of Ucs or latent content from the manifest or Cs con-tent. For MG, dream content is imagery deposited in the normal process of object-formation exposed in the absence of initial and final sensory mod-eling. Sexual content is not blocked from Csness, but owes much to state specificity, preliminary cognition, and affective tonality, and undergoes distortion not unlike that for other memories. Yet there is little doubt that the continuum from selective amnesia to normal forgetting requires further elucidation.

This is not to say that painful experiences may be denied, selectively forgotten or otherwise unavailable to Csness, but that there is no agency to prevent Cs recall. The representation of repressed sexual ideation, to the ex-tent that it is real, is a magnification of normal forgetting, while derailments given a sexual interpretation are not dissimilar from other displacements in early cognition. Further, the investment of drive-energy, libidinal or other, is not all-or-none; it is not attached and withdrawn from traces or ideas, but it is ingredient in the categorical object the idea represents. Though the con-cept of repression has clinical utility, simplicity and appeal, it is more likely that the saliency of Ucs contents is a function of the affective and contextual relations to which they (like all mental contents) are bound. The affective accompaniment of all memories and ideas and their contextual relevance determine their accessibility.

One may reasonably ask: why does sexual trauma in childhood un-dergo expression in symbolic form, or recur as neurotic displacement, while similar trauma in the adult can be recollected with intensity? Is PTSD in the adult a symptomatic equivalent of sexual neurosis from childhood? Perhaps retrograde amnesia is a model for childhood forgetting. A harrowing experience may be hard to forget in adulthood, but if it occurs early in childhood, it is more likely not recalled because of the "entrapment" of the memory, as in a dream, or in a preliminary cognition that in childhood is the dominant form of the mental state. A real or imagined sexual trauma submerged in Ucs thought is buried like a hypnotic suggestion, a fugue state or bout of intoxication. Free association might, through chance activation by a partially-related category, lead to the arousal of the content in Csness. Another possibility is that early non-sexual trauma is sexualized in the analysis itself. If, as Freud quipped, a cigar can be just a cigar, what conditions allow for sexual interpretation? MG provides a general theory of recollection and forgetting in relation to resemblance in state recurrence and drive-based feeling, rather than, as in PSA, the blocking or unblocking of selective contents in the Ucs.

For PSA, the analysis of dream reports in the regression of Pre-conscious (Pcs) day residues to early cognition validated the interpretation of the source of conscious pathology. In sum, the attachment and withdrawal of cathexis in one mental compartment or another and the specificity of cathectic charge account for a variety of neurotic illnesses, as well as hallucinatory phenomena. For MG, hallucinations are attenuated perceptions that occur with diminished or absent sensation, or when the substrates of imagery are aroused. Hallucinations replace perceptions. One cannot hallucinate and perceive at the same time in the same locus of the visual field. Auditory hallucination, then, replaces auditory perception. In dream, hallucination combines perceptual imagery with content from memory; memories are incomplete perceptions. The revival of the memory image realizes a phase of dream-awareness. Distortion (fusion, substitution, etc.) is characteristic of early cognition.

2. Drives

In PSA, instincts are divided into sexual (libido) and ego (self-preservation, hunger). Over Freud's protests, Jung tried to unify libido as primal energy, which distributes into sexual and non-sexual contents. In either case, libido is conceived as circulating drive energy that becomes attached to (cathects) certain memory images. How drive-energy finds the memory image, or how the image attracts or lures the energy, is undetermined. Is childhood trauma painful because it is initially libidinally-charged? Does it remain painful once it is de-cathected, or by virtue of continuing anti-cathexis? In what sense is it painful, if it is Ucs? Why is it displaced to neurotic symptoms that may also be distressing? Is there a pool of affect that is individuated by the idea, or is libidinal energy specified into affects in advance? In what manner does drive energy circulate to find the corresponding trace? The main point is that PSA postulates an association between energy and trace, without any explanation as to how this comes about.

In MG, every act of cognition begins with instinctual drive, which is the affective tonality of a category or concept. The directional feeling of drive, its subjective aim, evolves from the non-directional energy of inorganic entities. Drive concentrates feeling in an object-category; the category is derived to the subjective aim of the drive as the frame of instinctual feeling. *Feeling and idea do not come together at some point; rather, they are part of the same construct from the beginning.* Initially, the primary drive is that of hunger, and its aggressive and defensive vectors. This is obvious in animals, where hunger and thirst, and their defensive reactions, are the daily motivations of behavior. Over time, this complex fractionates to sexual drive. In animals, hunger is primary and continuous; sexuality comes later and is periodic. In children, with the appearance of sexual drive, elements of hunger such as oral and anal phenomena—ingestion and evacuation—become sexualized. For PSA, defenses against the drives of the Oedipal complex appear at the genital stage of puberty, when they are revived in relation to sexual instinct.

For MG, hunger and sexuality are not parallel (ego, sexual) instincts, but develop in succession; drive categories are bound together with feeling from the onset. In both, what is need in the Ucs becomes desire in Csness. Hunger fractionates to sexual drive, which then partitions to desire and conceptual feeling. Hunger has its active and passive vectors, or aggression and defense, in predation. In behavior, hunger evolves to greed, ambition or gluttony for the aggressive direction, and timidity, fear and the like for the defensive vector. In the derivation to sexuality, predation and avoidance become pursuit and dominance or escape and submission, while sadism and masochism accentuate one of these directions. In a word, the sexual instinct individuates out of the hunger instinct, as many of the latter's features (oral, anal) become sexualized. Put differently, the "apparatus" dedicated to the hunger drive is employed—preserved and transformed—to adapt to the needs of the sexual drive, while the latter is pruned to desire and the variety of affects and ideas.

Thus, the construct of feeling and category in drive partitions to the desire and concept that accompany the development of an object. The feeling of desire is the affective charge; its object is the concept or category toward which the feeling is directed. The feeling combined with a pre-object develops to the value or worth of external objects. In MG, the transition from the instinctual core to the outer world is a becoming-into-being, in which feeling is becoming and category is being. Feeling and pre-object-concept differ at successive phases in the micro-transition: for example, food is the object of hunger; mating and copulation are the objects of sexuality; an absent object is the aim of desire, and the value of an external object carried out into the world. Central to MG, but not part of PSA, is the micro-temporal process that accounts for self—and object-realization. In MG, cognition is not an open-ended serial or causal chain, but an iterative sequence over phases. The initial drive of hunger and its self-preservative aspects (eat or be eaten) is essential to the recurrence of the organism. Food is energy for auto-replication. Sexual reproduction is proxy-replication. Hunger and sexuality sustain recurrence, hunger individually, sexuality through progeny.

3. Repression

Freud wrote, ". . . the doctrine of repression is the foundation-stone on which the whole structure of psycho-analysis rests."[2] I have written in a similar way regarding the theory of perception. Let us consider repression and its relation to MG. The difficulties involved with the concept of repression as the de-cathexis of inert traces have already been discussed. If we set aside the account in the metapsychology, and consider repression as selective inhibition, there is a relation to MG in the concept of sculpting, parcellation or pruning. The transition over phases in the mental state is an iterated process of qualitative specification, in which wholes or categories partition to member-items. This intra-psychic process of individuation is derived from the evolutionary process of elimination of unfit organisms; that is, the environmental sculpting of organisms corresponds to the morphogenetic process of parcellation, in which exuberant growth is trimmed to specificity. This pattern in phylogeny and ontogeny is replicated in the elicitation of items from background categories and the elimination of redundant, irrelevant or maladaptive alternatives. There is coherence and parsimony in this account, with a continuation of the same pattern in evolutionary growth repeated in maturation and the process of cognition.

For Freud, ". . . repression is essentially a process affecting ideas, on the border between the system Ucs and Pcs (Cs)." From the standpoint of MG, repression is an instance of selective inhibition at successive phases

---

2. Freud, S. (1924) *Collected Papers*, Vol. 1, *On the history of the psycho-analytic movement*. P. 297, Hogarth, London

in the realization of the mental state. The drives partition to the desires, which partition to object concepts and value. The "Cs veto" postulated in studies of pre-activation confirms that the sculpting that begins in the core of mind is repeated over phases, culminating in Csness and the world surface. The cascade of qualitative whole/part shifts leads to a final sculpting of pre-object gestalts into external objects at the sensory surface of the mental state. On this way of thinking, repression is analogous to the elimination of early maladaptive content.

If the repression of maladaptive content in the Ucs is an instance of suppression or inhibition related to pruning, the symptoms that trace from the submerged content would represent discharged ideas or behaviors that are symbolic or metaphorical equivalents of the inhibited content. However, it is difficult to see how neurotic symptoms, which can be disabling, would be less maladaptive than the repressed traces from which they are presumed to arise.

I have avoided discussion of the id, ego and superego, which are reminiscent of faculty psychology and as such, in my view, are largely indefensible. However, for MG the conscience or superego would correspond to the constraints of character and value that condition the mental state at its inception, and guide the process to actuality. Values are the moral attitudes that go into habitual acts, as well as conscious decisions. Conscience is not a conscious negation, but an effect of the parsing of unacceptable thoughts and acts due to constraints of early-instilled beliefs and values.

4

Illusion and Reality[1]

SUMMARY

THIS ESSAY CONTINUES THE discussion of the preceding sections, by exploring the relation of a mental representation of the world to the inferred physical reality it represents. The interpretation of perception as a mental image, and the world as an image in outer-mind, assumes a subjectivity inconsistent with 3rd person externalism and the reduction of mind to material process. The articulation of external space early in infancy through the effects of sensation, and the subsequent partition of inner mind to self and the consciousness of mental events (thoughts, feelings) by the sculpting of categories, seem to give precedence to the impact of an independent outer world on the shaping of the mind, while the phenomenal quality and intermittency of events in the inner world of the mind appear contingent and secondary.

INTRODUCTION

It is said, and I have said it as well, that all mental phenomena are illusory, but what does this actually mean? What are illusions and how do they relate to perception and reality? First, we can distinguish pathological illusions, such as those of delirium tremens in alcohol withdrawal, which show optical relations to the viewer: that is, they enlarge with increasing distance from the projection surface, and disappear with the eyes closed. Other illusions

1. See: Brown, J.W. (2004) *The illusory and the real. Mind and Matter* 2:37–59

caused by brain damage include micropsia and macropsia (objects getting smaller or larger), rotation, acceleration and deceleration. These changes differ from hallucinations or dreams, which occur with eyes closed and do not alter with projection distance, though they undergo spontaneous change in size and shape. Hallucinations are fully autochthonous and in- dependent of the world, with a content that is often multi-modal, involving experiential and meaning relations, while illusions involve object-relations and tend to be unique in terms of modality, with concealment or disruption of perceptual features. Some illusions that are perceived in the world—a stick in the water that appears to be bent, a rainbow, the horizon effect of a setting sun—we recognize as unreal, but are powerless to suspend by mental effort. One way to think of this distinction is that in object formation, the "physical" features of illusion—as well as eidetic and after-images—point to a dominant locus close to the perceptual surface, while the memory-based affective quality of hallucination points to a dominant locus at a greater depth. In the first case, the image is object-like; in the latter, memory-like. The difference between hallucination and illusion is the depth of the point of origin in the perceptual process.

The question is this: are hallucination and illusion structural features or perturbations of a perceptual process that actualizes a real world, or, regardless of the degree of realness, are they evidence that all perceptual and related phenomena are illusory? In a word, is the world of perception a grand illusion, the Maya of Indian philosophy, or are illusions a disruption, or necessary feature, of the perception of an actual physical world? If percep- tions are mental images that approximate reality, how are we to understand them? Is our picture of the world like a waking dream, which adapts through sensation to the momentary surround? If an illusion is recognized by lack of coherence within or across modalities, or lack of correspondence with external objects, what would suffice to conclude that ordinary perception— indeed, every mental event—is illusory? A thought seems real enough to the thinker, but its shifting and evanescent nature and insubstantiality erode confidence in it as a judgment of reality, at least until ideation transitions to speech or action; but then, to what reality are acts and objects compared to form a judgment as to their real or phenomenal status? What can we say of the correspondence of propositions to world events? If there is no reality to which we can appeal with certainty for verification, we are comparing one psychic phenomenon to another.

As previously discussed, the progression from hallucination to illusion exposes phases in object development from inner to outer, from a mental image to one that is fully external. Intra-psychic alterations or illusory effects cease at the point when the object externalizes and is part of public space.

At this point, any change in the image is perceived to occur in the object, not in the mind; that is, the nature of an alteration at successive segments in object development will depend on the depth of the uncovered segment: hallucination early, illusion later, and change in the external object once it is independent. If hallucination and illusion are exposed phases in the perceptual process, and if perception develops over segments that are revealed in hallucinatory and illusory phenomena, the process of image formation would approach externality in phases, with an outcome that is also a mental image, but one that has been fashioned by sensation to mirror reality. The world is a mental image at the endpoint of waking perception, and grows to an object out of the unreal images of dream, while illusory deformities of mental objects point to alterations at the final phase of externalization.

What is the alternative to this account? If the physical and mental features of objects are assembled in the brain, do we not still have to deal with a perceptual world that comes to exist "inside our head" and serves as a model or mirror of the physical world outside? Is the inner world constructed and then projected outward? Do we perceive the external world directly by means of perceptual processes? Do we perceive the internal model or its outward projection? These possibilities imply the perception of multiple worlds: one assembled in the brain; another projected outside; and yet another noumenal world that is inaccessible. In all instances, the world of perception is an image in mind/brain that can be termed illusory, because it is not physically real but corresponds to or approximates an inferred consensual reality. If a local illusion is a discrepancy between the mental and the perceptual, an illusion of the world would imply a discrepancy between perception and the physical world it represents.

For idealism, the non-existence or lack of direct knowledge of physical reality leaves perception in the status of an hallucinatory image without a knowable world as template or representation. For Berkeley, the world is an idea posited in god's mind. In Indian philosophy, the Brahma dreams a world for millions of years, awakes and the world disappears, and a new world begins when he closes his eyes and dreams another world. Yet in spite of the intuition of a subjective world, we are accustomed to scientific demonstrations of the properties of a physical world, even though it cannot be directly perceived and is inferred to approximate (but model) perception. The distinction between subjective and objective is reinforced by instrumentation and physical science, which can give a compelling account of extra-psychic events such as gravity, electricity, planetary motion, sonar or infrared, leading us to postulate that the world of science is identical to, though more deeply investigated than, the world of perception. Another way to think of these demonstrations is that they augment sensation to refine the perceptual model. They do not bypass illusion or increase access to the physical, but are aids to or extensions of perception, and thus continue to reflect its limitations.

For objectivist accounts, descriptions of behavior that are imaginatively positioned outside the mind still enlist the subjectivity of the observer to record acts of mind-external in others. The subjectivity of the other who is being observed, when denied by the observer, cannot fail to influence the presumed objectivity of the observer's descriptions, including theoretical bias, truth claims and so on. Put differently, the externalist brings his own subjectivity to bear on a description of other minds, the subjectivity of which is ignored. Any distinction between purposeful, intentional and/or freely decided acts is thus obscured in a strict externalism, including the mental events that precede a behavior. Indeed, the entire process of thought and object development, or the becoming of intra—and extra-personal phenomena, is erased by a fully objectivist stance, while the description of others depends on subjective features of the observer's mind that permeate his objectivism. This approach is based on a materialism that reduces all aspects of mind to brain activity. In the identification with brain, mind is eliminated or treated as epiphenomenal, such that its inner workings—the dynamic infrastructure of thought, action and perception—are irrelevant to its output. The elimination of the mental also disposes of the problem of illusion, since the perceptible world is not conceived as a product of mind but as real and independent.

THE SIGNIFICANCE OF ILLUSION

Our image of the world is so close to physical reality—otherwise, we would not survive—that the question as to whether or not perception is illusory, in its very nature, has little practical import. This is the assumption of the externalist, though it engenders many philosophical problems. When he was near death, Kant, who had consolidated Plato's distinction of image and reality, was said to have suffered from hallucinations of insects on his body (vermification), and his terror was doubtless not mollified by his knowledge that they were unreal. If the world is a conceptual model shaped by sensation to veridicality—that is, if perceptual objects map to real entities—the formation of a perceptual image might well accompany the insertion into the physical of psychic ingredients, either because they are necessary to the perception of the world, or because they serve as accessories to make life meaningful. Certain of these features no doubt evolved because they are essential to the elaboration of mental objects and thus sustain life. This includes the exportation of purposefulness, consciousness, value and meaning into the outer world. For example, value as intra-psychic feeling is bound up with the aims of drive and the objects of desire, but it accompanies the image or pre-object outward to settle in the object as worth. The problem arises: at what point and with respect to what properties can we separate out the psychic excess or distortion in perception, or the infusion of the external with subjectivity, from a putative reality that is mind-independent?

Ordinarily, the physical refers to the material composition of organisms or complex systems by more elementary or basic elements. In theory, organic systems can be decomposed to constituents and then reconstructed to the original system. The difficulty occurs at both ends of the scale. In the human mind, many phenomena are not explicable on a physical basis, such as beauty, justice, intentionality and meaning, nor are proto-psychic features inherent in elementary entities or the objects of microphysics. Generally, the more basic the physical entity, the more hypothetical or inferential its status. Indeed, perplexities in quantum physics that suggest dependence on an observer imply that subjectivity is at play even on the most basic level.

How do mind and behavior fit into this picture? In order to safely navigate the world, the past—not conscious recollection but the assimilated past of experience, learning and memory—must invade perception, minimally, for object-recognition, awareness, category-formation and value. We conceive these qualities as psychic in origin and not part of the physical world, but is this entirely the case? We can demonstrate drive-categories in the brains of primitive organisms that are part of physical nature, such as things to eat and situations to avoid, while categories in animals are sufficiently plastic to adapt to changing conditions, such as objects not edible in times of plenty that become edible in times of scarcity.

Some mental phenomena, such as consciousness and the desire for absent objects, do not have obvious correlates in the world (though there are precursors), and their influence in the world is unpredictable. What we take to be mental values are commonly reduced to physical effects and interpreted as the output of mechanical, computational or robotic systems. On a process view, however, conceptual and affective features permeate object formation and are exported to mind-external. These features may not be ingredient in the physical nature of the object, though precursors can be identified that prefigure the psychic contribution to a representation of the real. In the human mind, such additions or distortions to the psychic mirror—love, meaning—give focus and significance to life. In this respect, the model is richer than what it represents. But unless the model—the illusion of reality—is fully explanatory on a physical basis, where does mind leave off and reality begin? That is, if the proto-psychic is essential to physical nature, how can we separate the mental contribution to phenomena such as object-stability, valuation, coping strategies, social cohesion and the belief in outer reality from a world that is illusory and mind-dependent?

In some religions and philosophies, an insight into the surplus that psyche brings to perception, especially desire and concepts, has led to a doctrine of self-denial and disavowal of the psychic contribution. If desire is a derivative of drive, with value the continuation of feeling into objects, and if concepts are the categories through which objects actualize, the relinquishment of concepts and desires would strip objects of mentation, and lay bare the actual world through direct contact with the real. Even if this were possible, it would not be enlightenment but suicide, since the cognitive process is a transition over concepts or categories with a parcellation of wholes to parts. To relinquish concepts entails an arrest of the becoming, both of the observer and his world. There is an irony here, in that the search for knowledge of an absolute or extra-psychic reality is itself quixotic, if not illusory, since the elimination of what is supplementary—the illusory veil that obscures the real world—also eliminates the structure and process through which the world is perceived. The feeling that goes into the world as value, the meaning that goes outward as purpose or signification, the categories that bundle experience into relational configurations, are obligatory features of perception, without which we would not even be part of a nature that exhibits these attributes. Moreover, as the outer world appears real even to those who believe it to be illusory, what is the guarantee that a confrontation with physical reality or a mystical descent to oneness with nature is not just another illusion?

The central question is this: if physical reality consists in micro-physics, superstrings and the physical attributes of inorganic entities, to what extent can this account for more advanced organisms? Surely viruses, unicellular organisms, slime mold, vegetation and primitive life forms are part of physical nature, but what of actions guided by purpose in a purposeless universe? What of maternal and other instincts, individual and social behaviors, problem-solving and creativity? How are these guided by physical laws? Teleology and final cause have been excised from evolutionary biology as inconsistent with material process, but these are things that figure importantly in the behavior of higher animals, certainly Homo sapiens, as evolution follows a path to successively higher and more complex forms.

PHYSICAL AND MENTAL

It is beyond argument that the physical world includes proto-psychic features intrinsic to nature that evolve to complex phenomena in higher organisms. The question is, what are those features and in what way do they exhibit attributes of mentality? This is not pan-psychism, but an openness to the possibility that certain features of basic entities expand in the organism to account for the origins and evolution of life, as well as the continuity from physical to mental and the growth of complexity. Among these features are energy and the process of becoming. Most would also agree that isotropic energy is a core ingredient of physical reality. The evolution of energy in organic forms to anisotropic or unidirectional feeling, that is, to becoming and subjective aim, might still qualify as physical process. If primitive feeling evolves to drive or will and associated behaviors, at what point does the explanation depart from a purely physical description? To the extent that behavior is generated by a nervous system, the physical reactions that constitute behavior, excluding the mental correlates through which the function of brain is understood, can be conceived as part of reality, at least until the stage of conscious mind, which is problematic, to say the least, in terms of physical law.

Is a comprehensive account of a living organism by physics even possible? Partly, this depends on establishing proto-psychic features at the most elementary stage, and partly in replacing causation with a model of becoming that is conceptualized as a relation of potential to actual. If change is not a causal passage from one state to the next, but involves the becoming of entities and their replacement, could we still maintain that only behavior grounded in causation is explicable in terms of physical science? The boundary that would divide a presumably naked entity, a "purely" physical object, from an object that is mind-dependent is less definite than it is often assumed to be.

If we invert the question and ask how closely a physical entity maps to a mental object, beginning with the material "building blocks" of complex entities, how far can one go without invoking subjective qualities; rather, at what point of complexity does a description of a brain or nervous system fail to account for mental states? As mind is a realization of process in nature, properties of mind as evolutionary outcomes must be grounded in physical process, which implies that attributes of proto-mind are ingredient in nature, and not that attributes are merely appended to substances that lack inherent proto-psychic features, which would be, at least in my view, fictitious. The point is this, that if we begin with mind we cannot descend to physical process without a substantial psychic remainder, and if we begin, hypothetically, with material process, say the laws of physics, we cannot account for the development of mind. A reduction or identification of mind to brain or to gene is a facile maneuver with little explanatory power, especially since mind cannot be reconstituted from the lower level.

Consider the duration of the present moment in the human mind. The present presumably does not exist in nature, but it is unlikely to have arisen without evolutionary precursors. If we accept, following Whitehead, that all entities need to have a minimal duration to complete one cycle of becoming, then the duration of that one cycle could be undergoing expansion over the mammalian series. When the duration is that of a human mind/brain state, a Rubicon is crossed and a present is possible. If all entities consist in a becoming-into-being, the envelope over which the entity becomes is a category that encloses ingredients that are virtual until the epoch actualizes. This envelope is a categorical frame through which categories individuate to parts or members. The specification of categories is equivalent to the relation of duration to instant, or the present to the events it encloses. Here, a property of basic entities evolves into an illusory feature of the human mind.

A phenomenal present in man that develops out of the duration of becoming in other organisms or physical entities allows the eventual liberation of organism from an earlier/later succession of mental simultaneities to a temporally-ordered series, in which the just-before is observer to the just-after, within a now that encloses "before" and "after" in a conscious moment, the "now." The passage from onset to termination of the mental state, or from potential to actual, is a before/after or earlier/later series that, on completion, elaborates a present in which, over a series of states, the earlier is witness to the later. In effect, the simultaneity of the transition to actuality becomes a relation of past to present (the past within the state is the core of the self, the after is an object or conscious content), which is felt as a succession in time. The self is experienced as the recipient of its own objects, and as antecedent to choice and action. This requires a "now" in which antecedent and consequent have a virtual separation, giving a self that is prior to choice, though self and choice are embedded in the same state. In the shift from simultaneity to temporal order, segments are felt as successive, with agency (attributed to the self as antecedent) having a causal influence on consequent phases that actualize in the same series.

Features of human mentation, such as consciousness and intentionality, represent a further development of animal awareness and purposeful behavior. Immediate awareness becomes consciousness-of when duration permits a distinction of self and object, or a perceived relation of inner and outer mind. The intentional represents the arc from self as observer to image or object as subjective aim. The "about-ness" of the intentional is this trajectory, given over to deliberation. As to feeling, drive has a subjective aim and, like desire, is for objects in the future, though in stalking a prey, or searching for shelter, the animal is presumably not conscious of the aim, but is motivated by drive and guided by sensation. Desire depends on imagination, thus pre-object imagery. As previously explained, the course of feeling runs from there in tandem with the formation of the object.

THE ARCHITECTURE OF THE SUBJECTIVE

A naïve realism that holds the outer world to be a perception of objective nature follows a machine theory of mentality. Such a theory, in the attempt to be quantitative, ignores the diachronic or retrospective history through which the perceived world actualizes. But how would an objective world first develop out of the subjectivity of inner mind? What is the course of object formation in the infant, and what can we learn from this of the subject/object divide? Presumably, the extra-personal portion of the infant's subjectivity initially incorporates the breast (or nutrient object) centered in bodily space. This subjective field is gradually punctuated by other objects, which begins to articulate a proximate spatial field that extends to the limb perimeter, finally to a fully extra-personal field. Consistent with the rapid individuation of the world in animals and the presumed absence of an interior life, the articulation of the outer field occurs early in life and precedes the partition of mind-internal.

Over years, the generalized or diffuse subjectivity of mind-internal, unaided by sensation, also undergoes an articulation that individuates a self that is conscious of objects, thoughts and feelings. The expansion and specification of the outer field is propelled by adaptive necessity and sensation; the inner field, unique to human mentation, individuates by endogenous sculpting. Over time, there is a coalescence of self and a discovery of introspection. It may be that the recurrence over successive states of the deep structure of character, along with the iteration of drive categories and consolidation of personal identity through habit and repetition, configures a self-concept that embodies core beliefs, values and dispositions. In sum, first there is immediate awareness of objects and activity; then consciousness of the outer world; then over time the inner field partitions to a self in relation to introspective content: inner speech, spatial thought and visualization.

The priority and rapid development of the outer field reinforce the sense of object-independence. The growth of the field from bodily space to the boundary of limb action (the space of the congenitally blind), and then to an external space that seems endless, illustrates the expansion of a subjective field outward from the observer. The space of perception is not simply "out there" waiting to be perceived, but develops from the body outward in the course of maturation. The early specification of objects in the outer field, which is essential for survival, replicates the pattern of animal perception. The specification of the self within human mind, along with the sense of personhood and consciousness of introspective content, arise as neotenous retardations of pre-terminal phases.

The pattern of rapid articulation of mind-external in animals continues in human infants. Animal and child awareness are roughly similar (Piaget). To paraphrase Kant, a new world appears with the "I" when object-awareness develops to a consciousness-of that is distinct from mere animal awareness. Gradually, the distinction of subject and object grows to a subjective contrast of self and mental content in the context of consciousness of an object world. With a feeling of agency, the self assumes responsibility for its acts and decisions and, to a lesser extent, its images and options. Though decision and action are implementations of the self, the self has a limited sense of responsibility for images (that is, these are "my" thoughts, though I may not feel responsible for generating them), and none for objects (that is, when I see a dog, I do not usually think of this as "my" perception of a dog, but rather attribute the causality of the percept to its real presence in the world).

Agency is bound up with intentionality, with interest that is directed to an object or idea. While the imagination can range freely, and is not often felt as self-initiated, still, in the narrowing down of choice to decision, contingency shifts to a subjective aim and sharpens the focus of volition. The sense of control requires partition to a definite aim. The progression to definiteness over a multitude of replications narrows the scope of self-actualization, with each realization a compromise of possibility and exactness. In contrast, awareness in very young children is without a self that is conscious of inner-mind, or even conscious of immediate object-awareness. A baseline awareness of objects is continuously present in normal waking adults. The self is also conscious of perceiving objects, but the consciousness of introspective content is a developed capacity, unequally distributed in the population, perhaps less prevalent in the action-oriented and more pronounced in those with a contemplative attitude.

ILLUSION AND THE SELF

Self is the enemy of self (Manjusri). Consistent with Buddhist thought, one should rather say the self is the enemy of non-self. The Anatman doctrine of non-self has been critiqued elsewhere; here we consider the fact that each instance of self, or the category of interwoven self-realizations, negates the potential for a range of other expressions. A commitment to a self-of-occasion is a bias to a certain outcome. A self that is pacific or aggressive, timid or ambitious, will usually forecast the outcome and eventuate in acts that are consistent with these attributes. Moreover, each manifestation of self is often in tacit conflict with other potential selves or agencies that may well conceal a deeper unity, perhaps a more genuine and generic self-concept, possibly one closer to its roots in drive and the animal inheritance. The self, as an amalgam of values and beliefs, arises out of the core. Mystical descent to the foundations of the self may not always result in a beatific vision, but rather in an encounter with the rudiments of an egocentric core, which can give an experience that can be enlightening, terrifying or repellant. One interpretation of the myth of Perseus and the Gorgon Medusa (according to which Perseus was advised by Athena to gaze at the Medusa only in reflection in his shield, to avoid being turned into stone by her gaze) is that perception is a mirror of reality, which is deadly when it is perceived directly. The meaning is that direct confrontation with physical matter is only possible in the dissolution of mind, its petrification, the end of all process. Thus, in a similar vein, Schiller wrote that knowledge must be death.

Can we examine the self apart from the needs, desires, values and beliefs that inhere in every act, or the attributes of traits left behind in each new arising? Recurrent patterns of self-implementation reinforce certain expressions of self, while others are subdued or erased in repeated instantiations. The lost potential in the self-of-occasion is the ground of regret in later life, nostalgia for what might have been, dissatisfaction that the full potential of the self was not adequately exploited. The world shapes the finalities of self-expression, but self-expression can, to an extent, shape the world. Still, the search for authenticity and contact with a sphere beyond the ordinary explains the retreat from mind-external, in order to access the potential of inner mind. To surrender the dominant or quotidian self in the expectation of greater insight into personhood is to explore the possibilities of alternative modes of self-expression and discover the limits of self-renewal.

The presence of a self is relatively uniform in waking life, but consciousness of self is intermittent, while consciousness of mental content is mostly infrequent. Unlike the incessant confrontation with the world, the consciousness of self and waking images is largely a potential resource that arises when there is obstruction or difficulty in spontaneous action, or in states of reverie or creative thought. As an instance of possibility, the self as observer explains the futility of self-description beyond the sum of its replications. For self-description, the self must not only describe itself in the act of describing but describe the ground out of which the self develops. Yet the self is not the totality of identity. Selves that are unborn, selves bypassed or inhibited, those disavowed or obscured in succeeding revivals, along with the thoughts, images and hopes that flow from the momentary self-concept, are also descriptors of character and personality. There are many instantiations of self but one realization of the world, excluding worlds unseen or parallel universes. The objects of mind-external follow a course independent of the self, even if the self is an agent for some of the images that precede the object world. That is, segments of choice or decision are not instigators but conduits for an agency that derives from earlier segments.

If the world arises from the self, an illusory self would give an illusory world. On the other hand, if the self is real, the world cannot be illusory, but an objective world does not require a real self as observer. We know from pathological studies that the self will not survive if the world is lost. If the world disappears in a state of pure subjectivity limited to inner-mind, as in deep meditation, the self will also be lost, especially if the state is prolonged. If one falls into the well of world-negation, the self is lost if the world is not soon regained.

WHAT DIFFERENCE DOES IT MAKE?

The value of pathology lies in the dissection and uncovering of submerged or unconscious pre-processing phases in the actualization of perception. This allows an alignment of phases and corresponding brain regions to re-capture the sequence of normal segments in object development. Based on such findings, as we have seen so far, the dynamic infrastructure of percep-tion can be described as a recurrent process of self and world creation over stages in the evolution of forebrain, leading in a continuous sheet of menta-tion from instinct at the physiological core through the subjectivity of self and thought to an external and ostensibly independent world. There seems little doubt that the world of perception is the outcome of an endogenous process in which memory, conceptual feeling, value and meaning infiltrate a gestalt-like configuration, which undergoes a final adaptive specification to reality by the sensory trimming of irrelevancy. The momentary outcome, then, is a fairly exact model or representation of the middle-sized objects that constitute the daily environment.

The transmission of feeling, concepts and memory into the model, along with consciousness of objects and an intentional relation to inner and outer content, may be additions to physical reality that increase but do not appear to materially alter the ability of the organism to navigate and survive in a threatening environment. This implies that the mental representation of reality—the niche filled by the organism—must be a close approximation to an essentially unknowable world of physical process, *die Dinge an sich*. The question is, if the perceptual world is illusory, that is, if it is a subjective model of outer reality, what aspects of cognition genuinely reflect physical reality, and what would a perception of the world be like if mental qualities are subtracted from that which physical reality supplies?

Any epistemology has ontological consequences. If the ultimate constituents of reality are not things, substances, being, but processes of becoming, that is, a relational and not atomic ground, such an account of physical nature will run through all of its evolved manifestations. The higher aspects of human mentality can be described in relational terms. Awareness is a subject/object relation. Consciousness and intentionality entail the relation of self to objects or mental contents. Meaning exists in the relation among words or images within or across categories, which are also relational groupings, which is to say, members in a category are inter-related by way of shared predicates or attributes. The partition of wholes entails a relation of parts to antecedent contexts. The relation is not just between parts; rather, process theory (unlike atomic theories, which postulate causal relations, i.e. forces, operating between objects, conceived as stochastic solids) entails a relation of potential to actual within the object itself, with relationality residing in the actualization, not in the final object, which perishes on achieving actuality.

If we conceive the most elementary particles as processes or relations, and likewise their derivations to the highest level, the question then becomes, what is the nature of a reality that consists of relations, not things, and what is the nature of a mind that mirrors the relational quality of the world? If there is no solid foundation to the physical or mental, if mental objects are, in Bergson's words, "logical solids", or if, as Whitehead put it, "process is reality," the illusion of the world is not just the perceptual screen or surrogate of the physical world, but the process of category-formation and the derivation to an epoch of actuality that constitutes an object or entity.

The primary activity of mind is the elaboration of categories and their specification to acts, objects and words. The category stabilizes the object over successive occasions and maintains its identity across instances of continuous change. If the contents of mind are the derivations of categories, and are themselves resting points in an ascent or regress of whole/part relations—between the super-ordinate and sub-ordinate—and if sameness is not an attribute of self or object but depends on objects belonging to the same category, the appearance of reality as a collection of mostly solid objects is not the reality of its intrinsic nature. The objects of perception are unreal, in this sense, that they are models of reality and present as solids composed of smaller solids, while their true nature as momentary instances in category realization is imperceptible. That is, if the primary illusion is the mental representation of the world, the secondary illusion is the solid foundation of nature and the invisibility of the relational quality of mind and the physical world.

The illusory veil is transparent, imperceptible: (1) because of the exactness of its fit to physical nature, (2) because the extra-personal is felt as extra-psychic, (3) because of the sharp divide between subject and object, mind and world, (4) because the perceptual events in illusions and dreams are interpreted as distortions of real perception, not as something ingredient in all psychic images, (5) because transition in the object is stabilized and rendered invisible by the persistence of the category, (6) because the penetration of the physical by mind is largely inconsequential for ordinary life, and (7) because the physical world is not an aggregate of inanimate elements, but exhibits properties that anticipate human mentality.

The contextual or relational aspect of all mental content develops out of precursors in the most elementary entities. As energy develops to feeling, feeling develops to drive and desire, to constitute the becoming of objects and organisms. There is a parallel evolution from the periodicity of basic entities to the duration necessary for an occasion of existence, as well as the duration of category formation and the cascade of specification eventuating in the duration of a present that enfolds consciousness-of, introspection and agency. That is, the duration of the present traces back to the periodicity of ancestral physical entities. Consciousness, meaning, value, choice, all depend on categories. There are no entities at an instant. Feeling is the becoming of an entity, category is the substance. Put differently, category is the being that feeling becomes. These features do not appear de novo in the human mind, but are realizations of process in physical nature, and form a consistent pattern over the evolutionary sequence. Features of human mentality are not emergent aspects of a physical nature that lacks psychic attributes, but are the consequence of evolutionary forerunners that exhibit proto-psychic features; in this respect, such features are as much a part of nature as their predecessors.

Insight into the illusory nature of mind and perception depends on the acquisition of attributes that are the natural progression of evolutionary process, as much a part of nature as the "tooth and claw" of Darwinian theory. The features of human cognition engaged in questioning our perception of nature are themselves part—albeit a developed and exclusive part—of the relation to nature they are invoked to describe. This implies that perceptions in non-human organisms are also illusory, even if the phenomenal nature of mind is not evident to the organism. Clearly, the advent of consciousness and the attributes it incorporates permits, but does not promote, a realization of illusory mind, for a person who is continuously aware of the illusory nature of the surrounding world would be psychotic, and probably unable to survive. Epistemology is an atavistic byproduct of an evolutionary advance that, barring introspective excess, favors the survival of humans in a world where mentality matters more than physicality.

Clearly, a phenomenon can appear real to an organism yet be an illusion, so that consciousness of illusion and the distinction of illusion and reality is not essential to this insight. We do not think a lion stalking a gazelle is involved in an illusory hunt, nor is a spider building an illusory web. Perhaps to human observation these activities can be termed illusory, but not from the standpoint of the organism. Why should this be so, if intermittent awareness of illusion is inessential to everyday action? At what point does an organism cease to be simply a part of physical reality and begin to elaborate a mental representation of the world, with an awareness that is not yet consciousness-of? If human mentality is continuous with that of earlier forms down to organisms ingredient in reality, the world will incorporate these organisms, which, in turn, exhibit mentality at a stage where the subjective grows out of physical nature—or rather, where physical nature grows out of subjectivity to reciprocally shape the organism's mind. If physical nature evolves to assimilate features of human mentality, the nature of mind is such that the capacity to observe and reflect on nature is itself an outcome of natural process. We perceive through that which nature proffers to engage physical process, unaware that the world we perceive is the source of the mentality by which the world itself is perceived.

The conclusion of this line of thought is that nature incorporates attributes of mentality that are conceived as distinct from the world, just as the world is conceived as distinct from mind. This implies that cognitive attributes at the highest level are as much a part of the physical world as the physical processes described by natural science. We apprehend our mentality as discontinuous with nature, not as an evolutionary outcome of physical process. Mind inhabits nature not as a ghostly presence or adventitious property but an inherent feature of process, that is, as the outcome of process in human mind/brain that is no less part of nature than the rocks and trees. The intuition of mentality in nature, the growth of process to the presence of mind in the world, is displayed in the intuition of divinity in nature, a spiritual force or impersonal god, in which the mind of nature is the equivalent of the mind in the brain.

To flesh out this idea with greater precision, the mapping of mind to world presumes a correlation of some but not all features of mind with physical nature, that is, with objects and events but not with consciousness, meaning and value; these features are only possible, however, because they represent the outcome of a proto-psychic process that begins in physical entities and transforms over evolutionary time to a pinnacle of realization in human mind/brain, which is part of the physical world it is designed to reflect. The implication is that the higher features of human subjectivity are part of the objective world from which they arise, and that the intuition of this fact leads to the awareness of mind in nature, from early religions with multiple gods, to monotheism, totemic beliefs, myth, magic, spiritualism and superstition, to the Jung-Pauli account of synchronicity and the anthropic principle of Wheeler. From this standpoint, the illusion of nature is a mental representation of the physical world but also a subtler manifestation of the outer world in human mind, which can lead to a deeper understanding of the relation of mentality to physical science. The argument is for mind in nature, which can be termed the spirit or soul of nature, but not a personal god, which is an objectification as deity of the physical process that leads to mentality.

5

Memory and Thought

SUMMARY

THIS ESSAY ON THOUGHT and memory has several goals: (1) to discuss some of the complexities of memory that are glossed over in cognitive theory, particularly the continuity of thought and perception, (2) to argue that the endogenous substrate of perception is memory-based, with conscious thought occurring as an enhancement (by retardation or neoteny of process) at pre-terminal phases in revival, (3) to show that the memory trace cannot refer to a localized store in the brain, but repeats the trajectory of the actualization process in the original perceptual experience, and (4) to further the idea (advanced in previous chapters) that forgetting is incomplete revival, not decay.

The distinction between thought and memory depends not only on novelty and a divergence from reproduction, but also on a feeling of presentness for thought, even for an idea that is being revived, and a feeling of pastness for memory. A thought image felt in the present has some feeling of agency, which occurs primarily due to the lack of resolution or completion and/or to an orientation towards the future, while the pastness of memory deprives the image of agency, though a sense of effort can accompany the attempt to recall a past experience. An analysis of the *déjà vu* experience is relevant to this distinction.

INTRODUCTION

If thought is thinking about what is possible, memory seems to consist in irrevocable fact. Memory depends on fidelity to experience or replication; thought includes dream, daydream, fantasy, imagination, planning, problem-solving, contemplation, rational and irrational ideation—basically, almost anything in the mind, apart from feeling, that is something other than memory. Inaccurate recall becomes thought when it produces new content. While memory is judged by the exactness with which it re-actualizes experience (*wie es eigentlich gewesen ist*), thought is mental activity that is itself an experience, not the recreation of one. Memory becomes thought when it branches out to novelty; thought reverts to memory when it is forgotten or revived. Since we recollect ideas and can, to some extent, revive feelings, memory is not limited to external experience. Neither does it require consciousness of mental content: quotidian behavior is dominated by the recurrent or habitual, which approximates memory to the extent that novelty is excluded. This is captured in the distinction between representational and procedural memory. Memory as conscious representation (or unconscious, e.g. dream) is close to thinking; thought that is unconscious or implicit relies on memory, but differs in the novelty of outcome. Further, what begins as thought inevitably becomes memory, as in learning a skill or acquiring a habit. Thought must be replaced by memory, or we would be overwhelmed on every occasion by having to think through again, from the beginning, even the slightest decision.

Novelty in thought or imagination rests on the expansion or recombination of learned content, but even if the material of thought is given—say, words for Shakespeare, notes for Beethoven—thought is not mere rearrangement, but a novel pattern or perspective on what is available. Creative thinking results in truly novel forms. A favorite example of this is Coleridge's line, "the clock has gone mad; it has struck 1 four times." The statement is entirely composed of familiar, learned elements, but the outcome is wholly unanticipated. The intersection of differing lines of thought—insanity in a mechanical object—exposes the process within a frozen metaphor, such as a friendly bank, or an ironic simile, such as "crazy like a fox." Poetry is especially permeated by metaphor, in which disparate items come together on the basis of shared attributes.

Thought and memory, the productive and reproductive, are thus closely aligned, but seem to be opposing spheres, separated by imagination, by effort and voluntariness, degree of novelty, and a sense of past or present. There is also a difference in feeling. A new idea may be thrilling or frightening; an old memory can be painful or pleasurable. Nostalgia pertains to memory, not thought. A sustained memory may give pleasure, while sustained thought is difficult, even tiring. In the former, there is a struggle for precision, in the latter, for originality. Ideas can be recollected, while feelings, though remembered, are difficult to reproduce.

Thinking cannot readily be studied in animals except as problem-solving, where failures tend to be discarded and successes rewarded. Thought is also difficult to study in humans, for it is spontaneous, variable, and, unlike memory, cannot be verified by comparing recall to a known prompt, except as deviation from rote patterns and formulations. There is a good deal of experimental work on memory, with division into components and the attribution of these to specific brain areas. Research methodology also influences the way we interpret thought and memory. The interval or delay in recall, the time that lapses from exposure to recall, distraction, accuracy, repetition, the nature of what is recalled (e.g. whether physical features or meaning)—all these factors motivate the division of memory into a variety of components and set it apart from thought. In the study of memory, as in so many other areas of cognition and language, deconstruction into components replaces thoughtful understanding of the faculty itself. As to the reduction of memory or its constituents to brain or to genes, the road down is one thing, the road up (to cognition) another.

The highest reaches of thought are, arguably, in artistic, philosophical and mathematical genius, the lowest in those who are mentally challenged or live lives of dull routine (Thoreau's "quiet desperation," or Nietzsche's "herd mentality"). In genius, creative thought triumphs over memory; in dullness or habit it is the reverse. Yet a prodigious memory may not be conducive to original thought, while thinking suffers when thought retreats to the habitual or over-learned. Indeed, an overactive memory can interfere with the reception, isolation and formulation of novel concepts. A photographic memory may be exhaustive in its scope, but it is essentially replicative and may prevent the synthesis, propagation and pattern recognition necessary for productive thinking. This was described in a case study by Luria, and by Borges in his short story, "Funes the Memorious." Exceptional memory occurs in autistic savants, mnemonists, chanting monks, or those who have devoted many years to memorization, as in the recitation of lengthy biblical or Sanskrit texts.

Forgetting and the suppression of irrelevancy are essential to selective recall and concept formation. In some fields, such as chess or music, accomplished masters can recall lengthy games or scores after a single exposure, but such performances (in chess) are largely reconstructions based on strategy and patterns of attack or defense, not rote learning. Recently, in a drowsy or dream state, I heard much of the Brahms Piano Trio #1 in my mind, several months after attending a performance, even though it is not possible for me to play or hum such a complex piece. Such an occurrence is not unusual in the artistically gifted, for example, Wagner's composition of the Prelude to *Das Rheingold*, or Coleridge writing *Kublai Khan* in a dream or transitional state. This shows that memory is not easily fractured into components or interpreted as storage in a computer file, but rather something far more complex.

Perception is largely memory constrained and externalized by sensation, though vivid memory can achieve actuality as a mode of perceptual experience, as in the case of the "flashbacks" symptomatic of post-traumatic stress disorder. Hallucination and eidetic phenomena occur in the transition from the image to the object and the reverse. Veridical perception depends on memory as antecedent process, without which no meaning or recognition can occur in a changing object world. When perception deviates from the norm, as in psychosis and other pathologies, memory becomes thought-like in its novelty, and the reality of objects is altered. But we are not usually aware of memory as a substrate of perception—indeed, memory itself is most easily understood as something that is entirely post-perceptual, a recollection of a perception that took place in the past. The passage of objects in formation from immediate experience to "working" memory to external perceptions, which is recaptured in forgetting, remains invisible, because the memory process is pre-empted by object development and only reappears, in reverse, when the perception is incompletely revived. It is not memory but the substrate of the memory that transforms to perception. Once the memory image becomes a conscious actuality, it no longer figures in perception. This is true of thought, which is conceived as largely conscious, even though unconscious thinking occurs in dream, in spontaneous decision and insight, and in artistic or other work, where the emphasis is on invention. Unlike memory, which is essential to recognition and the application of learning to sensory experience, unconscious thought remains submerged, and only its outcome reaches perceptual clarity. Moreover, memory qua instinct is the primitive capacity from which thought develops, as an improvisation that is inexplicable on the basis of inherited routines.

Lacking an inner life, animals do not have a thought process similar to that of humans; rather, their mentation is closer to spontaneous invention, tacit decision or trial and error, when instinct fails to provide a solution. In animals, instinctual drive governs most behavior, with a small window of originality where something innovative or unanticipated may interrupt, according to the vicissitudes of circumstance. Instinct is the inheritance of memory and its implementation, with some deviation attributable to learning and/or implicit thought. In animals, the relative fixity of behavioral repertoires reflects the movement of drive as memory into action. In humans, also, remembered patterns also constitute the larger part of behavior; life is mostly habit penetrated by moments of imagination. Most decisions are unsurprising. Thinking "outside the box" is a creative act. For most of us, most of the time, decisions follow well-worn habitual paths, even if they are not repetitive in every detail. It would be a strange world indeed if decisions were constantly unpredictable.

The immediately preceding and the deep experiential are revived in what conventional theory takes to be a "naked" object, that is, the thing itself, absent any interpretation. Personal knowledge and experience form the foundation of the object, infusing it with meaning and relevance. The transition to actuality is from before to after, but once it is complete, and over a series of states, a present is created in the disparity between what is being remembered and what is being perceived—the past and the present—in relation to the incompleteness of revival. The state develops over the still-incomplete prior state, allowing for preservation (continuous revival) of early segments of self, character, core beliefs and values. When the developing configuration or gestalt reaches a penultimate phase, it is analyzed into featural details and detaches from the inner world in the form of an object world, with antecedent segments constituting its memory-based infrastructure.

Unlike objects, which externalize, actions do not detach from the mind of the actor. This preserves the feeling that the action belongs to the self, which is the basis of the feeling of agency. Both the perceptual quality of hallucination and its origins in memory confirm the hypothesis that memory underlies perception, with the application of sensory constraints on endogenous process. That is, the endogenous revival of memory content, beginning with instinctual drive categories, forms a substrate that is shaped to perception by sensibility. Perception unfolds over a memory infrastructure that is uncovered in forgetting. The sense of ownership and personal value of intra-psychic process undergo a transition to the impersonality of the external and the varieties of intrinsic worth. Sensation carves adaptation out of memory.

We tend to interpret dream as a play of memories, but fusion, displacement and condensation of images (Freud's dreamwork) occur as well in the waking imagination, especially in creative thought, which taps certain aspects of dream cognition. The novelty of dream usually surpasses that of wakefulness, but the loss of the free range of dream is compensated by the adaptation and publicity of thought. Dreams are symbolic and thematic representations, rarely copies of prior experience. In this, they reveal the rudiments of productive thinking. They are not wishes, but embodiments of feeling, as much what is feared as what is desired, as much thought as memory, as much what is possible as what is sheer fantasy. Freud's concept of wish-fulfillment derives from the actualization of dream at an intra-psychic phase close to drive and desire. The involuntary nature of dream, or spontaneous recollection, nullifies the selectivity of volition and opens the door to contingency.

PAST AND PRESENT, RECEPTIVENESS AND AGENCY

Apart from documentation, photographs and witnesses, which we do not rely on for personal memory, how do we know that what we remember re-ally happened? Put differently, how do we distinguish a memory of an event from a thought, a dream or an imaginary occurrence? I have had occasions of uncertainty as to whether I was remembering a dream or an actual expe-rience, as well as whether a thought was original, a prior idea, or something I had read or heard. These confusions point to subtle continuities between these phenomena. The piecemeal approach of cognitive science attempts to sequester only those aspects which continuity can explain. A related ques-tion is how we know memory is true to experience, incomplete or inaccu-rate. If details are forgotten, clearly memory or its narration is incomplete, but how do we know events and their sequence are accurately remembered?

Since an experience in waking memory depends on the content re-called, such as taking a walk to the park, what besides the recollection attests to its actuality? Does the feeling of a match of recall and the actual events reflect a background potential in relation to what is elicited? In all aspects of cognition, only a fraction of potential is realized. Warren McCullough (1965) described a mason who, under hypnosis, could recall every brick in a wall laid decades before. Even in recalling a walk we do not remember every step, tree, leaf or branch. Or do we? Is a limited, often fragmentary, re-membrance compared to an undischarged potential for exhaustive recall to determine whether the remembrance is accurate? Is the intuition of unsatis-fied potential the basis for knowing a memory is incomplete, or even that there is a memory—the potential to remember—that cannot be realized at this particular moment. Is this what is lost in those who do not even know they have forgotten?

The illiterate native who can enter a Brazilian rain forest and circle around for two hours before returning to the same point, without relying on moss or lichen and unable to see above the canopy, has a capacity to form a mental map that may well be a potential in all individuals, but is lost in the context of literacy and education. Similarly, the fact that incidental or un-noticed events reappear in dream implies a greater potential for recall than what is consciously remembered. Presumably, the withdrawal in dream (or hypnotic trance) to a pre-perceptual phase allows the elicitation of other-wise unremembered items from the potential in the configural precursors of conscious recall. This raises a question: if dreams are memories, what happens to the dream content once it is forgotten? Does it persist, like a memory in wakefulness, never to be realized again, or does it fade forever into the shadows?

On the materialist account, an experience that is encoded in the brain is distinct from its conscious "retrieval", stored like a computer file that persists after each occasion of access. The existence of the file might then account for the sense of having a memory of something even when it can-not be recalled at will. An experience exists for the individual when it is recalled or, indirectly, when it influences other thoughts or behaviors, yet we presume that memory persists long after it has been forgotten, no less than before it is recalled. This supports the idea of consolidation, storage or a last-ing physical trace that, to date, has eluded localization. Stimulation of the brain may arouse a memory or an epileptic aura, but the aura or memory re-curs after the stimulated area is excised. Holographic theory postulates the generation of memory throughout the brain. Is the trace localized or every-where? What is a neural memory if not a latent configuration or potential for recall that rests in the relative strengths of innumerable synapses? The configuration has the potential for activation if one segment is aroused. The trace is modeled on the original perception; that is, the process of percep-tion constitutes the trace, the distal portions of which perish or are erased by the oncoming state. The trace must be non-local, for it is doubtful that the sounds, sights, conversations and feelings on a walk, that is, the entire perceptual experience, is "stored" in the same place. One can say that the memory trace is a distributed pattern of synaptic relations recruited over the same path as the original experience.

Presumably, the derivation from one configuration to another in the sequence of recall or perception implies a figural prominence that privileges the elicitation of one sub-set over another. An ingredient of the experience, a tree, a bench, can revive the memory, just as the memory can elicit the in-gredient. Put differently, the whole gives the parts, but a part can refresh the whole. A memory cannot be recalled all at once; portions become active or conscious before others. An effort can be made to evoke events selectively or in order of occurrence, usually generating one item to reconstitute the expe-rience. The more emphatic the memory for one event, the less pronounced for others. As a single word can be unpacked to a book, the totality of an experience can be collapsed to an event. Initially, recall approximates experience; then it fades so only the salient events are revived. It is difficult to imagine a fragmentation of the trace over time such that what is recalled is what is left in the trace, especially when long forgotten events are later recalled, some as habit, some spontaneously, others in daytime reverie, or symbolically in dream, or in a trance-like state. More likely, events "drop out" or are revived in relation to personal meaning or affective tone.

In recall, as in perception, the transmission from one configuration to the next is like a travelling wave, with the pattern of derivation comparable to that of a category/member relation. A neural configuration can be said to correspond to a category if sub-sets individuate as members. Presumably, the affective tonality or relevance to a context or situation is apportioned to virtual items in such a way as to bias the arousal of the sub-set, with a falling-away of less salient constituents by an inhibitory surround. The sub-set is then the next configuration (sub-category) to undergo partition. Initial partitions are determined by affective and meaning-relations, such as those that deposit in dream; subsequent partitions reflect "physical" relations to the original percept.

The relation of memory to a memory, a capacity or competence to a performance, is similar to that of *la memoire* to *le souvenir* in French, memory as potential and a memory as an actuality. The potential for total recall in near-death or trance-state experience (*Lebensfilm*, picture strip theory) is a mark of the coherence and pictorial quality of initial renewal, while the categorical nature of revival incorporates the multi-modality and serial unfolding of memorial content. On the other hand, the concept of a static trace that is looked-up and retrieved, as Lashley famously noted, has too many problems to be seriously considered; he emphasized the need for mechanisms that scan not only serial order, but also plasticity, decay, continuity with the before and after of the recollected event as well as with other phenomena, the often fragile nature of recall, recurrence in dream or trance, integration with cognition more generally, how the trace is found or selected, and so on.

When I remember walking to the park yesterday, what provides the assurance that my recollection is for an actual experience, that is, a faithful representation of what happened, and that it occurred yesterday and not last week? Can we know a memory is inaccurate without supplementary access to the events on which it is based? Is incompleteness or inaccuracy felt in a way that is independent of the experience to which it is compared? Does memory just feel right or accurate, and if so, then how? How is the memory of an experience compared to the experience if the experience gives the memory, or if the memory—"memory trace"—is all we have of the experience? Does partial recall reflect a partial trace, and if not, what determines what part of the trace recurs? If the memory is felt as more or less adequate to the experience or if nothing essential is left out in recall, how does this occur, since all there is in consciousness is what is recollected? Does a present memory realize another deeper memory that is an implicit record of what occurred?

As noted, what survives is a fraction of what transpired, since in the parsing to precision the elicitation of one item requires the suppression of others, so that much is lost in each instance of recall, or remains as potential for later visitation. Likely, it is the potential to generate a memory that permits one to know the memory is "there" but unavailable. In pathological memory, the person is usually unaware of having forgotten. In the amnesia of Korsakoff syndrome, or confabulation, or in the megalomania and exaggeration of syphilitic dementia, the person is usually not aware that remembrance is inaccurate, even false; embellishments often have a grain of plausibility. Typically, in Alzheimer's disease, the family, not the patient, is concerned about failing memory. If the patient is unaware of memory loss, what has been lost, the memory, the revival or the unconscious record?

These questions go to the problem of an occasional confusion of dream and thought. How do I know a false memory was not implanted in my brain, or developed spontaneously, or is mixed with imagination or thought, or arose in therapy or suggestion? Is the difference between a false memory and delusion the belief in its veracity? Is delusion a false belief or does it entail a strong belief in a false memory or thought? When is the problem that of belief or judgment? Fixed delusional beliefs often accompany a loss of memory. The person does not know if the memory or idea is true to experience, as the failure in recall permits only a rudimentary revival to a level of dream cognition, where novel contents arise without critical judgment in relation to affective needs. The delusion of thought-transference, that one sends or receives thoughts to and from others, is common in psychosis; mind-reading and telepathy are correlates in the popular imagination.

We can recall an event many times and it still remains a memory, but if the event recurs many times it loses its temporal locus and becomes part of experience. Once the episodic relation of memory is lost, that is, the temporal tagging of an event, as in learning a word, a skill, a route, general knowledge, or after many repetitions, the content is no longer felt as a memory but a part of one's personal or world knowledge. In this way, memory passes into thought. Events that are redundant, good or bad, or cannot be recalled, especially for early life, go into the formation of personality. This is why memories of early childhood are often misrepresented. They are in a more superficial relation to the personality. In a very real sense, what is forgotten is what one becomes. I often have the feeling that parts of my life not witnessed might as well never have occurred. Such reflections raise a still deeper question: what is the difference between a real and a fictitious life?

If I recall a walk and consider what other events might have occurred, or did not occur, there is a mix of memory and thought, as well as a feeling of some intent and digression in the present. Even with digression, the reproductive portion is felt as past and the digression is felt as present. When I recall a tree that I passed on the walk, it is a memory, felt as belonging to the past, but when I wonder at the beauty or age of the tree or imagine resting for a while beneath its shade, it is a thought, something that I feel as present. The term "reflection" applies to thought and memory. Thought is deviation in recall, or the revival of the memorial when it is unhinged from experience. This shift to a sampling of world knowledge is accompanied by a shift from the past to the present, from a backward look to a forward glance, from spontaneity or passivity to agency and purposefulness. Knowledge is termed "semantic memory," but actually memory becomes knowledge when it is unmoored from the temporal point of its acquisition. This liberation of memory from experience leaves the past in favor of the present, and shifts passive recollection to volitional thought.

Agency is not confined to action, presentness is not restricted to thought or perception; both are prominent in thought imagery, as in picturing a mouse crawling on the back of an elephant. The images are learned, and in that sense reproductive, but the experience is that of thought, thus it is felt in the present. The image can be "manipulated" at will. Agency is an intra-psychic experience that is lost when images externalize, but retained in actions—speech, motion—that engage the body and are partially intra-psychic. The relation of self to an intra-psychic image is critical. Agency for the body depends on the "body image," which, unlike objects, remains partly interior. We lift the hand volitionally, but the hand lifting the cup is an outcome. Volition and effort do not seem to appreciably aid recall, as in the common experience of searching for a name unsuccessfully until attention is diverted. The involuntariness of imagery in memory is parsed to necessity in perception. In volition, the image must be directed to the future, because agency cannot affect the past. The involuntary precedes detachment; agency is lost for ordinary objects that act on us causally, but not as a result of personal volition.

The simple response to the question of why memory carries a feeling of the past, and thinking is felt in the present, is that the sense of pastness relates to the awareness of prior experience, or that the object-experience is not happening now, or that it represents an absence of presentness, or the content is felt as familiar or reproductive. How then do we know that what we take for a present experience is not a recurrence of a previous thought? This does not require forgetting the prior thought so thinking will not be apprehended as recall since we can revisit a thought many times but do not feel the thought is a memory, even if thinking on a problem requires constant revival. Perhaps for a recurrent thought to be felt as a memory, or to convey a feeling of pastness, it first has to be a perception. Once the memory is elaborated as thought, it loses its experiential ground and thus its relation to re-perception (memory).

Perception is the realization of memory sculpted by sensation with a sense of increasing passivity until the image detaches as an independent object. The passivity relates to pastness and lack of agency for present experience. The final outcome of the pastness and passivity of memory is the detachment, immediacy and presentness of objects. The present becomes the past in forgetting; the past becomes the present in perceiving. Different phenomena occur at successive planes in the passage of memory to perception or past to present. In one such phenomena, déjà vu, past and present are confused, so a present occasion is felt as past or having previously occurred. A recurrent event in thought or imagination that is experienced as novel is not necessarily felt as past, nor are the daily repetitions of life, while in *déjà vu* a unique experience is felt as a memory. The problem of how we know an experience that we remember has actually happened is the opposite of the problem of how we have (the feeling of) a memory for an experience that has not occurred (that is, the *déjà vu* experience).

Agency or volition entails an arc from self to act, to object or image (such as a proposition). The feeling of volition is primed when it passes through an implicit phase of choice, or a delay that involves inhibiting a spontaneous reaction, whether instinctive or overlearned. Most often, the active and passive are merged. My writing is an active performance in which I feel myself the agent, but the words arise passively, without conscious control. The process of word production is actually involuntary, with a feeling of agency appearing only in the final act of writing or in revision. In fact, revision is felt as more volitional than original writing, which is largely a passive experience. Memory rises to perception as the actualization of past in present, while action carries a feeling of volition outward into the present occasion. Agency requires a forward surge in the isolation of the part out of the whole. This accounts for the intentional quality of feeling in the subjective aim. Choice heightens agency in the selection of content, in the resolution of potential, and in the conscious accentuation of partition.

We may have an experience of uncertainty as to whether a dream is a remembrance, but while in progress, the dream is felt as a present occasion.

There is no past or future. A waking recollection of a past event is a present experience, though memory carries a feeling of pastness into the present. A dream may be about a past event, but when it happens, it is felt in the present. Memory and dream both actualize in the present: memory renews a past experience of perception, while dream is a species of hallucination, but the former is transformed by sensation. In other words, memory achieves a present immediacy on becoming a perception, and perception takes on the quality of memory in the incompleteness of revival to an object. Dream content arises passively and involuntarily as an elaboration of thought and memory experienced in the "now" of the dream. The self of dream is passive in respect to the imagery, with a contracted sense of the present moment and without any feeling of past or future. The transience of the present is due to the truncation of the state, the absence of revival, the lack of disparity between perception and forgetting—there is no sense of forgetting within the dream—and the presentness of all dream experience. Memory experienced in dream is often based on actual occurrences, particularly fragments of daytime perception. Ordinary memory is for—or about—an actual experience; dream is an elaboration or symbolic representation that is itself apprehended as an experience. We say, "I remember that walk" and "I remember that dream," as though remembering meant the same in each instance. Why should a dream, even one that is relatively veridical, be felt as an experience, and not as the memory or thought of an experience? On waking, a lucid or realistic dream may be felt as faithful to a past experience, but the dream—within the dream—is not felt as recollection.

There can even be confusion as to whether dreams are thoughts received from others or are one's own. William James wondered if he was getting mixed up in other people's dreams.

Memory develops through unconscious phases to appear in conscious recall, while the unconscious origin of dream affects how we assess its unreality. If the unconscious origin of dream heightens the feeling of unreality, does our unawareness of the unconscious segments of memory support the feeling of its realness? Certainly, a dream that veers from waking reality implies a psychological distance from actual experience, but dreams that revive an experience are not confused with the memory of that experience. If I dream of walking to the park, I do not confuse the ongoing dream content with a waking memory. In one instance, I remember the walk; in the other I remember a dream of the walk. Is this the main difference? Unlike dream, memory is contextually real: that is, there is a before and after that supports the reality of the memory, even if recall is incomplete or erroneous. Dream is unconscious and recollected in consciousness; it is the conscious reconstruction or narrative of the imagery, not necessarily the actual dream that is recalled. The order of dream events is often uncertain in the dream, which consists of the replacement of one image by another without immediate memory, giving the "dream story" a recurrent character. Serial order is most likely imposed on the waking narration.

MEMORY, THOUGHT AND EXISTENCE

Existence is more than being; it is the recurrence of an epoch of becoming over successive states, such that the process of recurrence, together with the categories that actualize, constitutes a world-becoming, that is, a moment of existence for all constituents. Recurrence in a primitive entity is essentially just replication with minimal novelty. Rocks and elementary particles do not merely persist, but undergo continuous iteration to be what they are. A single becoming is insufficient to establish existence. A thing does not appear out of nothing; there is a before and an after. The shift from before to after could be a causal sequence or iteration, a boxcar of change or a fountain of recurrence. According to causal theory, one state is carried into the next. The transmission that preserves the cause in the effect, or carries the past into the future, can be interpreted as the revival of an antecedent state in a consequent one. In this respect, in the assimilation of the consequent to the antecedent, the effect "remembers" the cause. In recurrence theory, the "after" is not a direct result of the "before," but develops over its residue. The prior state can be said to be a memory in the current state. While the origin of change is uncertain in the causal account (the effect incorporates much of the cause, but the transmission is uncertain), with recurrence change occurs in the transition from potential to actual. Change is not from state to state or cause to effect, but within the state itself, as the just-after is derived over the just-before.

Memory is recurrence. The revolution of an electron in a hypothetical atom is a mode of physical memory that reinstates the being of the atom. So too are the physical forces that govern the process. Becoming is a recurrence of the memory of being, while being is the substance (category) realized in becoming. In the example above, the category—the atom—is a complete revolution that enfolds all phases in the orbit of an electron. In the human mind, being refers to a fully-derived mental state that actualizes on completion. Being is not a product or output of becoming, since it is an indivisible compilation of all phases in its realization. Put differently, an entity becomes what it is when all phases actualize one cycle of becoming.

From its lowly origin in physical entities, the pattern of continuous replication passes to plants and primitive organic forms. The concealed replication of organism is secreted in the DNA for auto-replication and the reproduction of like-others. Memory is transmitted to progeny in the self-replication of individual becoming; that is, reproduction is an overt manifestation of the implicit replication of the individual organism, and the revival of perception as memory is an extension into mentation of the reproductive nature of existence. The evolutionary series is a continuous reinstatement of organism in a non-conscious resurgence of form, until finally the cycles of replication develop to human mind, as unconscious revival is revealed in conscious imagery. This constitutes an endpoint in the transformation of memory into perception, or the uncovering, in memory, of the process of recurrence that underlies life and change.

Once memory becomes perception, or the reverse, the arousal of imagery—as an embedded pre-object—permits consciousness of memory content as a preliminary to thought. Non-conscious entities, and the worlds in which they are ingredient, are precursors to conscious mind as an iteration of instinctual memory, primarily in auto-recurrence, secondarily in progeny, with all instances of recurrence serving as modes of organic recall. Every act of memory is forged into a world of perception that re-creates itself to exist, whether as a conceptual or mind-independent entity. An organism is not just what it is; it is remembered into existence.

Creativity in perception is attributed to the world, as though it were the source of beauty, innovation and surprise, and not the inner process of reproduction which gives a novel world and organism in each iteration. Inexactness in renewal is the starting point for thought and creative imagination. In the revival of memory, the transition is from the distant past of animal inheritance to a more recent past of personal experience to a final phase of recall that approximates objectivity, at which point it ceases to be memory and transforms, through sensation, to perception. In this objectification, a present moment and an external world are created. The past, in relation to memory, experience, feeling and knowledge, produces thought as a branching to novelty at submerged phases. The direction is from an evolutionary and experiential past to the immediacy of the now, with an intuition of the future in the forward surge to the present. In this way, the replication of the past gives way to innovation in the future.

Individuals with a great capacity for thought, or the ability to use memory in the service of the creative, may have ideas that change the world. The world of the ordinary is the surface toward which the process is striving. The evolutionary objective of memory is not conscious revival, but its loss in the growth of thought, as the fading of the present prepares for the state that follows. While perception occurs as an endpoint in the development of memory, thought arises in its infrastructure. If the perceptible world is created out of the adaptation of memory to sensation, thought arises as incompleteness in the realization of memory content. As memory disappears in perception, thought is a replacement of its penultimate phases. The perceptual exists in a confrontation of adaptation with recurrence. We exist in the evolution of memory to thought. The creativity that begins in the world shifts to mind-internal when imagery takes the place of objects as the vehicle of originality. The genius creates a subjective world as companion to a world of strident objectivity.

An escape from repetition is a goal of thought. Other goals are solutions or useful actions. In most organisms, this amounts to little more than feeding, avoiding predators, nesting, care of young and navigating in a habitat. Thought appears in the cracks of contingency, when memory no longer assures survival. The pragmatics of thought adapt to the environment, that is, to the world that memory creates, to which thought, however abstract, eventually yields.

Thought entails the capacity to think, but the organism is not thought up in the same way it is reinstated by memory. Thinking is predicated on memory; thinking that something exists is predicated on its existence. Memory is a "knowing what"; thinking is a "knowing that." Memory reinstates its object, while the object of thought is distinct from the act of thinking. The only existence created by thought is the thought itself. If thinking were the equivalent of existing, existence would depend on an act of thought or its content. An organism lacking or deprived of thought still exists, no less than one that thinks. Consciousness of existence as a class of thought implies that existence is something that consciousness is about. The paradox is that thinking as a creative act depends on implicit memory to create the organism that thinks.

6

Subjectivity[1]

SUMMARY

THE DISTINCTION BETWEEN THE perceiver and the perceived in perception is the source of the contrast between the subjective and objective, in which the relation of self to object is generalized to the relation of an inner-field of mind or personal experience to an outer field of objects or physical reality. At one extreme, subjectivity is tied to waking and perhaps dream consciousness, the "what it's like" of private experience, qualia and so on, while at the other end, the inference of subjectivity from behavior can be said to begin with the reaction to pain and fear as the most primitive manifestations of an internal life. Pain is primitive sensation; fear is an affective state. Pain is displeasure in the body; sexual activity is bodily pleasure. The development of feeling in the body into affect in the mind corresponds to the progression in becoming from drive-categories bound up with the body-schema to their derivations and partitions into conceptual feelings and mental imagery, or from the intensity of bodily-centered feeling to the diversity of mind-centered affects.

At a deeper level, the subjective is the intrinsic becoming of an epoch of existence for an organism or basic entity. The expansion of the duration of becoming in successive life forms accounts for the transition from proto-psychic properties in physical entities to an expansion of psychic attributes

---

1. See Schilder, P. (1935) *Image and Appearance of the Human Body.* Kegan, London; Brown, J. (1999) Neuropsychology of the self-concept. *Journal of Nervous and Mental Disease,* 187:131–141.

in primitive and advanced organisms, a process that culminates in the duration of the human present.

INTRODUCTION

To begin with, it is essential to define precisely the difference between subjective and objective, since this distinction loses its force in primitive organisms and certainly in physical entities. I would say that the objective consists in the description of a physical entity, depicted from an extrinsic standpoint, as an atomic substance-like thing, possessing measurable quantitative values and involved in causal relations. In contrast, the subjective refers to a qualitative description of an intrinsic becoming from potential to actual, in which change is best described as a recurrence by and through constraints, rather than a progression from cause to effect. A subjective object or state is a dynamic actualization over a diachronic series of internal phases that realize an epoch of momentary existence, in which the duration of the epoch constitutes the entire sequence over which the object becomes what it is. The revolution of an electron in a hypothetical atom is an example of an internal series that aims to a completion that actualizes one epoch. This description applies to primitive organisms as well as elementary particles.

The fundamental transition from an object that appears to be merely a physical entity to one that seems to be an organism entails a shift from non-directional energy to directional feeling. From an interior standpoint, the continuum from basic entities to complex organisms involves expansion, coherence, greater complexity and extension of the subjective aim, in which an energetic process transforms to the feeling that leads from the inception of the epoch to its completion. The proto-psychic attributes of physical entities develop into the psychic qualities of an organism. Such qualities are only comprehensible from an internal perspective, in which a recurrent dynamic of form-creation is the prime requisite for the existence of an organism. The rejection of subjectivity depends on a resolutely extrinsic point of view that eliminates process in favor of a scientific description of things as they are, and does not interest itself in how they come into being; that is, externalism adheres to a present or predictive mode of description, denying interioricity and unwilling to explore the interior perspective, which requires a retrospective point of view on how things come into existence. The point here is that the self-sufficient being of particulars in a materialist perspective is the epochal coming-into-being of subjectivism.

The passage from primitive to advanced forms requires an expansion of the duration of becoming and an elaboration of the segments involved in actualization. In the most primitive forms of life, the duration of an epoch is quite brief; in advanced forms, duration enlarges. In humans, this duration is perhaps 1/10th of a second in clock time. Initially, feeling is not felt; it is closer to undirected and undifferentiated energy and the life force than to affect or emotion. Gradually, as organism evolves, there is a build-up through category/item specification of multiple segments or phases in becoming. These phases first realize the body-schema, allowing feeling to take on an affective quality, perhaps something like the hunger of the body for sustenance, but most strikingly in pain or its equivalent in behavior, that is, the reaction of the body-schema to disruption and a threat to its survival (see below).

The subjective is equivalent to mental events in inner—and, I would argue, outer-mind, in contrast with the objective, which by definition is fully extra-psychic, physical and external. For materialist doctrine, objects are a collection of constituent parts—smaller objects—each considered as an atomic element put in relation with other constituents through external bonds. Materialism further regards mental states as phenomena reducible to the physical substrates of the constituents, such that psyche, which arises from brain, can be ignored or eliminated as ultimately a property or manifestation of brain process. In contrast, for a process subjectivism, each constituent undergoes becoming in concert with the object or organism as a whole. The organism is not a collection of parts that have somehow agglomerated, but a unified system that recurs.

The subjectivity of an object is its mind-dependence; physical entities are extrinsic or mind-independent. Attempts to factor out the subjectivity of private experience naturally assume the objectivity of the perceptible world, in that the causal interaction of external entities is transposed to physicalist accounts of the mental state. That is, the physical entities of external reality are inserted in the mind/brain as material components of subjective experience. In the philosophy of mind, the distinction between subjective and objective is the basis for arguments in favor of realism or idealism, or first-person internalism and third-person externalism. The concentration in mind of a diffuse subjectivity, as in "mind dust" theory, is conceivable (James, Hartshorne)—the mind of god, or Eccles's psychons, or Teilhard's noosphere, a spirit Nature—but subjectivity is ordinarily conceived as dependent on consciousness, with mind understood as a population of contents and feelings, among which the self or self-concept is most prominent.

Much has been written on the self as illusory or non-existent on the one hand, or the nidus of the universe on the other, and much as well on the body image or schema as the basis of the self-concept, though the nature of the schema and the self, and the relation of self to body are seldom explored.

For animal mind, organism and bodily feeling—need and activity—are an indivisible unity. The instinctual drives of hunger, mating, defense, sleep and so on are embodiments of behavior. Feeling becomes urge, which discharges in activity; the urge is felt in the body, the activity is its implementation.

Internal feeling carries the body outward to action, with behavior appearing as the "output" of the body, though discharge in the body is the origin of behavior, while some degree of complexity of bodily activity is a criterion of mentality. In sub-primate mammals, discharge engages primarily the axial or midline musculature, and tends to be rhythmic or oscillatory, relating to earlier stages in forebrain growth. While the precursors of mentality are ingredient in animal mind, there is little evidence of a demonstrable cognitive residuum, apart from motility in relation to need and circumstance.

PAIN

The behavior that most strongly indicates subjectivity in animals is the affective response to pain as a manifestation of feeling. This response is not just avoidance of a painful stimulus, but an audible wailing that we take to be a sign of suffering. In part, there is projection of human emotion to animals, but when animals cry out in response to pain-inducing stimuli, it would be perverse to deny the impression that animal has felt pain, or to attribute the yelp, wail, or howl to an instinctual reaction or cerebral reflex. The cry of pain would not appear to be a behavior essential to survival in solitary animals, but in social animals it might serve to elicit a protective reaction from the group. Possibly the nature of pain differs in more primitive forms that lack the possibility of vocalization, such as fish. The cry reinforces the impression of pain, while its absence leads to uncertainty as to whether or not any pain is being felt. Yet even in fish some regard writhing in reaction to injury as an expression of pain, rather than instinctual avoidance behavior. One thinks of the birth cries of a human newborn, not to my knowledge seen in animals. Is it likely that birth is such a traumatic event that the infant feels physical or psychic pain? Crying begins with the first breath, and has the character of an automatic reaction, perhaps similar to the shock of a fish caught by an angler, as both fish and infant pass from an aquatic to a terrestrial environment.

We may be unsure of other animal feelings, but most agree that most mammals feel physical pain, and that higher mammals may suffer from a feeling of neglect, deprivation, isolation, loss and so on. For the most part, however, both the primacy of pain as a sign of feeling and the reality of the subjectivity implied by such a feeling are evidenced by bodily reactions. With superficial pain there are defensive reactions, fight/flight and evasion; with deep or internal pain, immobility. This is the typical response in humans as well. Some mammals appear to be in pain with the loss of significant others or infants. The animal is in distress; it appears to suffer, one could even say mourn. The yelping of a dog in pain is taken as a sign of suffering, and there seems little doubt this is true, but what does the reaction to pain in a dog, or the apparent grief in higher mammals in reaction to loss of a significant other, tell us about subjectivity? For some, animals are automata (Huxley). No one supposes that at rest a dog is thinking, or has memories or expectations. Loyalty is more likely an instinctual response—attachment to the pack leader—than an emotion. Animals at rest are unlikely to have feeling divorced from action, nor are they likely to refrain from action in the presence of feeling. Even humans during periods of repose have prolonged bouts of vacuity in which their mind "is a blank". Conversely, what can one conclude from the delight of a dog when excited at the prospect of a walk or upon being reunited with its master? When Fania Pascal, a friend of Wittgenstein, complained to him after a tonsillectomy that she "felt like a dog that has been run over," Wittgenstein said in reply "You don't know what a dog who has been run over feels like."

Excruciating pain can overwhelm an individual, but if I have a toothache the experience is something that I have, that happens to me, and not something that I am. In a dog, one supposes that physical or psychic pain, and perhaps joy as well, are the limits of the animal's affective experience. Unlike humans, animals do not laugh or cry. Nor is there an intentional relation to pain as a perceptual object. In humans, the quality of pain is more complex. In frontal lobotomy for chronic pain, the subject may say he still feels pain but is not bothered by it. This is a pain that is not painful. A similar response occurs in "pain asymbolia," even to loud noises, in which the feeling and meaning of pain are lacking. In research by Heinrich Klüver in the 1930s that led to the identification of the Klüver-Bucy syndrome, monkeys after bilateral resection of portions of the temporal lobes exhibited something he called "psychic blindness," that is, unawareness of the affective valence of external objects and events. This included the absence of fear, perhaps owing to non-recognition of danger. Thus snakes ordinarily elicit panic in monkeys, but after the procedure the monkeys examined them calmly. The condition occurs rarely in humans as a symptom of agnosia. In Klüver's monkeys, fear gives way to curiosity. One might say that avoidance is replaced by exploration, a negative by a positive reaction.

More generally, we may consider the significance of the observation that animals avoid dangerous and potentially painful situations: predators, cliffs, rivers and so on In what sense does the animal "know" such conditions are perilous? Usually, there is an innate sense of caution, but learning is involved, as in the cliff studies on infant kittens (Held). One-stage learning is common. A single encounter by a dog with a porcupine is usually enough. This effect reaches far down the evolutionary scale. Even frogs and butterflies have warning colors. Does the avoidance of danger indicate anticipation? Does the reflex-like or instinctive response to injury, which may or may not signal pain in different organisms, evolve to anticipatory behaviors in advanced forms? In higher mammals, delay before action indicates uncertainty, but not conscious choice. Uncertainty points to a lack of resolution among alternatives, with hesitation in bodily effectuation until an adaptive strategy appears; yet the organism is still one with behavior. The degree to which the behavior is instinctive or learned, or learning refines an instinctual bias, relates to the evolutionary recency of the organism. Some authors have speculated that higher-order responses are part of an approach/avoidance spectrum that is seen even in single-cell paramecia (Schneirla).

Often one hears of the pain/pleasure dichotomy, which pertains primarily to the pleasure of sexual activity, which, like pain, is felt in the body. Perhaps sexuality is transitional from bodily sensations to the psychic experience of fear and the varieties of non-sexual pleasures. This is not to say that deep brain substrates are not engaged in pleasure (Olds), though hypothalamic self-stimulation appears to induce feelings akin to sexual pleasure (Heath). However, the non-sexual varieties of pleasure and their intensities are so diverse (food, art, travel) that it seems implausible for pleasure—especially non-sexual—to be related to a small archaic area in the brain. Indeed, even in cases with stroke and total loss of language, individuals may show preserved aesthetic sense and continue to enjoy fine music.

Unlike pleasure, pain is near-universal, especially in mammals, without signs of pleasure. Animals instinctively devour food to avoid competitors, even a pet dog feeding alone, who has never had to deal with other dogs stealing its food. They give little evidence of pleasure in eating or mating. Is a purring cat happy? Is an iguana dozing in the sun having an enjoyable experience or merely warming up its body? Infants that engage in play that seems pleasurable are displaying instinct-driven behavior to acquire skills essential to survival.

There is no solid evidence beyond a weak analogy that emotional pain is derived from physical pain. Pain gives displeasure, but unhappiness is related to physical pain only in a metaphorical sense (suffering). Pain induces what appear to be affective reactions—anxiety, stress, suffering, fear—but apart from pain it is questionable if animals have other feelings. There is apparent grieving over loss, particularly in relation to maternal instinct, when the animal endures the death of infants or other members in a family structure. When an animal leaves or is ejected from a group, there is little if any reaction, and there may even be aggression if the animal attempts to return. This type of loss is not a source of grief. Such behavior occurs in social mammals that are part of a society, that is, herds, prides, or families. We see this behavior in whales, but not schools of fish or flocks of birds, so it seems to entail being part of a group in which individuality is shared or distributed.

We say, "words cannot express" the feeling of loss of loved ones. The grief is too much to be expressed in words, even if the pain of loss is "recollected in tranquility", in memory or in a literary, musical or other art work. Shostakovich said his notes were tombstones for lost friends. Loss and attendant grief may be trivialized by attempts to express feelings in words. Tears of sorrow are more eloquent than eulogies. This reminds us of animal grieving, such as distress in lions, elephants or chimpanzees on the loss of a juvenile. The reaction is pre-linguistic feeling in humans and animals. What do these observations say about subjective experience?

We say an animal feels pain when pain instigates vocalization or specific bodily actions. Why would an animal cry out in pain if it did not feel pain? If the organism cannot vocalize can it still feel pain? What quality of pain, if any, is felt by a worm on a hook, or an octopus that loses an arm? The question is not merely whether animals feel pain, but how this relates to the body image and the subjectivity of intra-psychic feeling. Pain is an intensification of the feeling that is the life force of organism. The nerve fibers that mediate pain, with little or no myelin sheathing, are the most archaic of pathways. Pain or its expectation is the primary warning or threat to survival. Pain is distress over bodily injury, but it is also necessary for bodily intactness. Rats with denervated forelimbs will chew off their paws, just as humans under dental anesthesia will bite their lips. Years ago, I described a young man with a congenital absence of pain. He felt nothing on drilling a tooth, and would jump off a roof and fracture his limbs, painlessly; yet persons with congenital absence of pain fibers have emotions.

Initially, feeling is raw experience that partitions to body segment and generalizes to states such as fear, which is avoidance of (potential) pain, or to the discomfort caused by hunger, thirst, cold and so on. When feeling is focused on an activity such as stalking or escape, the subjectivity of the organism is oriented to an external source or target, but feeling is still centered in the body. The organism feels the body and the bodily feeling is the inner-experience of the organism. The first sign of feeling as value in objects is existence. Feeling enlivens and awakens the body. Like action, it is deposited in a bodily object. Fear is the affective or emotional manifestation of the primitive nociceptive sense of pain. Fear is anxiety without pain, for which the visual, auditory or olfactory senses dominate. Pain is felt as though it existed in the body, while fear is entirely in the mind; one is a response to bodily injury, the other to external events. As pain focuses on a source in the body, vision and audition focus on threats and opportunities in the world. The body is one of a manifold of objects in the world to which action is directed, but action is first realized in the body. Some perceptions are identified with the body image—tactile, proprioceptive, vestibular, while others—auditory, visual—are relatively free of body-representation: one is not (usually) aware of the eye when seeing, or of the ear when hearing, but most of us are aware of the finger when touching.

Feeling is direction in the transformation of energy (Freud's libidinal Q in the metapsychology) as the vital force in organism. Whitehead wrote, ". . . the energetic activity considered in physics is the emotional intensity entertained in life."[2] The shift from isotropic energy to anisotropic feeling is the driving force of organism. Feeling as instinctual energy is palliated, diffused or de-focused upon consummation. The dissolution of hunger in satiation accompanies a generalization, not diminution, of feeling; feeling is no longer concentrated in a specific impulse or action. Like energy, it is conserved. That is, feeling intensifies with a focus or subjective aim, while a reduction in feeling points to redistribution. Feeling does not change, only its generality, partition, sequestration or transformation. In severe pain, feeling is allocated to the affected region; the nociceptive stimulus constrains feeling to the relevant body part, just as external sensory data constrain mentality to model the world.

In sum, subjectivity generated by feeling that develops from energy precedes organism, but the overt signs of subjectivity involve the response to painful injury. This represents the concentration of feeling in the organism as a whole or, in advanced organisms, in the body part. The body-schema absorbs the feeling as having an intensity that threatens survival. In humans, there is an intentional relation to pain as an internal object or state, analogous to the intentionality of fear as a reaction to a potentially harmful or painful event. In animals, the transition from pain in the body to the fear of a painful experience in the world is less clear, since we do not suppose that animals forecast future experiences. Pain as a disruption of the body-schema may transition through sexual pleasure, which also is feeling concentrated in the body.

2. Whitehead, A. N. (1934) *Nature and Life,* Cambridge University Press.

FROM ANIMAL TO HUMAN MIND

There is no reason to believe that subjectivity is unique to humans, especially since it does not develop *ex nihilo*, but on the basis of a more primitive, language-free mode of animal life. While feeling arises before awareness of inner and outer in animal mentality, pain in the body may serve to divide bodily experience from what is happening in the world. Initially, the outer is an extension of the inner, but is not recognized as a separate field, no more than the mental is recognized as distinct from the body. At this level of mentality, the outer world—*Umwelt*—is continuous with the organism; the body is incorporated in mentality even as the world separates, objectifies and becomes distinct. Perception provides objects for the effectuation of action, which begins as an impulse toward perception. The objects that perception creates are the targets toward which actions are directed. Though action seems to follow perception, objects and acts develop together, concurrently. Organism and behavior are bodily realizations, with action the primary instrument of feeling and implementation. Feeling is not "destitute of causal agency" (James), but rather provides the impulse to effectuation. Hume thought emotion, not reason, provides the impulse to action.

The organism is part of nature, as nature is part of the organism. The duality of mind and brain can be conceived as a division of the physical and mental, as of mind and world, or inner and outer. The relation of mind to the physical brain is analogous to the relation of mind to the physical world. In early stages, there is little awareness of the distinction of subject and object. Inner and outer, continuous in the human infant, retrace stages in animal mind, with an initial focus on bodily need and a limited engagement with the external, except as a source of satisfaction, or of threats to be evaded or overcome.

In human perception, the body seems independent of the objects the mind perceives; in action, the body is the object. One detaches; the other remains part of the self. Through perception and the arousal of pre-objects, a self is born in relation to an inner and outer world, leading to the recognition of a world independent of mind and a mind independent of body (brain).

The primary shift to human mind, then, is from an action-based body-centered mentality in animals to an object-centered perception-based mentality in humans. Action impacts objects without leaving the body. Perceptions leave the body as targets for motility. As objects externalize, they leave a residue of psychic content. The body-schema in animals, since it is bound up with motility, is incapable of more than a rudimentary inner life, which requires actualization of a mental state beyond the confines of drive-categories based on bodily feeling. These segments, derived from the instinctual inheritance, undergo an arrest (neoteny) in the process of object-formation, in order to lay down intra-psychic experience.

In an organism, subjectivity and the inner life are the criteria of mentality. The progression from a purely bodily experience of feeling as pain, through the bodily needs and excitements of hunger and sexual drive, to a sense of mind-internal (fear), corresponds to an extension of the subjective aim, such that early stages arise in relation to the body, while later or object-close stages, free of body-relatedness, lead to the experience of desire and conceptual feelings, inner content and a world that contains the body itself. The fractionation of the perceptible to an immense variety of objects precedes the partition of inner-mind to self and introspective content. Animals and humans feel the body, but humans perceive it. Consciousness recognizes the self that perceives. Mirror recognition of self in apes indicates a rudimentary self-concept. This capacity, along with the properties of mirror space, can be lost in dementia, though to my knowledge the status of self-awareness has not been studied.

In the course of actualization, the progression from categories to objects eventuates in substance (being); feeling, as part of the action development, constitutes process (becoming). Being is perceptual (assignment of the object to a category), while becoming is realized through action (feeling), though every pre-object has an affective tonality. The directionality of feeling (will) in animals, the subjective aim, leads to purposefulness in behavior. In humans, feeling passes through pre-perceptual categories to arouse intentional or volitional attitudes. Pre-perceptual levels serve as templates to realize intentional targets. Purposefulness becomes agency when the subjective aim is conscious.

The body image is a non-conscious "schema," not an actual image. Alteration of the schema occurs in pathology, such as lack of awareness of half the body (in anosognosia or hemispatial neglect), confusion as to the location of a body part (autotopagnosia) or involuntary actions that appear purposeful (alien hand). Most action occurs without consciousness of movement of the body itself, which suggests the body-schema actualizes automatically. In animals, bodily action with hesitation and the appearance of decision-making without deliberation may signal rudimentary thought in problem-solving. The schema is foundational to self and volition, with drive categories linked to bodily action realized through segments of object formation.

The infiltration of nature into primitive mind and its continuity with higher mentality convey the proto-psychic into animal and human cognition. So-called "brain-in-a-vat" arguments imply that the body exists for the individual as mental representation, or that bodily sensation is assimilated to a kind of picture of the body, at least its outer manifestations, while the body itself—a life-support system for the brain—is adventitious to mind, since mind persists when disconnected from sensation arising in or on the body surface, except for modalities relating to the external world. Thus, animals remain awake after cutting all but the trigeminal nerve, but once the nerve is severed they are unconscious. External sensibility is essential to the preservation of consciousness; endogenous sensation is essential to wakefulness. Consciousness persists in patients with cervical cord injury and loss of sensation and movement below the neck, though such individuals often go through a psychotic-like transition, with reorganization of the self-concept.

If sensation within the body can be lost with preservation of mentality, what is the contribution to the "schema" and its relation to mind? Kant wrote that his body served to carry his brain around. Some are anxious over the possibility of a failing brain, at least when it begins to fail, but most people are more concerned about bodily illness than mental illness. Death is annihilation of the body, the most palpable realization of individuality. Those who believe the soul survives are, one would think, less concerned about a loss of self or death of the brain. We are usually aggrieved by physical illness or injury and less distressed over mental impairment. Persons with failing memory are usually less aware of the problem than friends or family. The personal impact of disturbed mentality, in my experience, is proportionate to its development. A mild impairment in cognition is often of greater concern to those of higher intelligence than a more severe impairment to those with lower intellect.

Since the self-concept arises at archaic levels out of the categorical primes of instinctual drive, early phases are guided by instinctual needs. Whatever limits on freedom this origin poses, they are more than compensated by self-realization, through segments of choice and decision and the potential for liberation from instinct and the animal inheritance. Low levels of freedom entail willfulness, a semblance of choice and restriction of urge. The direction of feeling from self to image or object and the implementation of action by feeling (will) combine as a sense of purposefulness. Higher modes entail conscious choice and rational decision. While reason alone does not instigate action, thought is entrained by action to realize rational ends. The progression from instinctual drive early in the actualization to subsequent phases of imagination, choice and rational judgment gives greater latitude to actions that were formerly inhibited or precluded by drive.

When the discipline imposed on action by instinctual drive is relaxed in human cognition, through intra-psychic partition, the transition is oriented in a passage through segments of imagination and decision. From the rigid constraints of instinct to the endless possibilities of imagination, action is only limited by belief, values, will and physical potential. Absolute freedom exercised by a fully independent self would sever ties to experience, cultural tradition, loyalties, personal attitudes and social aims. An individual cannot exercise unlimited potential without conscious goals, which come from belief and experience, as the propellants of action and choice. We live between a commitment to ends of which we are often unaware and the possibilities of imagination, which, because of caution and dispassion, are rarely implemented. The spontaneity of animal mind is lost when conscious decision is employed. The cost of freedom from animal nature is thus reflection over actions, regrets, competing perspectives and uncertainty in conduct at the higher and more complex levels of human thought. Hamlet is the *locus classicus* for this.

Though reason is a watershed in human mentation, rational decision does not inevitably lead to personal satisfaction, since emotional and other needs may, of necessity, be sacrificed or unresolved. The compromise of feeling and responsibility tilts one way or another, depending on the insistence of emotionality and the resistance of reason. Decisions in which action veers to reason can leave a taste of the inauthentic unless accompanied by a supportive affective tone, since rationality and the public good are often opposed to individuality and personal satisfaction. It is one thing to compare the differing needs of two people and the needs of the individual in relation to society. If A loves B and B rejects A, or A neglects B, how can reason override feeling and experience in decision-making? Did Socrates, unjustly condemned to death by an Athenian jury, make the correct decision in awaiting execution in the jail, when his friends were prepared to engineer his release? Reason might compel me to sacrifice my life to save many others. The compassionate agency of the knowing self may be in conflict with what is best for the individual. That is why we are most at ease when behavior is automatic, since deliberation infects behavior with incompleteness or lack of the genuine.

THE PHILOSOPHY OF THE SUBJECTIVE

The seeds of subjectivity are sown in primitive organism and the landscape of animal mind, but the fruits of the subjective are in consciousness and rational choice, often involving conflict. The subjective is continuous with the physical—or with attributes of physical entities—such that a distinction depends on the priority of the endogenous, though interiorness is prior even to organism. We speak of the subjective with some certitude in its higher manifestations, though there are grades of subjectivity, all the way from automatism to creativity and deep reflection. When the self in contemplation turns from the external world to the interior of thought and memory, the subjective is enhanced by the prominence of intentionality and the exclusion of the external, as Schopenhauer came to realize, late in life. Perhaps this is its utmost point, though one could argue that dream, though non-intentional, in the absence of all external stimuli, is more fully subjective. If dream is pre-perception, sensation acts on a substrate of implicit imagery to create a dispersal into objects. If dream cognition or some features of the dream are the ground out of which waking consciousness evolves, the objectification of a subjective world imposes a burden of externality on the reach of consciousness. No matter how rich the inner life, no matter how intense are desire and meaning, the mind will always be found wanting in relation to the profligacy of nature, so much so that it seems incredible that nature could be a creation of mind, even if the creation is a subjective model of the external. Yet depth of thought, imagination and creativity are more than enough for any individual to feel the pulse of the active mind and know the reality of the inner life.

For externalist doctrine, human mind is like that imputed to animals, robotic, determined and reducible to brain. We are the sum of our acts, Sartre said, all the while employing his imagination to develop his philosophy. Actions specify categories and individuate contexts, but what is left behind or discarded, what is left unsaid, unwritten, imagined or considered, are no less part of what actualizes than the behavior that emerges from inner world to outer. A reliance on action focuses on the final definiteness of the mental state, excluding what went into an implicit or conscious decision to act. Actions often represent a compromise of intent with societal demands, of value and necessity, such that the latter become components of the action itself. All the reasons not to act, or to act differently, are part of what is decided on. While an objectivist account does not obviate the need to explain mental phenomena, the postulate of reducibility or elimination (Churchland) has the effect of collapsing psyche to brain and diluting the legitimacy of the subjective. However, subjectivity is not inconsistent with reduction or identity, since material entities exhibit subjective properties. Moreover, a theory on the primacy of the subjective might well be supported by arguing that, from a theoretical if not empirical perspective, it is more accurate to say that the mind is not in the brain, but the brain is in the mind (Kuhlenbeck).

A third-person approach is limited to accounts of minds other than that of the externalist, who is in the untenable position of employing his own subjectivity to deny it in others. Ideas brought to bear on the interpretation of other minds, for example, as causal outputs, are equally applicable to the mind of the externalist, whose consciousness, intentionality and ideation are engaged in a description of the robotic behavior of others. If the externalist philosopher is an automaton as well, what are we to make of his conclusions? Are they perspicacious, insightful, creative, or do they represent, as reduction entails, one robot deconstructing another? To what extent is the externalist subjugated to the *Zeitgeist* of trends, opinions and the attitudes of contemporary thinkers? Evolution is often cited as support for materialism, but this is not a settled issue (e.g. Whitehead). My own writings employ evolutionary concepts, but reach different conclusions. The impoverishment of externalism and the dispute over subjectivity reflect a willful neglect or ignorance of mental phenomena antecedent to "output", such that a description limited to performance trivializes the private states it neglects to describe.

The self and other mental contents are co-dependent: one does not occur without the other. The self is thought up as a contrast or foil to thought. What is the difference between the self as a thought (concept) and the thoughts the self thinks? In thinking, the contrast between self *qua* thought and thought *qua* content depends on the fact that the self is grounded in individuality, sameness of character and identity, while thought is fluid, changeable and ranges freely, and to an extent is independent of individuality. Self and thought are concepts or categories, the constancy of the self is a puzzle to be explained, the volatility of thought is a given. In other words, identity is a defining property of the self, and fluidity and scope are defining properties of thought. If diversity in thought emanates from a partition of the self, the paradox can be resolved by conceiving the self as a unified construct that elaborates, enfolds and binds together a range of potential thought content. The progression from the singularity and stability of the self to the almost limitless possibilities of thought and imagination suggests that there is a passage from the oneness of the core to multiplicity at the surface. The intra-psychic progression foreshadows a transition from the substrates of thinking to their still more diverse objectifications. In sum, the transition from the relative unity of the self to the moderate diversity of imagery to an infinite variety of objects is a continuous process of partition that is unbroken despite the apparent gap from mind to world.

An efflorescence of the self through imagination to the world is the rule, though the self can fracture or be deranged, and imagination can petrify in habit or obsession. Still, the passage ordinarily goes from unity to multiplicity, from relative stability of personality and character to a manifold of mental and world contents. The self creates diversity as spectator or participant on a spectrum from dissonance to compatibility, a transition that is prefigured by a tension of self and idea, of category and member, of self-realization and choice, or authenticity and submission or compromise. When the self fails to accommodate to its own model of the world, or rather, when sensibility generates a world that deviates from the desires and expectations of the self, the potential for self-transformation is obstructed.

Sensation has such a grip on mind that the tension between the apparent persistence of external objects and the tenuousness of thought and life does not ordinarily invade our concepts of objects until perception is compromised. Merely to experience vertigo is to know that the stability of the world is fragile, with a layer of imagination just beneath a veneer of objects that only seem to orient themselves in relation to a stable horizon. Hallucination provides the same insight. In fact, caloric stimulation (hot or cold water put into the ear canal) in persons with visual hallucination induces vertiginous rotation of the hallucinatory images, as well as perceptual objects, a clinical observation which points to the commonality of image and object, and the underpinning of perception in hallucinatory phenomena. While the finality of perception—the living reality of life in actuality—is attenuated by altered states, without a healthy and active self-concept the weight of the external and the slow erosion of mental faculties in aging can readily overwhelm and disempower the inner voice.

The objectification of the world creates a fissure in the connectedness of self and object, the continuity of which, recovered in animism and pathology, is increasingly fractured by the onslaught of sensory data and the compartmentalization of feeling that are so common in modern life. The immediacy of contact and the seductiveness of the external mitigate reflection and imagination for a worldly life. While the transition is continuous, we perceive a sharp divide between inner and outer, largely due to the massive amount of sensory processing applied to pre-object gestalts and the lack of awareness or even deletion of (potentially) conscious antecedents. Mind-external dominates mind-internal. The primacy of the world and the early articulation of object space have a long evolutionary history essential for organisms to flourish and survive, while the partition of mind into self and thought is a relatively recent and perhaps not universal phenomenon. Moreover, with the advent of evolutionary theory and the dominance of analytical philosophy and materialism, the theory of mind automates mind, which assumes a subsidiary role in physical doctrine, which, considering how little we really know of the brain, is based more on opinion than fact.

Still, there are contradictory theories as to whether: (1) mind can be reduced to the material, and exemplifies or is continuous with physical nature, (2) the continuum of mind and world is subjective, or (3) if there is an irreconcilable split between the subjective and objective. A material continuum from brain to world would not necessarily entail conflict between psyche and nature, or between a self and a physical world. The conflict, or distinction, of inner subjectivity and outer objectivity should not necessarily be problematic for a relation of one mechanical entity (brain) with another (world), yet the subject/object divide is pivotal. As to intra-psychic conflict, this usually represents indecisiveness in a course of action, difficult to describe or explain from a materialist perspective, since the sources of conflict—an uncertain self, repressed ideas, memories—are not easy to isolate as physical entities, and are thus often conceived as illusory. Thus, the self—isolated, assertive, compliant or vulnerable—perceives a world that can be friendly, hostile or indifferent, a dreamscape or a mine field that is traversed with a combination of luck and skill. In animals, danger and opportunity accompany a tension between organism and world. Indecision, which is usually fatal in the wild, is the germ of thought, as deliberation replaces spontaneity.

In part, the question of the subjective arises when the internal life of the organism appears to be distinguishable from its material basis, especially in creativity, choice, reflection, consciousness, value, idealization and the feeling of the present moment. As the physical complexity of organism increases, so does the impression of subjectivity. Ordinarily, mentality or subjectivity is conceived as a function of some material substrate, but complexity in the subjective workings of organism implies that the material could evolve as a complement to the psychic. That is, an increase in the intricacy of mental operations might be an agent of material change, rather than the reverse. A continuum is implied in the assumption that the inner life incorporates the physicality of nature, since the substrates of mind-internal are stages in evolution confluent with natural process. Instinctual needs that externalize in animals remain internal in humans to give conceptual feelings. Drives as foundations of thought are the origin of conflict within and between the self and other.

The self/other relation is central in the confrontation with others; mate, child, community, nation, way of life. The affinity for otherness depends on worth and personal valuation, distribution of feeling and the internalization of the other, as in love or fear. The other can be trusted, alien or oppositional; it can be an illness, a person, an idea, a political doctrine; it can be concrete or conceptual, a group or a member of a group. In love, the other is a sole category that individuates in relation to its attributes. Otherness is not always apartness or hostility, but varies from objectification (the other as "it") to idealization (the other as "thou").

What is the role of teleology or final causation in the path from the primitive to the advanced? One possibility is the trend to increasing analysis (articulation of environment and organism), with gradual specification of intrinsic process (inside-out, so to speak), such that subjective antecedents undergo progressive individuation and complexity. The external in itself, Kant's *Dinge an sich*, is relatively stable; the world is what it is, though it is a different world for different organisms. Mental antecedents advance through whole/part transformations that amplify the inner through fractionation to successive categories.

What are the implications of creativity for materialism? On the one hand, the intuitive basis of creation implies that consciousness serves to edit what is unconsciously thought up, so as to actualize unconscious learning and innate tendencies. In creativity, unconscious process has a greater role than conscious imagination. The works of great artists are the antithesis of mechanical products, since they arise spontaneously through yet-unknown mechanisms or capacities that transcend causal linkage. If the creative is recombination, what guides the combinatory process? What is the physical basis of metaphorical spread or elaboration? Does brain process have a subjective aim? Evolution leads to consciousness, but does consciousness drive evolution?

This is not to argue a rupture of brain from thought, but to emphasize a quality of subjectivity in material nature that includes the brain: that is, the physical process of brain activity has subjective properties that are ubiquitous, yet it makes little sense to say that a brain thinks, loves, doubts or desires. This is the implication of reductionism, even if it were possible for a mental vocabulary to be replaced by a neural code. Does it make sense to say the genome thinks up the phenotype, if it gives rises to it? If epigenetic mechanisms lead to phenotypes, what mediates the translation of a brain code to psychic process? Psyche collapses to brain, yet brain cannot be identified with psyche. Is there an algorithm that translates mechanisms to subjectivity? Are brain and mental process isomorphic? This was argued by the gestalt psychologists. What is the brain correlate of aesthetic sensitivity? If consciousness is the arbiter of what the unconscious delivers, and material process is non-conscious, where does this leave us in a physical explanation of creativity? An explanation of creative process usually retreats to the analysis of a completed work, a move that misses the very process of creation itself.

7

Mind and Brain[1]

SUMMARY

THIS PAPER DESCRIBES THE categorical nature of the mind/brain state from its origins in drive to the refinements of human cognition. Categories are concepts with a broader scope. The virtual quality of the members of a category corresponds to the relation of whole to part. A successive individuation of categories is the foundational operation of the mind/brain state. There is a similarity to fractal theory and the mereology of wholes and parts, though categories are not sums or containers, members are virtual, and the whole/part specification is qualitative, unlike the self-similar replications of fractal theory.

The discussion takes up the problem of causal transmission between mind and brain, and within and across mental states, concluding that an assimilation model has more explanatory power than a strictly causal one, in keeping with the distinction between potential/actual and cause/effect. The idea that mind-brain interaction is causal introduces the possibility of subjectivity independent of material substrate. This leads to speculation on a world soul animating brain as part of nature, and conversely, the effort to erase all vestiges of spirit, leaving a purely material organism and universe. In reality, there is no bifurcation of mental and physical; rather, there is a graded series of stages, with properties of material and subjective entities that eventuate in human mentality. This conforms to a neutral monism.

1. Brown, J (2014) Mind and brain: a contribution from microgenetic theory, *Journal of Consciousness Studies*, 21:54–73; Brown, J (2010) Neuropsychological Foundations of Conscious Experience. Chromatika, Belgium.

Duration is inherent in nature and evolves in company with organisms of increasing complexity.

INTRODUCTION

This essay explores some aspects of the relation of mind to brain that follow on the preceding discussion. The various philosophical approaches to this topic do not unravel the problem, but tend to propose overarching "solutions"; for example, mind is eliminated, reduced or identical to brain function, conceived in terms of a dual-vocabulary, or construed as epiphenomenal or parallel to brain activity. I have speculated on a neutral monism. In most of these instances, there is a materialistic shift, with a focus less on mentality in relation to specific brain activity than on neuroscience and a faith in future brain research, the assumption being that one can ignore normal and abnormal psychology, or the infrastructure of cognition, in favor of generalities that reduce mind to brain, with the assumption that details will eventually be sorted out by objective science. Entire functions, capacities or classes of behavior are correlated with parts of the brain (love, moral sensibility), but specific performances give conflicting results (phonology, reading), while the correlation, even if reproducible, does not explain the function that is reduced.

Moreover, there is no concerted effort to specify the relation to underlying brain process, such as the neural systems involved in the experience of saying a word or seeing a particular object; rather, the focus is on general statements as to the relation of mind to brain, without regard for the attributes of mentality and how these might be realized in brain process. How does brain process create a category? What is the role of memory in thinking from a neural perspective? How do words arise without thinking about them? How does conversation express thought or belief, especially if one discovers the thought after the words are spoken? How do values, consciousness, intentionality or meanings correspond to patterns of neural firing? The approach is much like attributing schizophrenia or autism to a gene, a virus or toxin, with no explanation of the hallucinations or aberrant behavior that not only accompany the disorder, but in fact define it. The facile descent to a lower level or the simple collapse of mind to brain is not an explanation, but only a way to finesse the actual problem, which is less the brain substrate of mind than how the particulars of mind are generated.

One strategy is to extract general principles, even laws, of mental activity and speculate on how these principles might be instantiated in brain. One of the more important of these regularities is the universal problem of category. A category is a concept that includes more than one member. Items in a category are potential sub-categories for further partition, or they precipitate as finalities in the actualization process. A category thus encloses a multitude of unactualized members, which, once elicited, can deposit *inter alia* in action, perception or language, or serve as categories for subsequent partitions. The process of whole/part transition corresponds to an elicitation of items or members that, if not realized, retain the potential for further transformation. The category/member relation is comparable to that of whole to part, such that the progression from holistic to analytic is analogous to that from category to member. Many terms have been used to describe this process, including individuation, specification, differentiation, analysis, as well as frame/content, surround/center, ground/figure, lateral inhibition, sculpting, parcellation and trimming of redundancy. The central feature is the elimination or inhibition of irrelevance as a means to final precision or definiteness. The iteration of this process over phases lays down the mind/brain state. Moreover, the propagation of a thought from one phase to the next by way of categories, rather than modular elements, accounts for the experience that a fragmentary memory lasting a few seconds can serve to reprise an entire event-category.

The whole/part relation can be found in the most basic physical entities, but in more advanced organisms categorization is most evident in instinctual drive. In animals, the repertoire of behavior is limited mainly to predation, defense, mating and maternal care, which represent categories shaped by inherited constraints on instinctual drive. Such categories include predator/prey behavior, aggression, defense, food and mate selection. This foundation of behavior is reinforced by recurrent occasions of satisfaction, which serve to elicit action appropriate to external conditions and constrain random or maladaptive behavior. The categorical nature of drive allows a flexibility that is not self-evident in the fixity and necessity of cause and effect.

Drive-categories correspond to neural configurations with the potential to partition to sub-categories. For example, on one occasion, chasing and killing a gazelle is the primary option; on another, feeding on a dead carcass. On one occasion the animal feeds at the site of the kill, on another it conceals or removes its prey. A drive is not a rigid set of instructions, but a general framework for behaviors that, within limits, adapt to circumstance. Thus hunger leads to predation as drive partitions to various implementations; stalking, deference to the hierarchy in a group or feeding order. The category realizes paradigmatic features that expand or contract according to intrinsic (age, health) and extrinsic (abundance, scarcity) conditions. In human mind, these features and their neural correlates are derived through many subsequent partitions, such that the outcome—compassion, table manners—appears quite distant from the originating drive.[2]

The sexual urge or the feeling of hunger and its neural correlates generate virtual objects—instinctual, experiential—to satisfy categorical primitives that govern further transformations and prevent derailments or maladaptive associations. Hunger might develop into greed or acquisitiveness; sexuality, to a manifold of variations. Objects or goals relating to drive-based categories propagate by metaphorical extension or overlap of shared features. The difficulty for neuroscience to explicate this pattern is that brain process entails widely distributed wave or field effects, not dissimilar from those postulated in Gestalt theory, while research in neuroscience tends to involve single unit studies that sample a fraction of the configuration or distributed system. At the other extreme, metabolic studies focus mainly on whole behaviors, not local features of brain or mental activity.

Another source of category formation in brain comes from repetition, relative constancy of behavior, and the daily recurrence of environments, such that similar patterns recur to reinforce categorical groupings. The strategy employed by a lion pursuing a gazelle or a bird pouncing on a grub is sufficiently repetitive that the recurrence of neural activity underlying the behavior tends to accentuate the pattern. The play of infant animals and early training further reinforce drive categories. Trial and error helps to strengthen adaptive routines, increase fitness and eliminate maladaptive behaviors. The evolutionary principle that matches organism to surround continues in trial and error to map behavior to successful strategies. The instinctual category that propels behavior is reinforced and expanded by experience. The same process occurs in the pattern recognition of ethological studies, for example, a mouse or chicken reacting with threat-response behavior to a cardboard outline of a hawk.

The neural configuration that corresponds to patterns of behavior and object recognition is the equivalent of a category, in that it includes paradigmatic features, such as size, color or contour, but excludes non-matches or atypical features. The instinctual category leads to a behavioral response that ignores or suppresses competing stimuli outside the category boundary. The configural pattern is the basis of ensuing partitions. The onset of an act of cognition in instinctual drive establishes a categorical foundation

2. A simple example was provided by my one-year-old son, who was shown a ball and told the name, which he did not repeat until a later occasion, when a pea rolled off his plate. Clearly, the generalization of roundness to different objects conforms to the notion of early category formation. There are many such examples in the literature, including the kind of categorization described in operant conditioning.

that undergoes multiple partitions as it branches into finer derivations over phases in the mental state.

To my knowledge, the neural basis of drive categories has not been adequately researched. However, the bottom-up derivation of configural groupings mediated by myriad synapses over a wide area of brain can hardly be disputed. Perception and action arise out of instinctual categories that frame the actualization of a series of whole/part transitions that arborize into acts, objects and ideas. This sequence is the fundamental operation of the brain. The commonality of whole/part shifts implies some degree of isomorphism of neural and mental process, inferred from focal lesions that selectively expose preliminary phases (symptoms), revealing the category/member specifications. The conclusion is that a single process of qualitative whole/part or category/member specification, iterated at successive phases from instinct to final act or object, is the fundamental operation that governs the moment-to-moment derivation of the mind/brain state. In this respect, there is identity, but no reduction of mind to brain. The study of mind reveals the nature of brain, not the other way around.

COMMENTARY ON RESEARCH

Generally, philosophical speculation on the mind/brain takes a holistic approach, with brain as a global physical entity and mind as a generalized object. This is the most comfortable perspective for a third-person externalism, which can ignore mental function and subjectivity, as well as the details of psychological study and brain organization. For this approach, a slab of brain tissue might well elaborate a partial state of mind, since the structure of mind and brain is excluded from theory. For example, a concept of input and output ignores the complex multi-tiered organization that supports the development of the object and the act. No wonder that, for most externalists, it is irrelevant whether the physical substrate of mind is carbon or silicon.

The alternative is to explore the micro-structure of brain and the neural processes through which the attributes of mentality are generated. However, even this approach is dogged by an objectivism that does not take the subjective seriously. Partly this reflects dogma and the Zeitgeist, but also limits on methodologies. Among the strategies for brain study are imaging techniques, surgical procedures, brain stimulation, unit studies and, of most importance, pathological disruptions of process caused by focal lesions. Studies that look for correlations of local or distributed functional systems are incapable of the fine analysis of the systems they explore. A slight change of method, arousal or perturbation can lead to vast differences in correlations. For example, different studies of phonology have found activation in multiple areas. This is not taken as a refutation or critique of experimental method, but as indicating a network in which all locations are engaged. Focal activation is designed to support discrete or modular localization, whereas a widespread activation supports a distributed network. What would it take to refute these findings? In contrast, single unit studies which look at cell response to stimulation sample a limited number of units and are oblivious to observations inconsistent with expectations, such as cells in the visual area that respond to auditory stimulation, or sign language in the deaf that activates cells associated with auditory processing.

Of the various techniques to study mind and brain, those involving the symptoms of local brain lesion are typically considered the least scientific or reliable, often dismissed as observational, descriptive, anecdotal and non-repeatable. For these reasons, as well as the large corpus of clinical material that discourages careful study, there has been a concerted effort to turn descriptive psychology into a scientific discipline by delegitimizing a qualitative approach to symptoms, in favor of quantitative studies in which probe stimuli, so it is argued, yield a collection of correct and incorrect responses irrespective of error type, the goal of which, consistent with circuit board models of processors, inputs and outputs, is to obtain scores in which the measurement of performance replaces the nature of the performance being measured. Partly, the problem is a lack of theory concerning the origin and meaning of the symptom, and the presumption that errors, especially of language, are mere guesses of no interpretive value. A model of symptom formation and its relevance to mind/brain theory has been described in detail elsewhere (Brown & Pachalska, 2003), but the arguments confirm that whole/part transitions in mind/brain mediate the development of actions and objects.

UNCONSCIOUS MIND

There is such overwhelming evidence for unconscious cognition, inferred from its conscious products, that to deny its occurrence is either to willfully ignore the origins of conscious thought, or to assume the indefensible position that all thought arises in consciousness. Some philosophers (Searle) dismiss the unconscious as mere physiology. However, in addition to dream, unconscious cognition includes hypnotic, trance and mystical states, creativity, myth, non-intentional moods or objectless states, such as diffuse anxiety or unresolved conflict, drive and motivation, sleepwalking and other dissociative states, "slips of the tongue", obsessions and compulsions, right hemisphere cognition in a case of "split brain," not to mention the whole "storehouse" of grammar, memory, beliefs, presuppositions and values that account for thought, acts, objects and language. There are also experimental probes of non-conscious processes, such as masking, tachisto-scopic presentation (percept-genetic and related studies), priming, learning during anesthesia, incidental and procedural learning, conditioning, habit and skill formation. To dismiss the unconscious as physiology avoids the obligation to go beyond negation to a more exact account of the transition to consciousness, its immediate precursors and evolutionary ancestry.

In some respects, unconscious mind is of greater relevance to subjec-tivism than conscious mind, since the interpretation of the unconscious and its manifestations brings the relation of the physical brain to mentality into clear focus, whereas consciousness raises questions on dualism or epiphe-nomenalism that are not helpful in deciphering the mind/brain relation. Cognition in the absence of consciousness raises the question of the subjec-tivity of "physiological" process; that is, mentation without consciousness. While it is unlikely that animals have an unconscious stratum in relation to conscious awareness, or that they have a fraction of the complexity of content in the human unconscious (necessarily derived in large part from conscious experience), still, the mentality or subjectivity of brain activity independent of consciousness is supported by unconscious cognition in hu-mans. In sum, though the human unconscious depends heavily on material acquired during consciousness, which is unlikely in animals, the occurrence of unconscious mentation reinforces arguments for the existence of non-conscious mentality, and for the subjectivity of physical states in organism appearing prior to conscious awareness.

CAUSATION AND THE MIND/BRAIN STATE

It seems clear from the standpoint of identity or neutral monism that brain does not cause mental activity. Mind is not a causal object, and the neces-sity for a causal step from brain to mind, or the reverse, is unproven and probably unprovable. One—or two-way causation entails an interaction of mind and brain as separate and distinct "objects." The inference that brain activity causes mental activity appears to be a result of the assumption that the physical is primary and mentation a result of physical process, and the commonsense observation that mind causes behavior mediated by brain: specifically, the everyday experience that thoughts and feelings cause behav-ior, which implies that mind is a causal output of brain and, conversely, that mind acts on brain to cause behavior. The presumption is that if a mental state can cause a motor act, physical states can cause occasions of mind, that is, the mind-brain relation is causal in both directions. This may be plausible for some, but it is as difficult to explain how mental phenomena could act on a physical brain as it is to explain how the brain could cause mental states. For these and other reasons, a causal account of mind-brain interaction has little current support.

In prior discussions I have argued that the overlap of mind/brain states constrains consequent states to conform to prior ones, inducing the prior state to assimilate the state that follows. This preserves continuity across mind/brain states and explains the impact of the antecedent state on that which follows. As to the effect of will or thought on action, the hypothesis is that a configural bias precipitates a sequence of category/item transforms as a kind of psychic corridor traversed by states dedicated to action. The finalities of introspection that arise as a subjective aim form a bottom-up pathway—a set of constraints—through which the action develops.

Prior to achieving finality in a state of indecision, action is forestalled or uncertain, not necessarily because of conflict, but for lack of a singular template through which the act can be specified. The final sequence has insufficient specificity to serve as a track for the derivation of behavior. This means that decision does not implement action, but rather provides a con-figured sequence through which action is derived. It is hard to say whether or not the development of the action, which assimilates to the parallel process of thought development, is causal, but there is no direct linkage of thought, decision or judgment and behavior, which is why rational thought can be construed as a justification for action, not its immediate cause.

If causation is not between mind and brain, can it be posited across or within mind/brain states? Most accounts of transition postulate causal relations from one state to the next. In Buddhist thought, which has sup-port in some contemporary models, each state is an encapsulated moment (*ksana*) of arising and descending that passes to the next in a causal chain. The state develops, subsides and gives way to the ensuing state. Whether arising and subsidence are transmitted as a packet or only a portion, and what constitutes a state (its boundaries, contents, duration) are matters of infrequent commentary outside of microgenetic theory, for the most part not even discussed in causal accounts, despite constant speculation on the transition from cause to effect, what is carried over into the effect, the source of novelty, and so on.

The problem is still more complex. With overlap in succession, if the mind/brain state does not exist until it actualizes, how can early phases prior to completion cause early phases in the oncoming state? Indeed, if the ensu-ing state is activated before the prior state comes into existence, the ensuing state could exercise a mode of backward causation on the forming-but-not-yet-actual current state. The overlap of early segments, which preserves the identity, continuity and the stability of self, character and experience, can be conceived as an assimilation of T2 (the "after" time point) to T1 (the "before" time point)—or the reverse. Once the current state exists, it can serve as a causal entity, but how would causation call up the oncoming state if it is already in the process of actualizing?

This raises the problem of cause and effect in a replacement model. For one thing, if the assimilation of one state to another is guided by constraints, the transition would not conform to causal laws, since constraints are not causes in any obvious sense (Hume). The process account of the state—a becoming-into-being—is inconsistent with a substantive cause, especially if the actualized state includes the subsidence as well as the arising. If the state is a completed process of actualization, does the succession cause an ensuing state, or does it cause earlier, then later, phases in the antecedent state? In the replacement, the consequent state is generated by, and takes the place of, the antecedent one, such that distal segments of the earlier state vanish before those of the ensuing state occur. This means that distal segments, say for an act or external object, have no causal efficacy for distal phases in the ensuing state.

The base of the state instigates the "abiding" features of drive and personality through a replication by overlap of early phases, with final phases compelled by sensation to model the occasion. Only intermediate phases have some degree of plasticity; they are less adapted, less assimilated and of dubious causal effect. If causation between states occurs, it would be maximal early in the state by virtue of overlap and distance from sensation, but relaxed over pre-terminal segments. This implies that a completed state does not cause its successor, which begins prior to the actualization of its predecessor.

In a conversation on momentariness I had many years ago in Sikkim with a Buddhist monk on what happens between moments in the transmission from cause to effect, we reached an impasse on the explanation of continuity, change, and the distinction of cause from effect. On a process model, the continuous transition is relatively seamless. On an atomic or modular account, cause and effect are discrete, with a multitude of causal pairs in the succession leading to an infinite regress in the interstices of the micro-transition. In both instances, especially with a replacement model, there is a possibility of multiple minds and worlds between mental states.

For some philosophers, a mental state refers to content items—qualia, propositions—without regard for spatio-temporal context or antecedent history. The aim is to isolate the content as a mental solid that can, in principle, be related to local brain activity and other mental contents, which are also conceived as modular. A heuristic advantage means little if it leads to a false narrative. Qualia can be anything from an after-image or feeling to the entire perceptible world. It is odd that after-images are often employed as examples of qualia, since, following Emmert's law, they have physical features, unlike hallucinations or other forms of imagery. Moreover, their relation to palinopsia and flight of colors is ignored. As to propositions, a logical proposition, such as the redundant argument "grass is green iff grass is green" supposes considerable experiential knowledge that is divorced from the propositional content. Such statements are artificial implants in the mental state. With respect to brain correlation, the presumption is that the content represents a demarcated particular that reduces to local activity in brain. The presumed isolate is not psychologically real, however, and its presumed localization is a philosophical fantasy.

WHAT IS MIND?

Typically, mind is defined as that aspect of organism that exhibits thought, feeling and awareness, which includes our primate neighbors and possibly animals quite far down the evolutionary scale. At some level of primitive mind, say that of a bat or octopus, the relation of mind to brain is not a vexing problem, even if behavioral performances cannot be correlated with specific brain areas or processes. Since the self, consciousness, language, intentionality and other features of human mentation have not arisen, the inner life of the animal organism, if there is one, is inaccessible to us. In such animals we are generally content to identify mind with brain or nervous system, or the latter with behavior, which is interpreted as an implementation of neural connectivity, even if the precise correlates of neural networks with behavior are unknown.

As mentality increases in complexity, its correlation becomes more elusive, while in human mind, except for a rough approximation, it is largely opaque. Language is responsible for much of the distance from earlier forms, but it is likely that a feral child would have mental capacities beyond those of wild animals. The maturation of human and chimpanzee infants is roughly comparable in the first year of life, even favoring the chimp, but with the advent of language the intellect of the human child rapidly moves ahead. Clinical findings indicate that the productive and receptive aspects of language originate in relation to action and perception systems in brain. Language parasitizes existing systems; it is not exclusively neocortical, but develops over stages in evolutionary growth. Areas for speech production are proximate to those for oral and limb movement and vocalization, while those for speech perception involve regions also important for auditory and visual perception.

The temporal lobe in monkey is largely visual. Bilateral lesions give difficulty in selecting an object from a visual array. The deficit is neither solely of perception nor solely of memory, but appears to involve the intermediate phase of isolating an item within a group of other items. The problem in visual selection involves brain regions that in man underlie the process of word-selection. We know from pathological disruption that in humans these areas mediate the selection of a word from a category, or a phonemic string from a lexical frame. In addition, regions on the medial surface of the hemisphere involved in the isolation cry of the monkey are vital to the initiation of an utterance in man. In my view, language begins with the ability to name objects and the phonology necessary to produce the name in speech, with syntax coming later. The pattern of act, object and language formation in relation to evolutionary growth trends is essential to understanding the correlation of mind or behavior to local and widespread brain regions, a relation more complex than the assumption of mind/brain identity would entail.

What then is a mind or brain? Is the cardiac ganglion of a sea slug a brain, or the nerve cells in the limbs of an octopus? As the nervous system evolves to a brain, behavior evolves from relative automaticity to adaptive originality, at which point the evidence for a subjective component can be entertained. The subjective evolves with brain from a stage where brain and behavior are conceptually inseparable to one in which mind appears to exhibit non-physical properties. But the ingredients of brain linked to mind evolve together with their subjectivity.

The conditions for mind are present in elementary entities, protopsychic features that together with physical features evolve to primitive mentality. One can ask if a semblance of mind is present in every atom or cell in the body or brain? Is mind generated by brain as a whole or are only certain portions involved? Large areas of brain can be removed with little or no demonstrable effect on mentation, while some very local portions can be damaged with profound effects on specific cognitive functions. The conclusion is that what counts is less the brain region than the pattern of brain activity that makes consciousness and attendant capacities possible. Since the pattern is common to all brain systems, individual systems or components can be sacrificed and mentality goes on. The mind does not ordinarily regress to animal or childhood function; rather, basic attributes—consciousness, duration, a present moment, intentional thought, dream and the unconscious, aesthetic preferences and so on—are largely spared, even with a severe compromise of language, action or perception.

Language may be responsible for the unique character of human mind but, except for verbal thought, many attributes of mind persist when language is lost. More precisely, the actualization of each component of mentality suffices to sustain human psyche, even when there is disruption within a given component. In animals lacking the specialization of human brain, this commonality of pattern—category/item transition—survives multiple ablations. This has suggested mass action or equipotentiality (Lashley) or holographic organization (Pribram). The degree of vulnerability to focal lesion results from the sequestration of function in the human brain, which can be interpreted as a furtherance of whole/part analysis, but the non-specific or general features of human mentality are still evident.

MIND, SPIRIT, SOUL

The properties of organism that evolve to the attributes of human mentality (such as duration, becoming, the distribution of feeling into value, the forward surge to a subjective aim as the seed of purposefulness) are intrinsic to the material substrate through which they develop, while the pattern of actualization of the mental state, inferred from the analysis of defects, corresponds to the pattern of brain activity through which mentality is derived. Passage to finality carries the organism to an open future. Each instance of re-actualization is a kind of re-birth that gives the sense of a force or spirit through which life is sustained. The recapitulation of evolutionary growth trends in each recurrence propels brain process in the direction of phyletic advance. Each state surges into existence out of the shadows of the unconscious to the clarity of conscious thought and a motion to the future, a birth out of death from darkness to light, from the invisible sources of being to the palpable reality of existence.

As I have argued in the preceding chapters of this book, the diverse particulars generated in an act of perception appear to exist as independent objects, but arise from a unitary source in the human mind/brain. Could one say that nature—seen and unseen—also arises from a single source, the mind of deity or a collective spirit? The life and death of organism, the interdependence of organic forms, the multiplicity of the natural world, generates a universe out of a singularity in recurrent acts of creation. Does mind elaborate entities in nature, as the human mind elaborates objects in perception? If rudiments of human mind are present in nature, nature exhibits proto-mentality. An intuition of the proto-psychic in nature, along with the instantiation of subjectivity in human brain as part of physical nature, constitute the pillars of religious thought. This appears in the ancient belief—even in contemporary Hinduism—in a multitude of deities that correspond to mental attributes or human personality, in most instances felt as personal gods to those who fear or worship them. This same intuition is on display in totemic and other animistic beliefs, which presume a continuum of nature and mind and/or the presence in natural process of the very properties that account for the evolution of human mind.

The partition to diversity in the mental state, like that of evolutionary nature, the creation in mind of an object world along with the development of consciousness out of instinct and automatism, lead to the belief that nature itself has the ingredients of mentality. The gods that realize the traits of human mind are eventually replaced by a single all-knowing, all-powerful god outside nature, or by an impersonal spirit within natural process, an example of which is Whitehead's process god. The divine is conceived as an attribute or emergent of nature, not as a power external to the universe that controls the world machine or manipulates human destiny. Feelings of awe and the sublime, in which a point in time and space is felt in relation to eternity and infinity, evoke the overwhelming grandeur of the universe, in comparison to the animating spirit in each fleeting instance of life.

The sense of spirit in nature—élan vital, life force, divine impulse—derives from an attribution to nature of the recurrent surge of process in the mental state extracted from the embodiments of physical process. Spirit is an extract of human personality, which individuates a multiplicity of living gods. Among the attributes that consolidate a spirit-infused essence, the most fundamental is the soul, which is conceived as arising from physical process but transcending and surviving the death of the body. Deity abides in the passage of nature; soul abides in the passage of the self. The immersion of soul in the mind of nature, or its reunion with god, in returning to the nature from which it arose, is the reverse of the emergence of the self out of physical process. There is a parallel between the relation of mind to brain and that of god or spirit to nature. Those who reduce mind to brain would also reduce spirit to nature. Both approaches eliminate the element of mentality from physical mechanism.

The present moment can be interpreted as an instance of the eternal present of god's mind (Eckert), just as the category/member transition over ascending levels in the mind/brain can be extrapolated from inner world to outer world: that is, to the specification of particulars, including the human mind, out of the widest possible category, the all-inclusive mind of god. The universality of god, then, is to individualities as essentially boundless categories are to the proliferation of actualities in mind. I would stress that this is not an argument for the existence of a personal or anthropomorphic god, but for a continuum of the proto-psychic throughout physical nature, which opens the door to the possibility of spirit as one source of belief in god, and, with subjectivity now understood to be essential to the process of nature, a reverence for the divine.

TIME AND THE MENTAL STATE

The nature of time is interwoven with the problem of mind and brain, whether in causal theory or a concept of becoming, particularly in any kind of replacement theory, since duration is an inherent and essential feature of the mental state as such. Further, there is a distinction to be made here between the duration of becoming in physical entities and the mind/brain state, and the phenomenal duration of the present, both of which present a challenge to the usual assumption of physical instantaneity in material entities. Of the various perspectives on time, the most common are these:

- Newtonian absolute time, which has its application in local contexts as well as clock time;

- the relational time of Einstein, which has greater import in cosmic or macro-system analysis;

- the mode of time discussed in this section, subjective time experience, which accounts *inter alia* for the duration of the present and the ordered series of events from past to future.

In physical theory, time is a dimension of space, while subjective time depends on memory. Since Heraclitus and Parmenides, time has been conceived as either instantaneous or continuous, that is, as a series of discrete instants or points, or as an unbroken flow or stream. An alternative to these concepts, which reflects the way time is modeled in the brain, is a process of recurrence in a motionless point that is replaced, which makes the passage of time more like the movement of water in a fountain than the flow of a river.

The concept of recurrence is deeply ingrained in the cyclical nature of life: circadian, lunar, seasonal, sleep/wake, vibratory and other periodic processes, the oscillatory nature of respiration, ambulation, and the rhythmic structure of speech, as well as the vibratory foundations of inorganic matter. These periodic or recurrent processes differ in scale, but all of them give evidence for the centrality of iteration in cognition and in the psychology of time experience. Specifically, moments in time actualize through a becoming into existence, such that each actualization comprises phases of transition within an encapsulated point. The actuality is a recurrence that exists as a moment in time, or a time-creating moment when the becoming is complete. As Whitehead put it, "half a wave tells only half the story"[3]. An instant refers to an isolable slice of process; a moment refers to the minimal duration of a thing, or one cycle of its existence.

The actualization of a moment, like the surge of a fountain, is a non-temporal succession with an epochal character. A moment in the subjective life of an organism is a becoming-into-being. Being is the frame, category is a collection of all the phases that constitute the process of becoming. The incompleteness of becoming is necessary for the miscibility—the becoming part of—one state in another. The continuity of adjacent states is a resolution of becoming with a momentary epoch. Time feels continuous, since we cannot grasp and hold the individual moment, when one state blends into the next. The replacement of actualities differs from a causal sequence of atomic instants, since states are assimilated prior to their existence; that is, the antecedent assimilates to the consequent, and the reverse, before either exist, each becoming an existent only after it is replaced. Again Whitehead: "each occasion presupposes the antecedent world as active in its own nature."[4] The sequence of mental states entails a replacement of irreducible packets of becoming that collectively are minimal units or "drops" of experience (James).

Things become what they are, and in the course of becoming are replaced. A forward-moving present is replaced by an oncoming future that actualizes part of an ensuing state that is a constituent of early segments in the present state, and then lapses to a layered succession of a more or less distant past. The immediate future is in the present before the present becomes what it is, such that the leading edge of the present always incorporates the state that follows. The present becomes past by failing to achieve actuality in successive revivals. In this way, the immediate future becomes the past on further replacement, with each new present immediately swallowed up by memory. We experience clock time, but moments are not experienced, nor do we experience the present as it rolls into the future, consuming the oncoming events in which it is embedded. We live in a present moment we are unable to grasp, much as we cannot catch a perception (Hume). Experience in each present incorporates a series of states, none of which can be experienced in and of itself, nor can boundaries be demarcated, nor their constituents isolated. States (epochs) overlap, so do

3. Whitehead, A. N. (1934) *Nature and Life*, Cambridge U. Press. p. 35
4. ibid, p. 88–89

durations, with no anterior or posterior limits. Durations and moments are categories transformed in the exchange of ingredients.

The forward motion of the present is due to novel replacement. Would the feeling of motion differ if each moment was the same as the preceding one? Most likely, it is less the novelty in experience that accounts for forward movement than the fading of the present. If events were unchanging, identical oncoming moments would impact the past as much as the future, since each present would be all there is without a past for comparison. In rare cases of bilateral temporal lobe damage from encephalitis, the immediate past is lost. The person lives in a shrunken present. Without duration there is no implicit relation to a past, that is, to incompletely revived former presents, so that redundancy or novelty cannot be established. Consciousness in such a person is a rapid replacement of duration-less states. The person lives on the knife edge of passage in a state of disorientation, with a stroboscopic now. A present that consists of one or a few states allows one to listen to music, but to hear only the immediate tones, without recollection or sense of continuity with what came before. When the disparity of perception and forgetting essential to duration is lost, the now is instantaneous, as in dream, and the self is carried along by events.

EVENTS

All objects are events—durations of change with arbitrary boundaries—that comprise a series of mental states. Are events in time, or is time in events? The variety in the events that constitute conscious experience implies that duration is a category for events of different epochal cycles, with recurrence governed by the cycle, not the events themselves; but from a subjective point of view, there can be neither timeless events nor time without events.

Though epochs enclose phases in succession, an actuality achieves temporal order over a series. The succession of phases within a mental state is non-temporal until completion, at which point the embedded segments unscroll in temporal order. A series of states is necessary to have incomplete revivals, which create posterior boundaries for the present. In objects such as trees and chairs, the sequence of states does not appear to change, because each state is a near-exact replica of the prior one. Change in a moving object, in speech or music, represents a novel sequence of overlapping epochs, though the change is occurring within the becoming, not in the difference from one epoch to another, which is an appearance of change spread out as a two-dimensional line over the replacement.

If all events ceased, including those in the brain, the world would come to a halt and time would cease as well. If time should stop, so would all events, but in some sense this happens every moment in the renewal of time and events by the oncoming state (mental state, state of the world). Time is suspended in the interstices of mental states, though the overlap of adjacencies prior to completion prevents a timeless interval. The effect is similar to the phi phenomenon, or a movie reel, where rapid replacement obscures the event-less gaps, but in the mental state it is not only the rapidity of replacement but the overlap that insures continuity (as well as personal identity and the preservation of core attributes of personality), which would be lost in a causal series of modular or atomic states. The difference is that with the phi phenomena or movie reel the mind "fills in" the intervals, but if continuity is generated independent of experiential content, what is the relation of time to events?

One speaks of objects, but all objects are events and all events are perceptions of the world. If a present duration is a few seconds of clock time (Pöppel), this would include 20–30 mental states, perhaps more, which is probably necessary for the recession of the past to form a moving boundary of the present. A disappearance of events, as in snow blindness, tends to produce hallucinations and disorientation: that is, incomplete objects and a degraded present. The absence of all events leads to sleep, while in dream, endogenous events create a brief duration that allows a fleeting consciousness and a passive self that perceives events but has no control over them.

The answer to the question of how time and events are related, then, is that mind requires events, in order to generate the duration necessary for self and consciousness. External events expand duration by carrying the state to an objective actuality. Without external objects, internal imagery has limited duration; there is a rudimentary self and consciousness, but no past, no future, no agency. Dream images do not behave like perceptions; there is no "decay", or at least it is insufficient to create a present duration essential for an experience of the past. The feeling of agency is also absent, since the future state always comes as a surprise.

The importance of events is not only to inject novelty into the present but, through forgetting, to create the duration necessary for novelty to be recognized. An animal past that consists only of learning, habit or incidental memory lacks the recurrence of past actualities as contents in consciousness. It is not essential for an animal to have an explicit recollection of the past, and for human mind it is also the implicit past, not the recollected past, that is most important in the experience of duration. Past states sink beneath the floor of recall in the progressive attenuation of revival. We can say that events create subjective time in two ways, by replacing the forward

edge of the occurrent state by novelty, and by establishing duration in fading to an unconscious level. A representational past is no less important to
the experience of time than events which, without a past, would exist in a
before/after relation without temporal awareness or episodic locus.

The duration of the present was termed specious by James, or considered virtual, phenomenal or illusory in my own prior writings, since
duration is presumed not to occur in the material world, and physical time
is conceived as "before" and "after," without a present or fixed point of reference. Perhaps we should think again about this distinction. The minimal
duration of becoming that is essential for physical entities to exist evolves
to more extensive durations in higher organisms, where existence refers to
the duration of a mental state. Duration is not an addition to nature, but an
inherent feature that expands over the evolutionary sequence. The primary
shift in human mind is that the duration of the mental state, or the duration required for the mental state to exist, includes prior states as receding
approximations to the occurrent one. This implies that human mind is not
set against physical nature, but is the known apex of evolutionary reach,
with features essential for mind being part of the inorganic world. To give
Whitehead the last word, "we should conceive mental operations as among
the factors which make up the constitution of Nature."[5]

5. Ibid p. 70–71

8

Being and Becoming

SUMMARY

THE RELATION OF BECOMING to consciousness and time is discussed in this chapter. The fine structure of becoming consists in the successive sculpting of forming objects through phases of experiential memory and object-concepts. In this process, feeling and concepts partition to increasing definiteness. Becoming is the process through which being is created; being is the entirety of an act of becoming.

Becoming entails physical passage to completion; feeling guides the process to a subjective aim. The outcome in human mind/brain is the duration of the now, which arises in an epochal state within the succession of before and after as a relation of observer to objects and mental contents. The microgenetic concept of forgetting as incomplete revival and the epochal nature of the mental state lead to a speculation on the fine structure of the shift from before/after to perspectival time.

INTRODUCTION

The topic of being and becoming, which goes back to Plato and before, is central to a metapsychology of process. The discussion in this chapter is in relation to human mind, though the inferences drawn here from the study of human cognition apply to all organic and inorganic entities. Before entering into this labyrinth of philosophical discourse, a reprise of the underlying metapsychology theory may be useful.

Becoming is the process of realization or auto-replication over phases in organisms and material entities; in the human mind/brain, it is the actualization and final specification of acts and objects. "Being" or "substance" refers to entities that become what they are; that is the nature of things that exist. Becoming is the process through which things come into existence. The implication is that things do not simply exist on their own, but exist, re-exist or continue existing through a process of near-replication. The concept of "being" refers to the ultimate constituents of nature: for some, isolated entities or solid particulars, for others, persistents or continua, for still others, dynamic processes, flux, momentary occasions that actualize, perish and are replaced. The problem of becoming and the character of being, topics of much abstract speculation in philosophical discourse, can be fleshed out in a reconstruction of sequential phases in the actualization process.

Becoming is the process through which objects become what they are, and being is the form that objects assume once their becoming is complete. Being and becoming are inseparable. Becoming extends from the inception of a particular state to its final actuality as an epoch of being. The periodicity of acts of becoming varies, from extreme brevity in elementary particles to a fraction of a second in the mental state. The process includes all phases in the formation of entities or objects; all the phases are ingredient in becoming as well as the entity that becomes. Until the becoming terminates as an actual object or entity, the process is non-temporal; the entity does not yet exist. Becoming is a forward motion to actuality, the fulfillment of a subjective aim. The process of becoming deposits an object and perishes on completion, to be replaced by its successor. Each act of completion or consummation entails a subsidence or relaxation as it is replaced, but subsidence is incompleteness of recurrence in the ensuing epoch. This means that every act of becoming revives incompletely actualized pre-objects of the prior state(s). The trace of a prior state is the track of its becoming: there is no static trace.

The uncertainty as to whether the becoming of a state incorporates its subsidence comes from the conception of a state as something that rises and falls, like an oscillating sine wave, in which the decline is a decay that is conceived as part of the epoch of the current state. The perishing and decline of the state—the incomplete revival of fading segments—are essential to the cycle of becoming. The process traverses—and revives—antecedent pre-objects, while the fading (forgetting) is partial revival in the state that follows. In this way, the current state "remembers" its antecedents and is remembered by those that follow. Things pulse into existence. Becoming is a forward surge that includes the subsidence of its immediate predecessors, with surge and subsidence merging in the oncoming state.

An account of becoming is a theory of being, since what becomes is not just the final segment or endpoint of a sequence, but the entirety of the process. Becoming is not a conveyer to output, but incorporates the full series of antecedent segments. Becoming revives precedents in decline; rather, the revival determines the degree of forgetting. An entity consists in this diachronic history. Once an object or entity deposits an endpoint, an epoch of becoming exists that encloses the succession through which it develops. Fading antecedents, revived in novel consequents, are ingredient in what becomes. Nothing, then, exists in isolation; all things develop over prior occasions. Recurrence is part of the present, while the present is revived as part of the immediate future, as proximal segments merge with those forthcoming. An act of becoming—the actualization of the mental state—unfolds over the residue of the prior epoch. Since a becoming does not arise from nothing, it must be derived over the remnants of its predecessor. The something that actualizes is the prior state embedded in the present one.

From the standpoint of human mind, a critical distinction has to be made at the point where an implicit duration in the cycle of actualizations shifts to the duration of a conscious present. Without duration there is no consciousness of past and future, agency or intentionality. Succession in a mental state is a residue of past occasions, aligned in a sequence that preserves the order of occurrence, though consciousness of temporal order is only achieved when the epoch actualizes. Put differently, the process from onset to actuality is a succession from before to after or earlier to later. Upon completion, the before/after relation is suspended in the epoch, such that the self, which is earlier in the mental state, is felt as the "before," while objects and images, which develop out of the self, are apprehended as the "after." Duration arises in the interstices of before/after, with perspectival time a pause in passage that undergoes illusory elongation in the epochal now of being.

The conscious present emerges in the disparity between an immediate actuality and the floor of revival. This conforms to the distal-after and the proximal-before, with time order filling the phenomenal gap between them. The knife-edge of physical passage expands to the perspectival time of conscious experience. The shift from the time-series of passage and the actualization of the mind/brain state to the duration of an epoch of being and the duration of a present is a movement from one time-series to another (McTaggart). This is what makes consciousness possible in the shift of implicit succession to serial order in consciousness. The stacking of segments—simultaneous and unconscious—is transposed in the present to a distal "before" and a proximate "after" as the limits of the now.

The shift from implicit to explicit, from unconscious learning to mental representation, requires a self in relation to phenomenal experience. To be conscious of a memory, a thought, an image or an object, is for the self to be an observer of its own derivations. Consciousness is the trajectory from self to mental or external events; it is not a faculty or function in itself, but a relation that spans the becoming. We get a sense of this in dream, where there is no past or future, only pure succession. The self is passive, without perspectival time or past recall, though the entirety of the dream, on waking, is potentially available. This supports the idea that events are stacked in the order of occurrence, not "spread out" from the recent past to immediate perception. The present of dream contracts in the lack of a perceptual surface as anterior boundary, and the absence of revival as a source of disparity from which duration is extracted. Still, succession in dream can be recalled on waking, as object perception is re-established, and the duration-less succession shifts to temporal order. The simultaneity of a "vertical" succession briefly becomes the seriality of a "linear" sequence. Dream events do not have perceptual objectivity, in contrast to memory content. Without external objects to anchor the forward edge of the now, dreams remain memories, and without direct experiential correlates are rapidly forgotten. There is a similarity between dream recall and rapid forgetting to iconic memory. This may also relate to the ability to apprehend the unconscious construction of an art work all at once, much as the whole of a dream is briefly recollected on waking and then rapidly dissolves.

Prior to completion, the passage from initiation to endpoint is non-temporal, thus non-existent until the outcome is decided, at which point the sequence takes on serial order, and events have a locus in time in relation to the now. Attention to the constituents of the present constitutes another present in another mental state. Events isolated with a selective focus, as in attending to an object, a word in a sentence or a tone in a melody, are novel mental states. The present cannot be partitioned into atomic instants, and does not have a fixed posterior boundary. Instants are briefer durations. The relation of a present to its constituents is comparable to that of a category to its members. The individual tones in a melody, or the individual words in a sentence, each have a beginning and an ending that can be roughly demarcated in clock time—but not in subjective experience.

Events in the now are in constant motion due to a continuous overlap of durations that incorporates changing epochs. Yet the now is apprehended all at once, as a static wholeness and a forward inclination. In the mental state, bottom-up actualization goes from the very recent past to an imminent future: the "saddleback" of William James. The now enfolds the past and an intimation of the future within its posterior and anterior boundaries, but attention to a past or ongoing event, as noted, constitutes another mental state. The non-local boundaries and forward motion of the now are constantly refreshed in the approach of novelty and the overlap of what is oncoming.

The before and after in the now is the before/after of passage, but with a suspension of the before as an earlier segment and the after as a later one. The before is immediate memory, the after is object perception. The perception of language or melody depends on this phenomenon, which does not just "hold" past events in memory—a simplistic way to describe the presentness of the immediate past—but revives memory to mirror past events. The derivation of perception out of successive phases of recency is also consistent with the basis of object perception in memory. The revival begins in the deep or instinctive unconscious and develops out of experiential or long-term memory, much of which is inaccessible, through recent events that become contents in the now, to the final perception. Through the now we perceive change in the present, but the now itself is indivisible.

BEING

The invisible transition in becoming gives being the appearance of stability. Put differently, a dynamic process deposits what appears to be a solid particular. How is this possible? If each actuality is replaced in the becoming of epochs, why do objects appear stable and unaffected by mind or observation? One reason for this is the imperceptibility of process and the relative stability of categories. For example, there is a tendency to conceive states in oppositional pairs: night/day, hot/cold, life/death, not mindful of the transition or gradient from one extreme to another. Mind is tethered to a logical solid at either end of a spectrum, largely oblivious to the continuum between them. Another reason for this is the transformation by sensation of (the substrates of) imagery to objects, which abruptly terminates in the final actuality. This combines with the ascription of mental phenomena to feeling and imagination, and external phenomena to reality. An object appears to be an independent entity in part because intra-psychic phases in becoming are imperceptible. We are conscious of the final object, not its formative process, and assume that the finality, not the formativeness, is the locus of change.

An account of causation in object change results from, and reinforces, this point of view. In passage, causation is presumed to be the basis of change across states, as the subsequent passes into the antecedent. The relative stability of entities is assumed even as a cause transitions to an effect.

On a modular theory of self-contained entities, change is not in the cause or the effect, but in the transition to the effect. Otherwise, entities or events would be arbitrary segments in a continuum of change. In continuous transition, entities seem to consolidate out of change. If cause and effect refer to the change in entities, and causation to the change between them, change would be continuous in the transition from cause to effect, over a gap or, some argue, simultaneous with the effect, though we are unaware of gaps in passage, whether modular, overlapping or continuous.

On these accounts, persistence represents minimal change from an entity at one point in time (T1) to the next (T2), such that each outcome is much the same as before. In "causal persistence"—for example in the sustained appearance of a tree or person—the entity is held to cause itself to recur. What then configures or demarcates an entity out of change? In a causal succession of instants, each state in transition is presumed to be discrete. Conversely, if time flows like a river and objects arise in relation to flow, like ripples in a stream, they would lack the solidity of perceptions and be in constant change. In a causal system, change is extrinsic, deflected to the transmission of one state to the next. If cause and effect are themselves changing, a changing cause merges with a changing effect and entities dissolve in change. If so, the assumption of solid isolates or atomic particulars is endangered.

In contrast, if the process of becoming lays down states (objects, events, the world), the sequence, if causal, is not across states but within them: that is, (causal) change occurs within the entity or its replacement, not from one state to another. Motion across appearances suggests causal transmission over events, but an object or event is an endpoint in becoming that includes the actualization sequence. This means the becoming in an object, not the final object, is the locus of change. States are epochal, thus atomic, but continuity is preserved by overlap, though it is uncertain if supplanting one actualization by another is a causal effect. Substitution of state T1 by T2 begins in the core, and T2 develops to some midway point before state T1 actualizes. Since T2 overlaps T1 only at segments prior to actualization, overlapped segments do not yet exist. Specifically, if existence pertains only to actualities, partial becoming would not give an existent. If the overlap is for the early segments in T1, their incorporation in T2 occurs before T1 actualizes, so that early segments are continuously reproduced in ongoing states without ever achieving existence. This accounts for the "persistence" of core features of personality, the perishing of objects and the creation of an unconscious, which refers to earlier phases that are replaced prior to actuality. Unconscious segments of psychic process impact subsequent ones, but do not, unlike the latter, have a claim on existence.

This might support the reluctance of some to attribute existence to unconscious content, such as that in dream. The advent of conscious duration opens the door to an unconscious. This is likely a specifically human phenomenon. We are only conscious of distal segments in becoming; some even argue that the existence of mind applies only to events in consciousness. But consciousness is an outcome of formative phases that do not achieve existence unless they are made finalities by pathology or in dream, and they are thought even then to have a somewhat tenuous hold on existence.

The history of an individual is revived in each becoming, as process goes from private (inner) space to public (outer) space, from the intra—to the extra-psychic and from archaic to recent in evolutionary growth and cognitive process. The floor of the mental state in drive and experiential memory is rooted in ancestral levels beneath conscious remembrance. This passes to recent memories that form the posterior limit of the now, then object perception. Overlap by a successor of early segments preserves those distant memories that form the basis of character and value. Subsequent phases revived in the now, particularly those proximate to the perceptual surface, actualize in the present; they recur but do not persist. The recurrence of an object—a tree, a chair—represents a similarity in development and parsing by sensation. We perceive the object to persist (recur), but what recurs is an ensuing state, including sensory modeling, not the particular that is its outcome. We do not go from one particular to another, but from one actualization to another, such that the actuality that individuates may or may not resemble the outcome it replaces. Thus, if the gaze is averted, other events are perceived, while the persistence of the tree or chair, once it is no longer in the field of vision, is inferred. The recurrence of the state, not the persistence of things, accounts for continuous novelty in content. The endpoint of the actualization—the object (world)—is the vanishing surface of the mental state, not the cause of the ensuing object.

If the actualization of perceptual objects is the furthermost development of becoming in human mind, it must occur to a variable extent in primitive organisms, even in physical entities. Things rise into existence through near replication. The content of an entity is not a final product, but the diachronic history of its derivation, a history that is not fixed in time until it actualizes. The derivation that is "summed" on reaching an outcome is obscured in the categorical nature of object stability. The non-temporal character of becoming, as Whitehead noted with respect to concrescence, is a paradoxical feature, with each instantiation incorporating a non-temporal, thus non-divisible, succession. This account helps to resolve a long-standing problem concerning before/after time, here referred to as passage, and past-present-future or perspectival time: the former characterizes the simultaneity of succession in a becoming-into-being, while in the latter, succession is allocated to perspectival time, in which the past—the greater part of perception—is co-present in the now.

In humans, being actualizes a perspective on past and present. The object accompanies the consciousness of present-ness. The recent past that is ingredient in the object and the remote past that is intrinsic to its infra-structure constitute the past of perspectival time, while forward change and expectation give the future. Unconscious succession is not only of events for potential recall; feeling invested in the event series combines to give the present a complex of accumulated sentiments. Unless the sub-surface complex is dominated by intense feeling, the common affect is a kind of mood that represents a mean of event-related feelings. Since conscious events in the present are recent—they constitute the immediate-before of perception—they are not necessarily viewed by the observer as memories. A melody or a sentence, when heard, does not seem to be a memory, but a present fact. When a past event is revived as a primary focus, the event occupies or becomes the actual object, while its pastness, recent or remote, is apprehended in a perspective on the past in relation to the now.

IMPLICATIONS

Those authors (such as Heidegger, Sartre and Merleau-Ponty) who dis-tinguish being-for-the-self and being-in-the-world, though differing in emphasis, refer self-consciousness and the belongingness of objects to a personal and impersonal field, with the observer a mode of being to which the field is in relation. An embodied self is the bridge to physical entities that, lacking a self, consist in a kind of concrete subjectivity that is mirrored at preliminary phases in the derivation to consciousness. This brings the personal subjectivity of the developing self into relation with the non-self of physical nature. Ultimately, all occasions and modes of being collapse to the fundamental nature of being itself, which in relational systems is an embedded feature of the whole. The being of a person, a self, exists as an im-mersion in the being of the world, while being-in-the-world is established by the now in the replication of the mental state. Individuals actualize for themselves, but the development of self in relation to otherness is essen-tial for self-realization. Individuality depends on relationality. There are no isolates—physical or mental—independent of otherness. Nor is being or existence dependent on the now (presentism). Existents do not exist only in the present; rather, the duration of the present evolves out of the duration over which being is created. The perspectival now is an extension of passage in animal mind in the absence of consciousness. The duration of actualization and the continuum in the evolution of organic systems to human mind imply a commonalty with primitive organism and basic entities.

The incorporation of being in the world, or of self in relation to others, physical and psychic, is not a result of combination or interaction of particulars or individualities to larger wholes; individuals are specifications of categories or hierarchies of backgrounds. The becoming of self and other jointly specifies a wider category in which they co-occur as virtual possibilities. Otherness is a web of potential relations from which oneness arises, just as the present is a category of virtual instants, each a constituent of a category of potential derivations. The categorical nature of duration and its constituents correspond to the categorical nature of objects, which enfold a multiplicity of parts, each a sub-category that can undergo endless partition. As with duration, object categories are roughly circumscribed potentials for individuation. Even in an atom, segments in the orbit of an electron can be conceived as members or constituents of the final entity, the atom, and themselves categories with a still deeper infrastructure.

This implies that objects and mind-independent entities are qualitative sets "contained" within larger wholes, as well as arbitrary way-stations in the potential for endless descent. The whole of my garden in relation to the manifold of the world is a field in my perception, a portion of which is the universe of a mole burrowed in the earth, still less to insect life on a plant, or the plant itself and its surround. A bacterium in the gut, a distant star, organic and physical, are modes of being that exist in relation to surrounds. We investigate the greater above and the limitless below, but we live in a world of middle-sized objects, upon which speculations on life and meaning depend. Self, surround, all individuations, are artificial dissections of an indivisible subjectivity, and momentary unities in a matrix of relationality.

The upshot of this line of thought is that being and its constituents are evanescent renewals of underlying relations, with individualities developing out of the bonds that join or separate them. The deeper the relations, the more the entity endures; the more superficial the relations, the more tenuous its identity. For the self, the potential in renewal is an occasion, a tacit opportunity for growth or decline. Generally, we speak of renewal in a moral or therapeutic context, but what exactly is renewed? The self, beliefs, values, outlook, behavior? Renewal is the conscious filtration of novelty in recurrence. The possibility of change or self-transformation is a social interpretation of replacement out of the deeper strata from which all things come into existence. Since every recurrence partitions to individuality, every renewal is a change in the totality of all particulars. Recurrence is not causal progression from one state or thing to another; it is the arising of a novel inter-related world.

This means that individualities continuously arise out of strata that enfold possibilities of becoming, including all selves and particulars. The insight that we are brief recurrences of sub-surface layers that arise in concert with the world and other selves, with a change in form or being in every recurrence, implies replacement rather than persistence, lack of substantiality and a shared ground of self with nature and others. A suspension of analytical thinking and its destination in partition and isolation, and a recognition of the common origin of things, that is, the awareness that all things are renewed out of potentiality, the sense of "connectedness" to nature and to others and the common struggle to re-exist, is the antidote to alienation and apartness. Atomicity is a recipe for conflict.

In contrast, becoming and consequent mutuality, if endorsed and deeply felt, mitigate the loneliness and vulnerability of an individuated life. From this point of view, the aesthetic is the satisfaction of the order and wholeness of all constituents of experience, such that the personal perspective of self as agent and observer can be resolved with an impersonal perspective, in which the self is a miniscule ingredient in a cosmic drama. Finally, insight on the relatedness of individuals and their inherence in nature takes evolutionary theory one step further, shifting slow evolutionary advance to the rapid evolution from a common source. Evolutionary process, the growth of novelty over time, is replicated each moment in the becoming of entities and organisms.

BECOMING-INTO-BEING

The deep source of surface content becomes evident when we observe behavior. In the sphere of action, the Moro reflex of infancy predicts handedness, indicating an axial or vestibular bias for asymmetric voluntary movement. The strength of grasping in infants predicts an outgoing active personality, while for children with hypotonia it is the reverse. Infantile reaching is the seed of the idea of causation and the future. Body-on-body action bound up with the autonomic nervous system forecasts limb action in the world. Rhythmic axial motility is the basis from which fine asymmetric actions develop. In the sphere of drive, the accoutrements of instinctual hunger pass to the secondary drive of sexuality in sucking, orality, aggressiveness and features of predation, which surface in desire, taste and refinements. In language, the underpinnings of action in respiratory timing and the rhythmic oscillators that give rise to music and the speech melody, finally to the temporal program of sound sequences, may arise out of animal calls and signaling. The point is, the ancient is not irretrievably lost somewhere in the past; on the contrary, it is the transformative basis of the present state.

To put this a little differently: the most ancient neural structures linked to ancestral behaviors mediate the earliest phases in the actualization of the self. There is a condensation of the main lines of evolutionary progression in the derivation of the mental state; the properties of becoming-into-being retrace phyletic history. Conversely, evolutionary growth can be seen as a recurrence of patterns in the elaboration of novelty that represent a kind of becoming over deep time—the being of ancestral organism—that collapses into the becoming where the submerged recent past develops into conscious duration. In other words, immediate experience generates a perspective that can be applied to events in the distant past of nature, and to becoming itself.

The process of becoming is an energic accompaniment to the partition of categories. In organic systems, feeling, as the analogue of energy, is the dynamic or affective tonality of drive-based pre-objects that constitute the substantive aspect of the becoming process. Organic categories develop as an envelope of phases, parts in transition subsumed in the actualization of the whole. Categories that pass from whole to part would be immobile without feeling, which propels division into category members. Stasis in a category is fulfilled in its implementation. A drive category such as hunger or sexuality encloses possibilities of individuation—food, mate—with feeling serving as the motive force that carries the category to final instantiation. Even the most intense feelings—hate, fear, love—have object or pre-object categories, while in the most abstract categories, feeling carries ideation into action.

For Plato, appetite and reason were distinct. Historical study in psychology seems to confirm the opinion that feeling and concept are independent, though how they come to be associated has not been resolved. One theory has it that libidinal drive energy attaches to the memory image to generate a drive representation or idea (Freud's cathexis). Behavioral neuroanatomy suggests that emotion originates in the limbic system, while thought arises in the neocortex. The conventional account leaves much to be desired. Even at the most preliminary stage, drive categories are activated by feeling, will or motivation. How does a specific feeling find and attach itself to an idea? If feeling is homogeneous, is it differentiated by idea? If feelings are specific, how do they evoke or map to the relevant idea? Do ideas have an address that lures, colors and specifies the feeling? The concept of autonomous ideas and distinct emotions is implausible. Categories without feeling are lifeless, non-existent; feelings without categories are shapeless bursts of energy. How category and feeling combine at every phase in becoming is unclear—though for microgenetic theory, feeling and category (concept) concur at the onset of the state and continue as process/content or becoming/being, to the endpoint in perception. In any event, a combination of feeling and concept is essential for things to exist, whether organic particulars infused with vitality or inorganic entities, conceived as masses of energy.

On death, we revert to the physical nature out of which we evolved. To become is to exist. The thrust of becoming is auto-replication, individuation of self or entity. The past, as the history of human consciousness, becomes upon realization an object of scrutiny. While becoming allows reclamation of historical events, it is the striving towards autonomy, towards particulars, through which the past is uncovered. While the ground of becoming embraces all possibilities, the subjective aim to definiteness is toxic to communality. The byproduct of individuation, incipient otherness, is lost in the drive to autonomy.

Human organism actualizes in itself as an entity or object for others, and it actualizes as an object for itself in self-realization. Consciousness of self and other is not accompanied by awareness of the process through which this consciousness occurs. The tension between the for-itself—thought, conscious observation—and the in-itself—non-conscious recurrence—is that of an object in a state of self-realization and an entity as material re-instantiation. Individual revival entails opposition to others that individuate in parallel for that moment. The self is what it is through specification and the trimming away of what it is not, the possibilities of which are limited by inner and outer constraints, as individuality is parsed by internal bias and defined by the surrounding field.

Shaping by otherness induces confrontation and curtailment of possibility as a ground of struggle or resignation. Conflict as a protest against limitation arises from hostility or insufficiency. The question, is it me or them, is not just an echo of self-awareness; it is an intuition of constraints on individuation in relation to the manifold of actualities that compete for primacy in the common now of a perceptual field. Each epoch of being is an adaptive becoming, through which a changing organism enters into new relations with a changing surround. The brutal struggle of organism to survive is tempered in humans in the direction of negotiation, compromise, uncertainty as to path, and an adaptive self in search of a core of authenticity. The hindrance to self-assertion arises as a result of doubt and lack of commitment, of disagreeable others, physical impediments and lack of opportunity, but the essential factor is the change in recurrence, of self and other, that necessitates constant adjustment and reconciliation, a condition unresolved even in withdrawal to a hermit's den.

Satisfaction in the for-itself is inevitably partial, since the potential that represents the full expression of possibility is shaved to definiteness in every adaptation. Intuition suggests that the tension of indecision, Hamlet's "to be or not to be", is the pressure towards an actual One out of a virtual Many, the selves that die stillborn; but this leaves a residue of what-if in every act. For most, introspection is an infrequent occupation amongst the spontaneity of daily action; such people—often in error, never in doubt—rarely question their choices, while others with an interior bent, attuned to the sources of commitment, especially in states of vulnerability when the mask of certainty is lifted, are aware that every motion, no matter how trivial, a singular act or a compound sequence, a turn to the right or left, a sideways glance, a gesture, a stare, can initiate a monumental change in a life. Continuous insight into the sources of every inclination can lead to the replacement of action by thought and eventual paralysis, for any uncertainty in the resolution of action is a byproduct of the self-doubt that goes to the core of who we are.

Thus, a life of dedication to self or others, to work, art or other pursuits, is often to be applauded even if it avoids some dangers of the unknown by a sustained detour to the familiar, while the uncommitted life, a life freely in the present, though lacking in purpose or unselfish aim, is open to possibilities. The essential condition for a successful life is not mere happiness or achievement, but a recurrence of the passage from virtuous character to decisive action, in which the implicit choices in becoming are decided by courage and concern, and the endpoint in being is a self of action and quality. Self-realization is the goal of becoming, which determines the full actualization of the self. Like a musician following the written notes on a musical score with a beginning and an ending and some flexibility in allotted time, we can live our lives ineptly or with virtuosity, even if we cannot change the notes.

SELF, BEING AND CATEGORY

Momentary actualization and recurrence provide opportunities for change, but the self as a singular category retains a stable identity over a lifetime, just as a tree, as a singular category, is the "same" over seasons. If we ask, what is the self, or what is the tree, we might say it is the sum of its occurrences: for a tree, the sum of its appearances; for a person, at least from a moral standpoint, the sum of his acts. Though each appearance of a tree is a novel occurrence—a sapling or hollowed stump, ice-weary in winter or glowing green in summer—the tree is self-identical as the sole member of an object-category. This is true for a self; each manifestation belongs to the category of that person. The upside of the categorical nature of the self is identity over time, as with a tree. The downside is guilt, remorse, and culpability for acts in the distant past, even if such acts would be strongly denounced by the self of the present. On this view, a near-infinite number of selves accumulate over a lifetime, each actualizing the category and contributing to the sum of the self to that moment, with no hope for redemption. An act-based account of the self has moral implications; indeed, it is a moral necessity, but from a psychological point of view, Buddhism and process theory are closer to the truth, in that the self is what it is at any given moment, the selves of prior moments having vanished: each self disappears in its successor, with only personal and communal memory keeping the past alive. Some people, as they grow older, look back at their own actions in the past, for better or for worse, with growing detachment, as though these were the actions of some other person; and their own motives in some past action are as opaque to them as though indeed they were the actions of some other person. Yet only in pathology does this detachment cause the self to doubt its identity with the self of the past.

As the category of becoming leads to the duration of the present, it also serves to enfold recurrent instantiations of self and object, accounting for recognition of the sameness of people, animals, objects over time. Categorization occurs in animals as well, with a sense of sameness and difference that is established or reinforced by olfaction and other senses. A dog shows recognition of sameness when it responds to its master, even after a long separation, and barks at strangers. Is this related to category formation or mere association? Interestingly enough, a dog may show greater excitement on reunion with its master after an absence of a few days than after a few hours, indicating a sense of duration. Perhaps this points to the delay in associative bonding, or greater priming by a long interval, but the stimulus-response relation—operant conditioning—can also be conceived as the arousal of members in a makeshift category, similar to the category-item transition that occurs in animal drive. In humans, of course, the categorical, especially with respect to language, undergoes expansion, until it becomes essential to a view of the world and ourselves.

The categorical that begins in drive undergoes whole/part specification, to become the object of the drive or the subjective aim. This transition, which is abbreviated in animals, expands in humans in a passage through object and semantic categories. Increasing complexity is a product of the multiplicity of whole/part shifts, from instinctual drive to the final act or object. The category of physical entities, which is the envelope of phases in recurrence, evolves to category/item specification at each phase, such that the object represents an irreducible or non-divisible category—a person, tree—as well as the sequence of specifications in its formation. In sum, becoming is the progressive individuation of successive categories, until the final category actualizes as being, along with the formative phases. In the course of this process, preliminary (psychic) phases may actualize as images within the framework of an object-experience. The self, an image or a thought, is the coming-to-the-fore of an insubstantial phase within a complete actualization. Yet all things, those that quickly pass and those that seem to endure, those that appear phenomenal and those that appear continuous, must be iterations of what they are in order to exist. Becoming is the energy, the feeling and the life of every object and entity, while being, as the outcome of becoming, is the category of phases in its actualization

If, from the standpoint of a perspectival now, the object world is the outer rim of the subjective, and if being includes the subjective antecedents of perceptual objects—phases of which we are ordinarily unaware—being would not apply to segments submerged in an object perception, since they do not achieve actuality, but it would apply to such segments when they come to the foreground in conscious introspection. If the perceived external world is subjective, the actualized precursors of the objective exist—physically and/or psychically—no less than the objects in which they terminate—unless being is attributed only to noumenal entities or to "solid persistents." More precisely, the memory content implicit in objects and ingredient in the being of those objects is a different mental state than it is when memory content itself is the focus of attention.

What is the difference, with respect to being or existence, of memory that is implicit in acts or objects, and memory that is a focus of attention? If I should withdraw from the world to memory, and deeper still to dream, at what point, if any, do mental contents cease to have being, and, in consequence, cease to exist? While the inclusion of subjective contents in the concept of being muddies the waters of physicalism, for which being refers to mind-independent particulars or atomic entities, even within physics the concept of atomicity is slippery, with the progression of ever-smaller particles seemingly bottomless. Moreover, the account of entities as proto-psychic, or of rudimentary subjectivity, brings the passage of nature into relation with the subjectivity underlying the conscious now.

The problem in conceiving psychic experience as being is the insubstantiality of thought, compared to the solidity of most everyday objects. For example, the real existence of ice and liquid water seems no less certain than that of glaciers and oceans, but we are less certain of the physicality of steam and vapor. We see and touch ice and water, but steam and vapor do not seem to actually occupy space, and thus have a tenuous hold on materiality. The difficulty is less in deciding what things constitute being than in determining the nature of being itself, which implies physical solids and tends to exclude non-solids and mental phenomena. Our concept of being is conditioned by vision and reinforced by collusion of the senses. Yet "being" does not refer to a substance or solid, but to the process of becoming through which things actualize and recur. Objects as categories retain the potential for further partition, but once an epoch actualizes it is a completed whole that only advances through iteration. Objects are the outward manifestations of a hierarchy of subordinate phases constituting the processual structure of the world, a series of rhythmic or vibratory elements forming a dynamic series of levels, from celestial bodies to superstrings.

An example of this rhythmic structure is the realization of language and music over a common system in brain activity. The progression begins with a slow frequency rhythm for the breath group that programs the expiratory pattern, organized around archaic systems in brain evolution. This passes to rhythmic derivatives, possibly harmonics, that mediate the speech melody or melodic contour of the language, which partition to the rapid sequence that mediates speech production. These levels constitute a set of kinetic or oscillatory rhythms, a vibratory structure in the brain, for language and music. In classical music, a simple opening theme or core musical idea is comparable to the kernel of a sentence that undergoes a complex development or transmutation. The growth of diversity out of unity or simplicity is an essential defining feature of the process theory of becoming. Levels in this dynamic structure can be interpreted as derivations of a fundamental frequency to its harmonics, combining the concept of a category/item sequence in becoming with the oscillatory or vibratory nature of content, and supporting the processual account of actualization as a model for mind and the universe

BEING IN-ITSELF AND FOR-ITSELF

Non-conscious entities, physical or organic, exist in-themselves, whether they are solitary or communal: an isolated crab, a school of fish, a cluster of barnacles. Becoming in entities or non-conscious objects, being in-itself, follows the same path as the for-itself, though in varying degrees. If perceptual objects are iterated and change is recurrent, what applies to human mind should apply to lower organisms and physical entities as well, given that the human brain, though perceived as an object, is a physical entity. Retracing the evolutionary sequence, we encounter organisms that change by way of recurrence through a minimal phase sequence, which progresses to basic life forms that undergo the same process, with becoming a category of change and being as the entity that recurs.

A person who is not attentive to self or mental content or not self-consciously aware of objects has a different brain state, perhaps one in which object development is not attenuated to articulate the mind with images. In a person unaware of present happenings, the present may be of briefer duration; conversely, someone caught up in mental imagery and not attendant to outward appearances may experience a feeling of "now" that engulfs and dwarfs the present. The occurrence of a self in a state of image or object consciousness is a discontinuous experience that depends on subtle features of the epochal sequence. Self-consciousness or consciousness of self in relation to objects and mental contents supplants the implicit, ready-to-be—awakened self as the perceptual center of experience. Just as the mental state can be drowsy or distracted, or incorporate remembrance and expectations, so the conscious self can be more or less prominent at a given moment.

9

Existence

SUMMARY

THIS CHAPTER CONTINUES WITH the exploration of some perplexities in thinking on the nature of existence, primarily the distinction of, and transition between, the subjective antecedents and objective realizations of perceptual objects, and the relation to the brain process through which they are derived. The subjective properties—formativeness, subjective aim and becoming—that precede and appear to persist in the object are an intrinsic part of—and exist as surely as—the final object itself. The temporal quality of existence is discussed in relation to recurrence as the basis of object stability and persistence, which presumably applies to the physical entities mirrored in perception.

INTRODUCTION

Confronted with divergent ways of conceptualizing existence, it seems to me we must first decide whether to begin deductively, with a definition or preconception, for example, that only causal objects, substances or properties exist, and bring the various phenomena that exhibit some mode of existence into relation with this definition, or inductively, as in this discussion, by exploring without preconceptions and in an inclusive manner the enormous complexity that is hidden in this seemingly innocuous term "existence," in the hope of arriving at some novel criteria that can accommodate a wide range of phenomena that lay claim to this designation.

One way to begin is by asking whether a thing can exist as a concept or mode of thought, and not as an ingredient of the physically real. Is this a binary choice? Is existence absolute, or are there forms or degrees? If we say everything exists, every thought, feeling, object, is there not some difference between a perceptual object, a physical entity, and its indefinite and/ or imaginary antecedents? If we say nothing exists, that objects are phenomenal veils that obscure reality, like a film of the real that is on-line with external events, one descends into the deepest skepticism. What precisely does it mean to exist? If causal relations are necessary, how would they apply to psychic experience or mental phenomena?

A footprint in the sand is a momentary depression that mirrors a foot, a negative image of the real that is washed away in the tide. Does the fleeting imprint differ in its existence from the object that shaped it? The fact that a foot is a solid object and the footprint is a cast, a depression or an outline, implies that solidity and stability impact existence. Is a footprint a copy of the real, like a shadow? The footprint is stationary, but disappears (unless it comes to be petrified, like a dinosaur footprint). The shadow comes and goes, changes. What does it mean to come into existence and then no longer exist? A shadow has no substance; a footprint is an empty space, the absence of matter in a place where matter would still be, if not for the foot. Does emptiness exist? The footprint is a construct, however brief, no less than a sandcastle. In contrast, a shadow is an absence of light. Are we saying that absence can exist? Mark Strand wrote, "In a field/ I am the absence/ of field." Does an existent replace an absence or can the absence be an existent? The space behind my head exists inferentially, while the space I see when my eyes are closed—the "visual gray"—is a perceptual existent. A shadow can affect the warmth of the earth or stone it covers, and attract organisms that avoid the sun.

If causal effect is necessary for existence, a footprint is causal like a shadow; in this respect, it exists no less than a reflection of a person in a mirror. We could say the person exists, but not the reflection, yet the reflection depends on the object reflected, as all things depend, for their perception, on the surface reflection of light on the retina. Like Escher's animals that parade behind a mirror, or Cocteau's world within mirror space, the interposition of the mirror between self and world gives a sense of a parallel world that is an artifact of perception. In one, there is self-reflection or the reflection of other objects that are identified with their reflection, as opposed to the ordinary reflection of light, while a mirror image is perceived as distinct from the person or object reflected. There is the person and the mirror reflection of the person. In effect, the person sees himself, while ordinarily he sees the reflection of light from other objects, just as he is a reflection for other observers. Does a reflection exist in some fashion like a perceived object? If we say that for a thing to exist it must have causal relations, a mirror image can cause a person to alter his appearance, as the image of Narcissus led him to abandon the activities of daily life and starve to death. The mirror reflection reminds us that a world of reflected light is not an actual world, though the world that is reflected is presumably the ultimately real.

We tend to think that objects in the world have a more certain existence than do mental phenomena, such as feelings and ideas, or that true facts exist in an manner utterly unlike false ones. Unicorns exist in drawings or as ideas, while horses exist as real things. If one thing exists as an idea, or as an idea of a non-existent object, in what sense does it exist as an actual object? A horse exists in actuality and a unicorn as an idea; what of the concept of a horse, which not only promulgates horses but informs us what a horse is? In terms of its existence, can a false or mythical concept be distinguished from a veridical one, or one that points to an actual object? A true concept differs from a false or imaginary one, but they are all concepts just the same, so if any concepts exist, all concepts exist, regardless of their content or what they refer to. The ontological problem of existence cannot be confounded, as it often is, with the epistemological problem of truth.

Every object appears for a moment and is replaced by the same or another object. The evanescence of a thing gives the impression of a fleeting or even questionable existence. Impermanence has a weaker claim on existence than an object that endures. However, from a mental standpoint, persistence is a recurrence of like instances, while the recurrence itself gives the object the impression of stability. The object—category of the object—recurs continuously, so we think the object is a solid thing, an existent independent of our perceiving it. Repeating a word does not increase its claim to existence, as does repeating a perception, as when the mind/brain revives a perceptual object, like a tree, in the process of perception. The tree seems to have an objective persistence that is lacking in the word "tree," especially since that substantial persistence is not dependent on the language used: that is, the realness of the tree does not seem to change if we call it *un arbre,* or *ein Baum,* or *drzewo.* A particle with a half-life of a fraction of a second exists for that fraction no less than the mulberry in my garden. In this respect it is like a footprint or a shadow.

As human history bears witness over millennia, an error or falsehood can have a more intense effect than a truth, a value more than a fact. If causal effect is essential, how do we understand the difference in causal power between truth and fiction? If errors and falsehoods do not point to true facts, what mode of existence do they share? Things of the imagination may seem more vivid and real than "solid" objects. Is inner speech (verbal thought) less real than vocalization? Where is the difference between formulating a sentence in the mind and producing it in speech? From a neural standpoint, the difference is passage to the articulatory apparatus, but this is only the final stage in the production of the utterance. A word spoken and then forgotten has a fleeting existence no less than its psychic precursors and physiological substrate. Words have causal effects, not just shared ideas or cries of "help," but even the little structural words that have no other function than grammaticality. A word uttered by a hermit in the solitude of the desert is no different than one spoken in conversation. Suppose mental telepathy were to be proven to occur. Would this mean that thoughts now have a causal existence, like words? Is the effect of a word what the word is, what it means, what it provokes or signals or what it points to?

Every act or object exists by being contrasted with other possible objects carved out of an antecedent yet unrealized potential, with the adaptive or relevant object "selected" to map to and represent what is otherwise imperceptible. All objects are impressions. Like footprints, they are negative images of the real. Adaptation conditions an object to fitness in a social or physical niche. The object becomes what it is by a process of elimination. It is what remains after all other possibilities—like those that appear in dream—are trimmed away. In this respect, the object is like the relief of an entity, the concave that appears convex. Assuming a physical reality mapped by appearance, the mental image of the world is not merely a copy of reality, but a reciprocal. An object does not replace what it represents, but is like a mask, an alternate if accurate representation of the outside world, a Rorschach of the real, like anti-matter—positron to electron, the levo to the dextro—a reflection of reality or its complement.

At this point it hardly needs to be repeated that the perceptual object is not the same thing as whatever it is that is physically there, *die Dinge an sich*. Apart from the temporal lag, constancy effects, and the reconciliation of the separate images of binocular disparity, the brain/mind inverts the retinal image as inverting lenses temporarily invert objects. The conscious object is a mental image that models and is slightly off-line with the physical entities it represents. In spite of this, immediacy of response is guaranteed by the activity of preliminary phases in image and act prior to conscious realization. At successive levels, sensory data bounce off the receptors to create a psychic replica of the physically real. The perceptual object is derived from mind as an endogenous category generated within the subjectivity of the observer and parsed at its endpoint to a virtual model of the world, but the true (yet inferred) source of the image is the relation to physical reality, as a mirror reflection of a world that may be either entirely unknowable or entirely noumenal.

As in the case of the preverbitum becoming speech, not only is there the contrast of an object with the physical entity it represents, there is the sculpting process that elaborates and is submerged in the object representation. Objects are reflections of something, and we call this something the reality behind or reflected in the object. The object representation is ordinarily identified with the reality that it actualizes. The image of the world, though we have come to realize that it is a copy and a result of impressions coming from physical entities, is felt as solid, real and tangible, not as a mental category that fractionates into featural detail, or an approximation to a reality that impacts the brain by way of the constraints of sensation. This mental image of the world, including the self, navigates through physical reality; survival depends on correspondence of what is perceived to what is really there, and on coherence of object and (re)action across serial occurrences. The reality to which objects correspond is imposed on the developing image; conscious life transpires in a mental bubble that maps to the physically real.

The perceptual model must be close to physical reality, or survival would be endangered. The match is such that objects are apprehended as direct perceptions of physical reality, independent of the subjectivity within and behind them or the process through which, like an utterance, they develop. In the normal waking state, sensation governs perception by exclusion, but the substance of the object is a series of mental configurations that, as potential or possibility, prefigure the final modeling. The object matches reality by virtue of the elimination of irrelevancy at successive phases, especially the final transition to independent existence; but the object world, though it is a field outside the observer, is fully subjective. Given that the major portion of the object is an intra-psychic process, with objectification by sensory pruning at its endpoint, the question of what constitutes existence for a perceptual object cannot focus on the outcome and ignore the inner derivation.

We can ask, does a forming object that is not yet existent—that is, it has the potential for it to be what it will become, which as potential or possibility is not identical to the outcome—exist in a manner comparable to the objectified endpoint of the becoming? Ostensibly, there is little relation between the early phases in object development and the final outcome, whether such phases are viewed, conventionally, as features to be assembled, or microgenetically, as categories to be partitioned. For standard theory, stages in the progression to an object are partial constructions. The microgenetic view of a succession of whole/part shifts has wholes as categories out of which parts, as sub-categories, devolve. Since pre-object categories are not containers of content, and members are unresolved unless they actualize, categories are better conceived as proclivities that are not fully predictable or even probable (at the point of passage) that trend to the definiteness of a subjective aim in the final qualitative partition.

For example, if one dreams of being stabbed by a unicorn as an unconscious image that foreshadows (or is a psychoanalytic interpretation of) a waking preoccupation, say a conscious fear of horses, perhaps with a sexual element, the unconscious image is a displacement in the broader category from which the conscious idea or feeling is derived. This is not to say the unconscious image is a transitional phase on the way to an object, but that the same "operation" that leads to the object is corrupted in the dream. A unicorn image does not persist in the final thought or object; the phase that actualized as a unicorn passes to an ensuing phase and is unrealized in the conscious outcome. The fusion of images in dream—unicorn, piercing, sexual connotation—can be related to conscious ideation, and thus illustrates the overlap or metaphorical extension of sub-surface categories that precipitate in dream. More generally, at every phase in thinking or object-development, virtual categories of object and word concepts and experiential memories achieve definiteness only when they actualize.

Memory and the creation of novel categories are records of object experience that figure in every perception. Memory can become perceptual; perception fades to memory. A relaxation of the sensory inflow that parses possibility to definiteness allows objects to withdraw to a field that is the ground of possibility, and the potential for creative advance and novel outcomes. Sensation is a two-edged sword. On the one hand, as we have seen, mind adapts to sensory data to individuate endogenous categories into an independent world. Without the final adaptation, life would be a dream and survival impossible. This is essentially what happens in prolonged sensory deprivation, and to a lesser extent in snow blindness, though a real world can still be recovered by unaffected modalities (auditory and tactile channels, etc.). On the other hand, sensation limits possibility by trimming the unexpected, narrowing contingency and restricting innovation. Thought and imagination are trimmed to necessity. The immediacy of sensory adaptation filters the image to the perceptible, elaborating thought and an interpretation of the environment in a sequence of world states to give an anticipatory response, as well as forming the mentation within multiplicity to gird perception with recognition, emotion and conceptual possibility. Early phases exhibit potential in fusion and displacement in proximity to experiential memory and feeling. The images and distortions of dream, fantasy and creative thought that crystallize in the mind in the relative abeyance of sensation give a picture of antecedent process through which veridical objects develop.

Possibility is the converse of the certainty that sensation imposes on novelty, though the certainty of the world is not apparent until it actualizes. We cannot say that the subjective process aims at a veridical world, since veridicality is impressed on subjective process at its culmination. Even the genesis of a veridical world shared by others differs in each observer as to conceptual content and value, which depend on the balance of mind-internal with sensation, a balance not between the inner and outer, but between concepts in the mind and the sensory data that rain down in each modality on developing configurations. In creative thought, the withdrawal from sensory input is intermittent; in psychosis, it is pervasive. In most, there is some balance in commitment to the external and relapse to the preliminary, reflecting the mitigation of a forward surge to completion by the prominence of pre-terminal phases.

The question may be asked, is the memory, meaning and feeling inherent in the object a continuation of mind into appearance? In other words, do subjective antecedents accompany the forming object outward in its development as psychic constituents, or does the object stand alone as an external product of antecedent phases, as its precursors fade away? Put yet differently: is the subjective diachronic or micro-temporal history of an object's development part of the object, or, once the object has fully developed and is "projected" outward, is the object a quasi-physical entity that exists independently of its formative or constructive history? On the standard view, in which objects are conceived as logical solids independent of their construction, value and meaning are projected onto it as extraneous attachments. While the featural contents—lines, angles, color, etc.—participate as elements in the construction of the object, like tires on a car, the psychic contents are typically seen as additions or supplements, not as pre-objects, categories or images. In principle, then, an incomplete object is, according to standard theory, a piecemeal construct still lacking certain yet-to-be-added elements, while for microgenetic theory, an incomplete object is a configuration with a subjective aim and an attenuated analysis, a figure not yet differentiated from ground.

From an objectivist point of view, the perceptual process is like a conveyer belt with a series of separate stages leading to the completed product. These stages are important as to their specific contribution, not to their order of assembly and not as continuants. The lines and angles of early process are building blocks in the final mosaic. Memory, concept and feeling are secondary additions, after object assembly, while the process through which the object exteriorizes remains opaque. Moreover, the mental activity that is presumed to assemble an object consists in identifying the properties of the object to be modeled. This assumes that object properties are installed in the brain or instantiated in nerve cells as constructive elements. On this view, the properties of the perceptual object are merely transferred to visual cortex as detectors of the very properties they duplicate.

For process theory, the object grows out of belief, value and memory as a configural precursor. As we have seen, the cognitive process iterates patterns of forebrain growth in phylogeny, while micro-temporal features continue the "force lines" of morphogenesis. We could ask the same question of a person as of an object: namely, in what sense does an individual here and now incorporate the prior states of a life? Is the person a composite of successive moments of existence, a reconstitution or revival of a history of instantiations? Otherwise, in the standard view, the individual at a given moment would be a logical solid, independent of its past states, such that the current state preempts or excludes the endogenous past through which it develops—which is not only counter-intuitive, it is patently absurd.

The fundamental question is this: is existence in mind part of the sum of what exists in nature, or is there an ontological distinction between subjectivity and the physical outside? While it is commonly held that the form of our knowledge originates in the mind, while the material is given from outside, with the properties of physical entities thought to exist differently than the properties that are mind-dependent, still, as Whitehead pointed out, all properties of matter are conceptual. The mental structure of an object, as much as a person, is its diachronic history. The fabric of external or physical structures—tissue, machine parts—consists of synchronic ingredients. One entails the becoming of an object in mind; the other the being of an object in the world. Does one set of constituents have priority over the other? Are the physical constituents of an object more real than the internal (cognitive) ones? What of the physical brain process through which the object is formed? Surely this exists even if it cannot be described. If we grant existence to the brain process that mediates the act and object development, then surely the mental events that accompany the brain process have an equal claim on existence. If, then, the mental phases that move from drive to concept to object correspond with neural activity—a series of physical events—the correlated mental events would have to exist, if only (in a materialist view) as indices of underlying brain events.

If a concept that actualizes as an object exists no less than the object that actualizes, what of transitional images, such as dreams and hallucinations that appear real but are not object-like in their realness? If intermediate segments in the transition actualize, or the endpoint deviates from the shackles of sensation and adaptation, or segments do not fully objectify, what share of existence attributed to an object rightfully belongs to its ante-cedents? Outside of perception, mental images do not persist, nor do they have a definite locus in space and time, nor do they necessarily correspond to anything in the world. The problem of the inner life is largely a problem of human mentality, since the presumed absence of an unconscious or sub-jective phenomena in animals implies that only action and its physiological correlates exist, though what a bat or horse perceives, what a dog smells and feels, and what a plant senses in the earth or sun may be said to exist as well. If we did not experience the foreshortened and palpable space and fluid image-transformation of dream, we would not have knowledge of an alter-nate, imaginary realm that foreshadows, sometimes very dimly, the visible world. We become aware that object space is an outcome of mental activity, and that what applies to dream, as a mode of perception not sanctioned by sensory data, also applies to waking perceptions that are constrained by adaptation.

Here the question is whether a subjective existence—or any existence at all—requires consciousness, that is, whether one must be conscious of a thing—mental or external—to say it exists. After all, a physical reality inaccessible to consciousness is presumed to exist—is possibly all that re-ally exists—including brain events that mediate conscious and unconscious phenomena. It would seem that the contribution of consciousness is not to confer existence, but to conceive the problem that existence poses, and to consider the distinction of at least two modes of existence, one for physi-cal entities and one for subjective phenomena. Without consciousness, one might have a mechanical universe that exists only in god's mind.

The converse to a mechanical, material universe to which mind is extraneous and quite possibly superfluous is the notion that everything which happens is part of reality, including mental events—conscious or unconscious, subjective or objective—even if reality is assumed to be mind-independent. Reality would then include the mental and brain events transpiring in each individual mind. One could argue that brain events are primary, so that mental events are collapsed or reduced to brain as second-ary or epiphenomenal; but why should the mental, of which we all have some direct knowledge, be deprived of reality in favor of the corresponding physiological events, of which we know so little? We might say that thought and feeling are real and exist, but what about every momentary individual perspective? Does what transpires in a momentary state of consciousness exist, or does it vanish when attention is diverted, like a thought that comes and goes? If an idea must be conscious to exist, what of the idea of the world? A continuous shift in attention gives us a world in constant change.

As mental events shift from one occasion to another, the reality to which mind is coupled is also in constant change.

When we perceive the world, we are not conscious of most of the detail within our perspective. The tree before me exists, even if I am not aware of every leaf and branch. When my attention is focused on a leaf, its structure surely exists, even if I am not aware of it. I do not have to take an object apart to know it has a structure, from the visible to the microscopic. A general knowledge of things obviates the necessity for the dissection of each individual object. The point is that a perception of the world as a whole cannot be conditional on, or even accompanied by, attention to individualities, or to the totality and multiplicity of embedded objects, not to mention the layered fabric of each item. Thus existence predicated on consciousness implies that what exists is the focus of momentary attention. Clearly, this places an extraordinary burden on consciousness, which, for the transient objects of attention, would be responsible for the existence of now one, now another, brief perception. The consciousness of a thing creates the problem of what the thing is and its dependence on conscious experience, but it is dubious that consciousness, though creating objects in the mind, confers existence on them.

Still, this raises the question whether every instant of mind and world at every moment in every consciousness is a new reality, and whether reality includes all prior instantiations. If reality is taken to consist of only the present occasion, then every event comes into existence in every present (a conscious present, since there is no present in nature), and ceases to exist, at least in the same form, in every ensuing present. This problem is resolved in mentation, not in physical nature, in the category-belongingness of objects that embodies successive appearances in a single reality. On this way of thinking, there is passage from one category to the next in the actualization of the mental state, which gives a present that is also categorical, namely, a virtual duration that encloses virtual instants. Since the present is illusory and presumably unique to human mind, and since existence means present existence, existence would be mind-dependent, or at least refer to events within a conscious present, specifically, a state of consciousness. The problem is to resolve the virtual now of human mind with the absence of a present or any sort of category formation in physical nature. If the present is unreal (illusory) and not part of physical nature, and if events in an illusory now are equally illusory, all events in the present are unreal, so the existence of objects in the phenomenal present is as illusory as the duration in which they are perceived.

The self has been defined here as a preliminary concept that overlaps prior instances of itself antecedent to full realization, but without existence unless in relation to actualized contents or objects. If the self is a categorical prime through which the mental state actualizes, then any illusory quality of the self would invalidate the reality of its products. Insofar as the derivations of the self and its ensuing categories result from progressive limitation of possibility, which is liberation from mechanical constraints, no actual contents pass from one phase to the next. If reality consists in the passing state, with the past forever gone and the future not-yet, a before and after in which the after continuously melts into the before, and all that exists, or all that has some constancy, occurs as a phenomenal appearance in a micro-temporal present in forward transition, reality would refer to a process of change or transition (see below), not a series of states from and into which the transition occurs, since existence of the duration or persistence necessary to have a state is conditioned on a bridge over passage in the now. The only knowable state that meets this criterion is the process of state creation and replacement in a human mind/brain, that is, the mental state that gives a conscious present spanning the before/after transition. From this standpoint, genuine change occurs in the realization of a perceptual moment, a mental state, not in the succession of replacements, i.e. the passage from one objectification to another, so the essential transition is the elaboration of appearances as present objects or events, not the presumed causal change from one conscious world to another.

Given continuous transition within or across putative states of the world—and the impossibility of describing any transition without aborting it—there is no solid, stable reality, no actual states, substances or static masses, only a process of change and recurrence, a flux well captured in Whitehead's remark that a rock is a mass of raging particles. We perceive objects in space as spatial objects, but in subjective time objects exist in the transposition of the before and after to a now. Objects are artificial demarcations in passage, since to delimit a state from the becoming through which it is realized severs transition in order to impose the arbitrary boundaries deemed necessary for analysis. Causal theory requires instantaneity, or stoppage, to circumvent the problem of transition across causal pairs, isolating states—causes, effects—at the cost of change between them. Private experience and public objects may be described in terms of logical solids, but these solid objects are illusory isolates in a dynamic of recurrent becoming.

In mind, objects are events, the nature of which depends on the scope of the category and the attention of the observer. An event can be the spark of a match or an evening by a campfire. A mountain looks to be the most solid and enduring of objects, and yet it is an event, which began with upthrust and will end when erosion displaces the last particle. At no point is there a pause in the transition from non-existence through becoming to non-existence. In nature, events are carved out of change by postulating the existence of atomic entities, that is, substances or discrete particulars that endure for a variable period of time. If time is the measure of motion, it is also the measure (container) of persistence.

In contrast, for process theory, the existence of an entity is the minimal period over which the entity can be said to exist, while persistence is the recurrence of the entity over some period of time. On this view, it is an open question as to whether the inferred duration of entities, e.g. arising, perishing, recurrence, is an application to the physical world of perceptual experience—a necessary postulate in process theory to achieve some sem-blance of stability—or if subjective duration is an evolved outcome in mind/brain process of the minimal duration of physical entities. Is the duration that is necessary for the actualization of the mental state, and the experi-ential duration of its outcome in the now, the basis of the hypothesis of the minimal duration in a physical entity needed for its existence in an objective world, or is the concept of a minimal duration a proto-psychic feature that evolves to that of the mental state? Clearly, animals exhibit category forma-tion, for example the category of things to eat or avoid, of same and different species, of suitable and unsuitable mating partners, and so on. The question is whether these drive-based categories arise from duration in physical enti-ties, and/or whether they develop to the object and lexical concepts in the human mind that provide a basis for the duration of the present.

For a long time, I presumed that entities enclose a process of becoming like that in mind, with a minimal duration to become what they are. I now see that the principal basis for this belief—which may well be true—is the (very real) possibility that inanimate nature exhibits proto-psychic features in the shift from isotropic energy to anisotropic feeling, such that entities require duration to achieve completion. Feeling strives to a subjective aim, undergoing progressive expansion over the evolutionary sequence. The be-coming of the mind/brain state and the category of a virtual present are the outcomes of the creation of entities out of flux.

It is difficult to conceive an ostensibly solid object (for example, a mountain) as a process of becoming, or to accept that mental categories delimit and stabilize objects and, to a lesser extent, mental contents. Change is conceived as something that happens to an object or what the object un-dergoes, not as a process through which the object comes into being. If there are no categories in physical nature save for those imposed by mind, and if categories are the foundation of durations that, like wholes, enclose virtual parts or instants, the absence of categories in the physical world entails the absence of duration and, by implication, entities stabilized by categories.

This is consistent with transition, becoming and relationality as the fundamental mechanisms of existence.

The insolubility of this problem has led, I think, to the temptation to ascribe reality to extra-psychic objects and events and deny it to mental phenomena or individual perspectives. What is perceived is taken to be mind-independent, regardless of its perceptual basis, with the act of perception independent of the object perceived and the diachronic progress of object formation. On this basis, a thought or a word achieves reality in action or speech, respectively, whereas objects, irrespective of perspective, are real existents, for all practical purposes identical to external physical entities. This gambit, which effectively identifies perception with reality, may ease the difficulty that a consideration of the nature of representation and object development create, but it eliminates mind from nature, with the result that even brain activity, which can be interpreted as wholly physical and external and separable from its appearance in conscious perception, cannot be partitioned into (putatively non-existent) psychic functions.

To make the objective primary, or to remove mind from nature, supposes that mental phenomena are secondary to sensation, since if we assign existence only to the objective, we are presuming that subjective phenomena are phantoms. This is largely a theory of provenance. For an externalist theory to be plausible, the sensation that guides perception has to be imported into the mind/brain to explain the slightest manifestation of preference or choice. This assumes an intrusion of sensory data into what is essentially a blank slate, with sensory association building up mental activity, or a compilation of physical reflexes accounting for the complexity of mind. Since brain facts cannot in the particulars be substituted for mental phenomena, this strategy holds only for those willing to overlook staggering explanatory gaps.

REALITY AND THE REAL

Is a thing that exists necessarily real and part of reality? How is the real established? What we see or experience as real does not ordinarily entail a judgment of its reality, but is a feeling of its realness. What is felt as real may not physically exist (rainbow, hologram); what exists may not be felt as real, or felt as unreal (events described in Mongolia or on the moon, in dream or hallucination, a film). This raises the question: what is the nature of the real, and its relation to reality? Since we cannot know physical reality, any determinant of the real will be a subjective judgment of how real the object or event appears, i.e. physically real, or conforming to our perceptual model of the world. We are misled by dream and hallucination, by feeling, and judgments of the character and motives of others, by perceptual constancies, mirror images and so on, but the main criterion of the real is its match, or closeness, to our ordinary perceptual model.

Reality and the real are not identical. There is a distinction of the real and the unreal in individual mind, and common sense holds that reality may include the mind, but it is not its product. Can we say that a thought is a part of reality, but not a judgment as to its function, truth or plausibility, or whether the criterion of reality is the meaning or correspondence of a concept? If I think about something, having the thought is a real event irrespective of what I think about. A thought may refer to a real horse or a unicorn, but the reality of the thought, which is all there is at that moment, is distinct from what the thought is about. To dissect a statement or concept as to what it is actually about may be necessary to tell us what exists within the concept, but not whether the concept exists. This is similar to the existence of a tree and the analysis of the tree into its visible and microscopic elements, each of which has existence as a feature or property of the tree. The content of an object can be deconstructed down to the constituent molecules and atoms that compose it, just as a concept can be analyzed into its formative, contextual and experiential history. The old concept of essences is replaced by an infinite descent of categories. Similarly, postulating that a thing exists, even if true, does not make the thing exist, it only accounts for the existence of the postulate. A thing is independent of what is said or thought about it, though what is said about it exists as a statement. The statement that unicorns do not exist exists as a statement regardless of the non-existence of unicorns. In the same way, the aboutness of the thought, its intentionality, is a mark of its conscious occurrence, a kind of arc from the self to an idea or object. This points to the relational quality of conscious experience, but the aboutness does not distinguish whether the thought exists or not.

For existence to be a property makes a thing independent of the property of existence. A horse that can jump has the property of jumping, but it is the horse or the jumping horse that exists empirically, not the property, no matter how essential or paradigmatic it may be. What would it mean for a property to exist apart from the thing to which the property pertains? How could "jumping" exist independent of objects that jump? Does each property designate a unique existent, or does the thing that possesses these properties exist independent of them? If having 4 legs and a tail, *inter alia*, is defining for a horse, it is the horse that exists, not the defining properties. If it is a property of a lion to be a carnivore, or of a dancer to be able to dance, what happens to the property when the lion or dancer is sleeping? Does the property cease to exist when it is inactive, or persist when not exercised? A horse that has lost a leg is still a horse, though it can no longer jump. What do descriptions or definitions add to the things they describe? One could say that a lion eating meat or a dancer dancing exhibit those properties, and then the property becomes part of the thing, but a lion and a dancer exist when these properties are not realized, or remain as potentials for future activity; and both lions and dancers perform other activities that we would not consider definitive for either category. There is confusion in a statement about a thing and the thing that is the topic of the statement, as in the relation of facts to truth judgments or propositions. A predicate is not the same as its subject; an utterance is not the same as its mental predecessors. The momentary form of the thing—a thought or an object—is what exists, a bird in flight or on a perch, a frivolous idea or a profound truth, and the momentary form is in change over time, so its existence, or what it is, is constantly changing as well. Things come into and out of existence, whether they die, transform or disappear.

Reality exists, though we cannot know it directly, but does existence refer to reality? The real exists even if it is unknowable, while the unreal may exist even if we cannot disconfirm it. There may be unicorns in some other galaxy, or living things composed of silicon. Appearance approximates reality, but cannot be an essential ingredient of it, since what appears real may be (indeed is) illusory, and the illusory would by definition not exist in physical nature. If the world of perception is an appearance, and a close approximation to some aspect of reality, and if an appearance as an approximation to physical reality is part of reality, then reality consists not only of what it is, which we can only approximate within the limits of our sensory organs, but of all occasions of the real that are approximations to a reality that can only be experienced through a simulacrum. No doubt, the degree to which perception maps to reality differs to some extent across individual human minds—certainly in relation to animal mind—but the mapping will never be exact in relation to the aspect of reality that is modeled, while the degree of precision will have infinitely many planes of definiteness. Perception is more exact than description, or opinion, which seeks to replace, record or express the facts of observation. Description is heavily influenced by belief, presupposition and the knowledge base, and is subject to test, dialogue and critique, in contrast to the effect on perception of sensory data in eliminating false or erroneous objects. Certainly, we want to believe in the existence of one reality or truth that is modeled in perception and communicated in language, but the varying degrees of clarity and accuracy, and the inexact proximity of a social and physical model of the world to physical reality, implies that reality is best described by physics or other material sciences independent of individual perspectives. Science can, of course, tell us the probable constituents of the material world, which in physics is generally taken as an account of the ultimate ground of reality. However, science cannot answer the question of whether the mind, which is after all the instrument of understanding the processes of nature, is also part of reality—though in microphysics, mind-dependent phenomena have been described (for example, the observer effect).

Particular things may seem more or less real, but not in relation to reality. The feeling of realness is not an indication of reality. Dreams and hallucinations seem real, but are questionable as elements of reality, while a movie, though it is not perceived as real, can be conceived as part of reality which, being known only through its perceptual model, cannot provide a standard for approximation. The irony is that the real is judged, or felt, in relation to the object world—a correspondence of one idea with another, or thought with appearance—while the actual world can only be judged as real by its coherence and testability in behavior. What is the relation of the involuntary or unconscious production of the world and the evident purposeless of nature? The appearance of the world in consciousness, and with agency, explains the impression of teleology in the world, god's aim or a final cause. As the subjective objectifies, it carries with it features of subjectivity. The tension of a subjective and objective point of view, and the possibility that an intuition of mind/brain process, which derives from nature, is conveyed back into nature, was addressed by Schelling,[1] who wrote that idealism brings forth realism, in that it materializes the laws of mind into the laws of nature.

A mirage appears real until it is sampled or matched to behavior. The real is not a substitute for reality; it is a feeling of completeness that comes of the coherence of perceptual modalities. In dream, the image can be seen, heard and experienced in other ways. As in waking, there is no sensory modality to disconfirm the others. Hallucination in one modality, e.g. a face, is usually recognized as unreal, until another modality is engaged, e.g. an imaginary face speaks. One can say that judgments of the real depend, for the most part, on the coherence of perceptions, while judgments of reality depend, so it is assumed, on the correspondence of concepts with objects. The real is an inner and usually implicit judgment based on a conspiracy of the senses, almost the literal meaning of "consensus." Reality is a relation of inner to outer that is grounded in common sense belief. If I am lost in philosophical speculation, what can bring me back to reality? Almost invariably, it will be something that intrudes on my attention, requiring an immediate

1. Schelling, F. (1800) *System of Transcendental Idealism*, English translated by Peter Heath, University of Virginia Press, Charlottesville

behavioral response: physical discomfort, a ringing telephone, the appearance of another person, etc. The return to reality entails taking some action to solve the immediate problem posed by the intrusion.

An anecdote of interest here has been preserved regarding the Renaissance humanist, Guillaume Bude. A servant entered his study when he was writing to inform the master that the house was on fire. Bude replied, "Go tell the mistress. You know I have nothing to do with running the household." He refused, in other words, to let reality intrude upon his thought.

If reality is inferred from the correspondence of a concept and an object, or an object and the entity it represents, even if the physical entity to which the object representation refers is screened from observation or knowledge, a judgment as to physical reality must depend on the adaptive value of the representation. In fact, a concept does not correspond uniquely to an object, but is a category out of which the object is derived. Even a simple proposition such as $1 + 1 = 2$, or grass is green, requires a mountain of proof or argument. There is no direct comparison of object (being) with its conceptual precursors, or the precursors with the outcome. The notion of correspondence replaces tracing the passage from mind to object in a becoming-into-being.

What, then, is the status of mental experience, finally, with respect to reality and existence? Are mental phenomena excluded from existence no matter how real they seem, even though the physical brain correlates of mental phenomena constitute part of the material world? If brain activity corresponds with mental activity, describing the mental is equivalent to describing the physical, but in a different vocabulary. That is, if every mental phenomenon traces, reduces to, or is identical with brain process, and there is no slippage between mind and brain events, the mental would be no less part of the world than the underlying brain activity through which it occurs. Except for a resolute and, in my view, indefensible realism as to the perceived world, there is no alternative but to attribute the same quality of existence or reality afforded to physical entities to object appearances, or hypotheses about such objects, or logical and mathematical accounts that substitute a method of analysis for the things analyzed. Once the door of idealism is opened to perceptible objects, i.e. appearances, their psychic precursors also pass through. Only the sharp separation of images and objects, the contrast with a non-veridical unconscious, and the transitional nature of thought assign reality to the outcomes of acts of cognition and not to the cognitive act itself.

Conversely, if appearance and the subjective are presumed not to exist, not only do we lose thought, imagination, feeling and the self, but also the world as a correlate elaborated in the brain and, for that matter, brain as well, and the whole of our knowledge base. Reality is a definite concept that refers to an experiential and inferred world, including everything that is, even if it is beyond individual experience or direct knowledge. Experiences that are more or less real, that fill and entertain our lives, a manifold of incomplete, fragmentary or erroneous phenomena, though part of reality, can be conceived as images of a parallel universe, a real mental world in relation to a real physical one, a realm of experienced subjectivity that models the unknown. The question is not so much what there is, or what exists, as the nature of existents in a subjective or physical manifold.

The argument that all happenings in all minds and entities exist and are constituents of reality, mental and physical, regardless of their origin, duration and illusory quality, leaves unanswered what it means for a categorical object to exist in the absence of essence, substance, spatial location and persistence. Existence is largely a temporal concept. To exist is to be in time. To be timeless or out of time is to not-exist. There are many ways of thinking about time or change that impact this concept: one is the brevity and variability in the minimal duration of a thing; another is change in an object in its development over that duration; still another, the possible interval between successive instantiations. An object and presumably an entity are bundled transitions with evanescent stability, which is attributed in part to a realization over a series of categories, and in part to the inapplicability of temporal analysis prior to completion. The transition is presumed to be a succession of earlier/later shifts, but the simultaneity of the unconscious does not allow a description of phases in the becoming. Once actualized, events take on temporal order in mind and world, and an object, retroactively, can be analyzed into a definite series. The becoming of an object is a dynamic process of transformation, depositing objects that comprise segments in change. Every existent has a micro-developmental history that achieves temporal order on actuality. The paradox is that the becoming of an object can be delineated only after the object exists or achieves momentary being, but once it exists it perishes in its replacement. Being is the illusion of persistence created by iterated replacement, while becoming is the reality of objects that exist as they vanish. In the rapid replacement of objects, we perceive change from one occasion or event-series to the next, when in fact we merely exchange the seamless recurrence of mental states for the appearance of persistence and stability.

Life, then, is the sum of the births and deaths of all momentary objects. If we assume that, like objects, entities arise and recur, the reality of things in the world is the invisible process of their creation, the transformation within an entity, not an entity itself, which is inert. Only by perishing does an object or entity make possible the novelty we find in its successor. The reality that is veiled by perception, were it perceptible, i.e. could we perceive physical entities, would still not consist of perceptions, but of the generative process through which they become what they are. Reality is doubly impenetrable: first, because we perceive appearances that are approximations; second, because entities consist of a becoming-into-existence that is itself imperceptible. Similarly, the change that is inside an object, which is the becoming what it is, is not only concealed within the final object appearance but, as process or transition, escapes detection.

The centrality of change in the transitional process and the ephemeral stability of particulars—the becoming and being of objects—has some resemblance to the wave/particle theory of light, though it is not clearly a dual-aspect concept. Still, a wave-like becoming creates momentary objects (modules, being, particulars) with recurrence, not continuity, the glue of passage, and overlap is the reciprocal of causation. However, as light has wave-like properties but requires a particle theory to explain other properties, the converse is true of objects, which appear as particulars that enclose an intrinsic dynamic. The processual or relational ground of reality encompasses all objects and entities. This leads to the conclusion that mind and nature, subjective phenomena and physical entities, exist as constituents of reality, while reality presumes a processual basis for all the entities it includes.

10

Moral Theory[1]

SUMMARY

THIS ESSAY EXAMINES SOME of the complexities of moral theory from the perspective of a process account of the mind/brain state. Many assumptions are questioned and reinterpreted from the standpoint of the category/member or whole/part transition through which the mental state actualizes. The relation of moral behavior to spontaneity and deliberation, or character and conduct, or subjectivity and action, or potential and self-realization, is explored from the same point of view. Value is discussed in relation to object formation, and is understood as a derivative of drive through conceptual-feeling and desire into the affective tonality of objects. The origin in energy of instinctual drive and feeling, and its inherent relation to phases in the development of actions and objects, constitute a becoming-into-being, as character and value are realized into conduct and social life. The chapter concludes with a speculation on the mental process underlying value and moral decision.

INTRODUCTION

The relationship between the philosophy of mind and the making of moral decisions has always been problematic. It is tempting for philosophy to postulate or advocate moral thinking that would be guided by logical thought

1. Brown, J. (2005) *Process and the Authentic Life*, Ontos-Verlag, Heusenstamm; Brown, J. (2012) *Love and Other Emotions, London, Karnac.*

and argumentation, not by instinctual drives, appetites, or aversions. The problems caused by the failure to take account of the nature of mental process, as the previous chapters have begun to elucidate, are manifold and serious. Before we can begin to construct a model of moral thinking based on a coherent theory of mind/brain process, it will be not only useful, but absolutely necessary, to confront these problems. Much of what follows over the next several pages may seem at best digressive, at worst offensive and amoral, but this is an unavoidable "deconstruction" of sorts, in order to make room for a moral theory grounded in a theory of mind/brain process.

Moral logic is frozen psychology, in which features of human thought are subordinate to rational judgments, which are conceived as the instigators of just action, rather than as rationalizations or exculpatory arguments for behaviors that in reality are guided by unconscious values and beliefs. Moral thinking is not merely a series of decisions as to what actions are best for most people, but also, in the diversity of occasions that confront and constrain individual choice, a determination as to whether or not rules or laws can be identified to guide human conduct. To alight on a maxim or principle and assume others will follow it, especially if it stems from a theory without religious or political support, or charismatic leaders who exhibit the desired qualities—that is, without a wellspring of powerful core beliefs—is less a recipe for good conduct than a commandment based on philosophical authority. Slogans such as the greater good, or putting oneself in another's shoes, do not extract those universals that are ingredient in individual and mass actions, and in their generality do not offer a prescription as to what one should do. The principle must either be a derivative of core values or appeal to them. In any event, a principle arrived at by philosophical argument does not ordinarily motivate behavior, unless reinforced by extrinsic evidence, belief or faith.

A utilitarian principle or one that is best for the majority does not prevent oppression by an intolerant society, tribe or community. What is good for all must be aligned with what is good for the individual. Even in a relatively just society, the notion of the general good does not prevent a vocal, intolerant or violent minority from provoking a dangerous reaction or a radical transformation worse than what it replaced. A doctrine that is acceptable to most individuals can still stoke radical upheaval, when every grievance leads to outrage, and simple acts of courtesy are trampled by certainty of belief, no matter how idealistic. Clearly, there is a case for a majority rule that respects minority rights; indeed, that is often the crux of moral decision, which requires a resolution of the often competing interests of the individual and the community (family, tribe, state, nation), or a reconciliation of personal agency with the collective will. Morality entails action involving self and other; thinking about an act involves the self alone. The relation of the individual to the community is an example of the part/whole problem to be discussed and implies conformance of the needs of one to those of another, an adjustment to some middle ground that entails a tolerance of differences that do not harm others. We tolerate diverse religions, lifestyles and politics, so long as they do not interfere with the rights of others. The tacit acceptance of diversities of various kinds becomes a moral issue when one belief system is imposed on members of the community who do not share those beliefs. A compromise may be found, but the downside of reconciliation is concession and relaxation of principle, a tricky issue for moral theory.

Usually, choices are not of one extreme or another, but involve minor differences that can be settled without much dissent. Yet there is no mean between good and evil, or right and wrong. An immoral act cannot be excused or tolerated by a just society without encouraging the very acts it condemns. From a different perspective, and apart from moral consequences, an innovative society is usually marked by unrest and extremes—think Periclean Athens, Renaissance Italy, Elizabethan England, fin-de-siècle Vienna—unlike a society with more homogeneity, which it achieves by diluting eccentricity and draining the creative impulse down to bland mediocrity.

More fundamental is the role of the informed judgment of a higher self—deity or ideal judge—that is compatible with reason and impartial decision, a worthy concept that takes on near mythic status. Is any decision impartial, that is, free of affective and cultural bias, loyalties, personal experience, tradition, legal precedent? The ideal judge would then be a computer—though programming would install prior bias—with human intervention only to insert mercy. Otherwise, one can ask whether or not moral propositions can be shown to be true. Or do they merely feel right or appeal to intuitions? Even in extreme cases of wide consensus, such as the prohibition of murder, there are exceptions, such as executions, self-defense, war, euthanasia, as well as an accepted view as to what constitutes murder, broadly defined as the taking of another life, whether due to depravity, jealous rage, vengeance, intent to kill for advantage, assisted suicide or psychosis.

For example, killing a fetus may or may not be an instance of murder, depending on whether it is considered the termination of a pregnancy or the killing of a baby, whether the fetus is normal or has a genetic anomaly, whether conception occurred because of rape, as well as on such factors as the length of the pregnancy, the health of the mother and so on; still, each instance is an act of murder, but with different justifications according to circumstance. Killing a stranger who is committing a robbery or one who threatens to kill or hurt a person in a dispute differs from killing someone who rapes or murders your wife, though if one is a spontaneous impulse and the other a planned aggression the implications will differ. Similarly, killing a burglar who climbs in the window differs from killing him on the way out. The circumstance is the context, the act is the instance, again a category/item relation. Moreover, in most instances the limits of rationality are disregarded under the impact of feeling, or necessity trumps reason, or one value is balanced against another.

Though a moral decision should be made on strictly rational grounds, it is questionable whether reason without feeling can impel action. If, as Hume thought, reason strives for truth, but feeling is essential to action, can choices ever be fully rational without some distortion or personal bias? The problem is that reason does not compel action, while emotion, which does, is not rational. Thus feeling is essential to action, but of dubious relevance to moral theory, since it can underlie, motivate or justify any action, even if it plays a large part in moral judgment, as in jealous rage, adulterous revenge, intent, compassion and so on. Ultimately, the diverse emotions are derived from the articulation of drive-feeling into value, need and desire. Even in the sphere of emotion, a specific affect individuates from a background of drive and need. A complement of feeling—as value—accounts for the power of rules or general principles to effect action, whether or not they convince the skeptics, the indifferent or the amoral, or apply only to the reasonable, or those with values that are malleable, or those in whom reasonableness owes to exerting or suppressing those values that determine the outcome in conscious thought and to which the individual is bound. In a legal setting, we take an oath to tell the truth. The oath establishes the grounds for perjury and the punishment of dishonesty but it also shows the need for external (religious) support, as in "so help me god". A moral principle—philosophical argument generally—has little impact when it stands alone. Conversely, a religious belief, deeply felt, good or bad, needs little rational support.

The complexities of choice and behavior through which an individual must navigate, even when decisions are more or less instantaneous, make a general rule applicable to only a sub-set of circumstances, while a moral principle is only as useful as those inclined to follow it, which depends on nurture and experience as much as moral instruction. There are many instances where a general principle does not apply or it is selectively applied or counter-productive, such as Kant's admonition against lying, so that moral judgments often appear ad hoc and conditional. Moreover, principles often collide. It may be a good principle to always be honest, but not if it is hurtful or puts others in danger. To kill an innocent person to save many others would violate the rule against murder, but sparing that person would violate the rule against allowing innocent people to die. To sacrifice one's child to save hundreds produces the same conflict, complicated by the obligations of parental feeling.

There is also a conflict of quality and quantity. On the one hand, all life has value, so we suppose, but the idea of unequal value introduces a qualitative measure. Do we not think that the life of a healthy young person is more valuable than that of a person who is old and/or infirm, a brilliant scholar more than a dullard or no-good, a model citizen more than a clod or truant? On a quantitative basis, and according to reason, five lives are worth more than one, *ceteris paribus*, but taking one life violates every moral code. The goal of moral theory is to arrive at just principles of conduct with universal applications that least modify or forfeit the natural expression of human needs. This balance of the many and the one, which is played out in most moral acts, is central to the role of equality in moral decision.

EQUALITY

A common and more general principle is that of equality, initially the equal value of human life, which extends to all life and, within humans, to equal opportunity, equal protection and treatment under the law and freedom from bias, all of which are foundational to most moral codes. The principle also extends to punishment, as in execution for murder, "an eye for an eye." The virtue of this principle is that it can be adapted to a variety of conditions, though equality of individual value is a qualitative judgment that may conflict with quantitative measures and rational conclusions, as in the examples given above. Decisions almost unthinkable 30 years ago, such as gay marriage, paternity leave, women in combat, hardly raise an eyebrow today, yet they are not grounded on any moral principle other than equality, which morphs into the irrelevance of gender, cultural or racial stereotypes or sexual preferences. Other applications of the value of equality to such problems as abortion, vagrancy, gun control, affirmative action, etc., remain unresolved. Overall, the concept of equality is an anodyne to disarm objectors in particular circumstances, since it ignores physical and cognitive differences, or considers them trivial in relation to the authority of the over-riding principle. When all such distinctions are dismissed, the principle becomes political correctness as a weapon against dissent.

Similarly, if we are all to be treated as equal, opportunity based on merit is a moral violation, since it rewards inequality of ability, intelligence, access or potential. Equal opportunity, were it be fully realized, would not need a legal mandate. Clearly there is not equal opportunity, not only because societies are intrinsically unjust, but because individuals are not equal. This was discussed by Aristotle as constitutional luck. Apart from genetic, environmental and other factors, the quality of parenting alone creates inequalities that effect accomplishment and potential. A meritocracy is desirable for its efficiency, but inherently unequal. In some countries, taking an obligatory examination at the age of 17 ranks intellect and/or rapid maturation over other qualities, and is an opportunity killer, in direct conflict with the motto of égalité. Such exceptions as affirmative action or a need for racial, religious or ethnic diversity may be useful measures but they also violate the principle in the opposite direction, by allowing for a preferential treatment that, in promoting the interests of certain groups perceived as the victims of oppression, limits the rights of deserving others.

The intent to right an historical wrong based on its alleged role in contemporary life reminds one of the philosopher Schiller, who said, "I ask for truth and they give me history!" To what extent are past abuses relevant to ongoing moral judgments? Is this a case of extracting one variable and explaining or justifying a complex situation in terms of it? Again, this points to the relation of part to whole in moral judgments. The Jew does not claim preference as a descendant of those lost in the holocaust, or the Armenian for the Turkish genocide, or the Japanese for incarceration during the war or the sins of their foregoers. There may be justification for trans-generational guilt and responsibility, but over how many generations? It is only when long past abuses are misconstrued as instrumental in the present—which is impossible to ascertain—that the principle of equality itself is abused. Even terminology—such as African—or Native-American—has the effect of reinforcing uniqueness and inequality and/or provoking sympathy—or discrimination. Some are darker or more native than others, but we are all descendants of Australopithecus, thus of African heritage, whether a million or a few hundred years ago.

Should a university or professional school strive for a meritocracy or for a proportional representation according to gender, ethnicity and so on? When I was a student, some medical schools had a quota on the top-heavy enrollment of Jewish applicants. Diversity at the price of equal opportunity is bias, even if it mutates to a worthy cause, namely, to preferentially aid the disadvantaged, though the public may suffer by the matriculation of less qualified individuals. We justify breaking the more rational and general principle for one that is local and has emotional appeal. Take the example of the age of consent for sex and/or marriage, which differ according to state and country, and intuitively for gender, but fail to recognize the early sexual profligacy of many youngsters. What is the difference if a 14—or 16-year—old girl consents to sex with a teenage boy or a 60-year-old man? Is sex that

comes of experimentation or "puppy love" in teenagers worse than seduc-
tion by an adult, or should the choices of a young girl be respected? Should
a teacher be punished for sexual contact with a 14-year-old boy who boasts
of his conquest? What precisely is the offense in marrying a step-daughter,
when the genetic taboo is not relevant? Are the genetic consequences of
consensual incest in closely-related adults worse than repeated pregnancies
in couples with a strongly penetrative gene for a devastating illness? One is
a taboo and/or unlawful, the other is referred for counseling. Does the state
have a right to regulate sexual activity or intrude on personal decisions that
victimize and disempower the young? Age of consent is arbitrary. In many
countries, a girl comes of age with menstruation. This is not about rape
or molestation, but depriving the young who have reached sexual (if not
cognitive) maturity the freedom to make sexual choices, especially when
the choices of adults are often just as foolish. Does the well-intentioned but
arbitrary aim of protecting the young violate equal rights? Perhaps it is appropriate to minimize unwanted pregnancies or single parents supported
by the state, but there are other ways to manage this problem—education,
responsible fathers, adoption, a creche, to cite only a few.

If these arguments make us uncomfortable, then we are forced to con-
cede that, in the end, all lives are evidently not equal, though the distinction among humans, and between human and non-human life, or among
all forms of life, is blurred. We could say all life has value, but would we
say some organisms are more human or more valuable than others? If we
restrict the concept of equality to all humans, it is clearly not a widely applicable principle. As noted, not everyone can take equal advantage of opportunity, though this is a bromide. At what level is this claim justified?
Children are born sickly or in health; they have different genetic endow-
ments, different parenting, good or bad luck. If just being alive is an entitle-
ment to equality, this applies to all living things, even unicellular organisms.
Is the life of a person who is severely mentally handicapped as valuable as
that of a genius, an ordinary person, a healthy young child, a senile old
man? Attractive people have greater opportunities. Is this just and fair? Is
equality conditional? Does it depend on the quantity of attributes, or is it
an arbitrary principle? Should the value of a life be central to assessing its
worth, or should a difference in value be ignored in favor of a principle that
is an obvious untruth?

As to the recognition of animal rights, this also depends on a concept
of equality, namely sparing all creatures from abuse or the fate of being
a meal at the dinner table. This applies only to human consumption, not
the predation of other animals. Apart from the preservation of species and
ecological balance—saving whales and guppies—what determines which

animals should be eaten? We might demur on whales and dolphins as mammals, but what of amphibians, fish, mussels? How far down does edibility go? We eat chicken with impunity, but would be criticized for eating a nightingale, or an eagle, endangered or not. What is the value of a chicken other than as food for humans or other predators? Would the common defenseless sheep survive evolutionary pressures without human cultivation? We might be too squeamish to eat a monkey, but the natives of the Amazon are not. A monkey may have too close a resemblance to humans, thus violate a taboo on cannibalism, but evolutionary relations exist all the way down the ancestral scale. Is cannibalism immoral? What is worse, to kill a person out of anger or, if one is starving, to kill for food? Both violate a powerful rule or taboo. It is a common practice for the Chamorro islanders to eat relatives, out of respect and the desire to acquire their qualities, sometimes deadly. Here, someone is not murdered but already deceased. Disgust over cannibalism was asserted by Lévi-Strauss to be a precursor to table manners. To draw a line between what is edible and what is not is comparable to an evolutionary Rubicon for consciousness or value. The higher the life form, the more protected. The alternative that avoids troublesome distinctions is to argue that equality takes the form of a respect for all living things. This is consistent with the panpsychic approach in philosophy of mind, with a Schweitzerian mode of thought, and with the Jain moral code holding that all living things are sacred, though a vegetarian who restricts his diet to plants should know that Stefano Mancuso and others have shown they have a primitive nervous system.

Is killing a gorilla an act of murder? The gorilla brain is larger than that of many Bushmen; their IQ is greater than the severely demented or mentally handicapped. Killing a gorilla is illegal; killing someone who is mentally handicapped or irreversibly comatose is murder. The punishments differ. Does human life merit special treatment? Why? Should the attributes of humanity be considered? If so, what of other animals down the evolutionary scale? Here we think more with our stomach than our brains. What principle should be used to decide? Is intelligence or closeness to human appearance a rational measure? Pigs are smarter than chickens, but eaten just the same. Equality can apply to race, gender, opportunity, freedom or all life forms. The principle taps human sentiment and leads to wide disparities in attributes and selective use. One could ask, should birds be free or kept in cages? Does keeping a pet undermine the natural order? Is selective breeding or domestication inhumane. Is it a form of animal slavery? Is it unconscionable to raise pets for amusement, or cattle for food, when such animals can no longer survive in the wild? Indeed, unless an animal works on a farm, or in hunting, or as a sled dog, pets are little more than emollients for loneliness and vanity. When I lived in Korea, the cows that worked in the rice paddies were kept in the house, while dogs, useless and needing to be fed, were eaten. Is this not more logical? In these examples, we have an instance and its relation to the context around it. One could say, a principle that is employed to interpret the instance replaces the context, again a category/member relation.

SPONTANEITY

Another difficulty is the clash of spontaneity and deliberation. Is a spontaneous act, whether egocentric or sacrificial, a surer mark of character than one that follows deliberation? Does spontaneity reveal the genuine self directly, without a detour through reflection? Is conscious deliberation the source of freedom, as Kant wrote, and spontaneity an automatic reaction? Or, as Schelling put it, is spontaneity the true freedom of the will? The person who, unthinking, dives into the rapids to save a drowning child, or someone who risks his life to push a stranger away from an oncoming car, or a soldier who falls on a grenade to protect his comrades, are occasions when immediate action is necessary and a moment's reflection would nullify the act. When we compare acts in which life is risked to save a stranger to acts that are less dramatic, that flow from conscious reflection and rational moral decision, we reach the core of a personal moral code, embedded in unconscious values and unadulterated by thought and attendant justifications.

Such cases lead us to ask what reason adds to moral behavior, if the most unselfish, virtuous and courageous of acts is done without thinking, especially when the readiness to sacrifice one's life is vitiated when it gives way to thought. Instances where immediacy and an impulse for the good merit admiration contrast with the inaction that comes of contemplation, which more often than not brings hesitation, reluctance, aversion to risk, mendacity and excuse, that is, it allows self-interest to predominate, leading to outcomes less costly to the individual. Spontaneity is absolute; contemplation may weaken resolve. We can ask if risking one's life for another, especially a stranger, is foolish or noble, but we honor the courage of someone who acts at once without deliberation. Spontaneity of this type depends on the implicit belief that all lives are equal, the subject no less than others. However, while it is unclear whether indifference to danger, a sense of invulnerability or belief in equality is instrumental in spontaneous altruism, if someone risks his life to save a drowning dog, depending on the context, we may be unsure if the person is a saint, a hero or a fool.

What is the distinction between spontaneity and automaticity? Learning a new skill is accompanied by deliberation, hesitation and consciousness of decision. Gradually, the skill becomes automatic and can be performed with little conscious thought. Is spontaneity the automatization of conscious instruction in values that become, as we say, second nature, a pure expression of values that are over-learned and habitual? This is similar to occasions when obstruction, uncertainty or complexity bring the over-learned skill back to the level of consciousness, just as ingrained values can rise to conscious deliberation when challenged by complex or novel circumstances. On such occasions—by aligning values with options—thought resolves the difficulties that skill confronts. Value is influenced by wider considerations than skills—whether playing a piece of music, climbing a mountain, or doing carpentry—which tend to be more narrowly focused, though every decision, however trivial, reflects a valuation. Skills involve choices that are relatively confined and may not pit the self against others. Still, the process through which the spontaneous expression of value, e.g. to put the other before the self, and the automatic expression of skill, as in playing a well-known tune, confront a novel challenge that, without resolution of a line of action, shifts immediacy to conscious reflection. In both instances, a course of action is selected from competing possibilities.

In most situations, contemplation more often leads to uncertainty or compromise, not decisiveness. If thought, as many including Freud have written, fills the delay before action, it is also a substitute for action, bringing the act to fruition in the mind, not in the world. The forthcoming act, along with other possibilities, crystallizes as psychic events that anticipate or foreclose actual conduct. To forestall action for deliberation, whether in solitary thought or in dialogue, is generally a strategy to avoid decision, or to shift necessity to probability, or the immediate to the incremental. Should deliberation influence what should be instinctive? Is compromise a good thing if a core value is weakened or abandoned? Spontaneity derailed by thought introduces perspectives and future possibilities that can impede doing what is necessary at the moment. Spontaneity realizes the morality or character of the individual; deliberation that is aimed to the good is an adaptive strategy. Put differently, spontaneity is an intrinsic relation of character to conduct; deliberation attenuates action by placing it in relation to logical self-interest, law and judgment. In this sense, the spontaneous is less inter-personal and closer to individual will, while deliberation and the indecision that is its companion, in exploring various (let us assume, well-meaning) options, are closer to the collective will, where consensus and compromise may take the place of a moral imperative when a guiding principle is no longer dominant.

This is the rationale for the morality of the state, but it can be that of an individual without a strong moral compass.

An act that is moral from the standpoint of the agent might, in deliberation, lead the subject to examine a risk/benefit ratio, or question whether a person who might be saved by a spontaneous act is worth saving or, in a thought experiment or in retrospect, ask if the one lost would have made a greater contribution to society or family than the one who is saved. Should a doctor, a teacher or mathematician be sacrificed for a dull, disabled or even an ordinary person? Is the life of an alcoholic, a wife-beater, a derelict or scoundrel, as valuable as any other life? When a doctor saves the life of a murderer condemned to execution, he acts spontaneously in relation to instilled values that allow him to avoid the effort and cost of deliberation. This is an habitual response that does not deserve moral credit. Should an exceptional person risk military combat, or be excused from service as too valuable to sacrifice? Suppose a doctor would save countless lives, a teacher would inspire innumerable students, or a mathematician would solve a vexing problem or devote his talents, like Turing, to breaking a code? All lives are clearly not of equal value, yet we persist in the comfort of this unfounded belief.

What is the difference between a person who does "the right thing" naturally, and one who succumbs to force, pressure or necessity? The psychological root of moral decision is evident when the character of a person who would ordinarily behave in an anti-social manner is inhibited by the implicit threat of punishment or retaliation. Take someone who wants to steal or cares little if someone is maimed or killed, but is fearful of capture or injury. If one judges a person solely by his acts, we might say the individual acts in a proper way in spite of an immoral wish. The fact that an inherently unkind person, a misanthrope, acts meritoriously though harboring malicious thoughts raises problems for an act-based theory of morality, when the immoral is prevented by consequence, or the person is not compelled to action. What of the distinction of moral action generated by habit, or deference due to insecurity, and that impelled by genuine goodness and moral principles? How does an impediment to malice correspond to an unconscious urge to the good? In these instances—impulse with obstruction, coercion with resistance, or automatic reactions—the self does not act freely, for there is no volition or awareness of voluntary choice. A truly moral act should have a feeling of agency in the resolution of unconscious value and conscious desire. This implies that the contextual bias of instilled values supports the derivation of conscious wish, that the spontaneity of early-acquired values partition to the conscious choice of mean-spirited or well-intentioned acts, and that the presence of choice coincides with the transformation of a single-minded purposefulness to a feeling of agency in decision.

What of occasions of inaction through fear in a person with a kind heart? Does one unkind or thoughtless act negate a good life? Do episodes of moral crisis outweigh little acts of generosity in everyday life? Should we praise the miser who is stingy in life and philanthropic after death? Francis Bacon criticized those who, for the sake of post-mortem generosity, deprived their heirs of their inheritance. What of a refusal to act, such as donating a kidney? Should it matter that one refuses a stranger, a friend or a relation? Equality of life and opportunity should blur the difference. How is moral action wedded to personal risk? What of politeness, manners, consideration or deference that come from training, not genuine concern? Is it the act that counts, or the feeling in the action? If compassion is, as Hegel thought, more idea than feeling, does the ideational content of the act increase its rational component, thus adding to its moral value, or is the lack of emotional commitment a factor in moral worth? If one does the right thing for the wrong reasons, is the moral value diminished?

INTENT AND OUTCOME

How does one weigh the outcome of a moral act or decision in comparison to the intent behind it? In some respects, this problem opposes theory to praxis. If a corrupt person accumulates wealth in order to improve the lives of many others in a mission of philanthropy, and if the wealth could only be accumulated by devious means, say, by defrauding rich investors, do the ends justify the means to their realization? If the means hurt a few slightly, and the ends help the many greatly, how do we judge this balance? The relation of means to ends is an important distinction in moral theory, but, as shown, this can readily be challenged, for example in social justice theories of income redistribution, Robinhood scenarios, munificence as a byproduct of greed, psychoanalytic interpretations as to the foundations of intent, resolution of conflict and the unconscious sources of conscious intentions, along with the usual impurities of motive. Consider the great benefit to the poor in India from the purely mercenary outsourcing that seeks higher profits and cheaper labor. The means can be intermediate to the ends, or mental stages to their realization. If intent to do good is essential to the judgment of ends, what of intent to do harm that does not materialize? If a person can be exonerated for good intentions, can he be prosecuted for malicious ones?

If a known murderer is set free on a technicality, a legal principle or insufficient evidence, with the expectation he will kill again, that is, understanding his intent—even compulsion—to kill, the decision might be narrowly justified but the effects will be catastrophic. Should the potential effect of a decision confined to a specific act, ignoring the likelihood of future misconduct, be part of the moral judgment? Should moral judgment be for acts in the near present, or should it be cumulative over a lifetime? The question is, should a judgment be independent of character and concerned solely with the act? We say someone "acts out of character" when there is a difference between conduct and expectation, or that he is "the last person one would suspect of such a crime," or "I didn't know he had it in him," all pointing to a dissociation of inferred character from unexpected acts. The opposite is perhaps less common, a poor character that surprises by an altruistic act, or one that remains ineffectual or reveals itself impulsively later in life.

Take the example of tracking a potential terrorist and doing nothing until the act is in progress, with the risk of being too late. How does the intent to do harm figure in a judgment when the act has not yet been committed? Suppose the person changes his mind at the last minute. Are outcomes the only arbiters of moral judgments? If a person declares intent, or if, with a future mind-reading machine, we could judge a person's character in the absence of action, would intervention and punishment be justified by character and intent alone? A harmful thought or wish tends to be excused, since we all have them now and then, but ordinarily do not act on them, so to what extent is morality hostage to action? If we could truly read the mind of another person, short of forecasting an outcome, how would this figure in judgment? To what extent should individuals be judged by prior acts and reasonable expectations? If judgment is deferred for lack of knowledge, or rejected as hypothetical or unfounded, or lacks strong evidence, does the one who judges have culpability no less than the one who is judged? To say or think, "I hope he dies," is not the same as killing him, but if a devoted friend overhears the comment and carries out the act, how is one to judge the wish that instigated the killing?

The delay before action that is occupied by thought can produce conduct that is or is not moral, or wanting in courage. The lack of a guarantee that reflection arrives at the best option raises questions as to the relevance of conscious deliberation prior to action? Deliberation may postpone impulse, but it does not necessarily allow for better choice; instead, as discussed, it may give time for choices that are devious or self-serving. This question goes to the impact of deliberation as a mode of action that is internal and un-actualized. From this perspective, options that are considered but unrealized provide insight to moral character no less than acts that are chosen. How are we to judge someone who decides on a good act but considers malicious choices, or chooses the lesser of two evils without entertaining better options? Ordinarily we choose among two or three options, not a range of alternatives, perhaps because of limits on the number of possibilities one can hold in the mind at the same time. Even the chess grandmaster usually considers no more than a handful of moves. Ironically, the feeling of agency is weaker with a menu of options and stronger with a limited number of choices.

Robbing a bank is a crime, but does it matter if the reason is to enrich the robber, to help the poor or pay for medical bills? The reasons for an action speak to character, and can harden or mitigate judgment of the merits of the act. An act-centered morality does not address these differences in intent or motive, presumably because it is difficult to infer the true intention of an individual prior to the act, or to separate the reason for the act from its nature, justifications and excuses. The premeditation that plays a role in punishment assumes that consciousness of choice will influence outcome, and that sudden impulse may, to an extent, be excusable, but it only begs the further question if conscious choice is implemented or only justified by deliberation. That is, do choices follow on conscious selection and directly provoke an action, or more likely, are they a result of unconscious beliefs, tendencies and presuppositions that specify as they surface, with reason serving to justify or explain unconscious bias?

A related question is whether a person is less moral in the absence of action than one who acts out of obedience, even with the absence of positive values. A fear of censure that figures in moral decision, in deceit or disguised malice, or other instances of a disconnect of action from thought or feeling, is captured in the "secret Nazi" paradigm, where, excluding those like Sartre who believe, arbitrarily I would say, that we are the sum of our acts, a failure to act does not excuse a hateful wish. Even the most virtuous have conflicts concealed beneath unimpeachable conduct. The latently immoral act can stem from unconscious tendency, suppression of benevolent impulse, lack of imagination, conformity, or the effort to maintain an egocentric sense of moral superiority, instead of being prompted by other-centered values.

Suppose a doctor keeps alive a person whom he dislikes in order to prolong his pain, or gives narcotics to a pleading addict that ensure further addiction, or withholds them, leading to misery in withdrawal when the addict is beyond help, or saves the life of a murderer, or prevents a death to guarantee a life of distress and helplessness. Clearly, one metric is applied to conduct and another to character, for good intentions can induce suffering and despair, while malicious intent can be subdued on occasions of goodness. In one instance, a moral act accompanies a malicious intent; in another, a harmful act accompanies unselfish motivations. Is the doctor who assists the suicide of a terminally ill person less or more kind than one who refuses? Morality might prompt the doctor to proceed, while professional ethics would say no. In the conflict between values, kindness can lead to hurt and the reverse.

Generally, the morality of action is judged primarily on conformance to social theory, to law, to conduct in relation to character or instilled values, needs and desires. But presuppositions, loyalties, cultural and other biases, possible genetic determinants and evolutionary precursors play a role. When discussion strays beyond the dictates of the Decalogue, the Golden Rule or Kant's maxim, which appear reasonable but are otherwise not forcefully grounded, or depend on social and political norms, or derive from (justified by) a general theory, such as evolution or Marxism, arguments for what is good inevitably depend upon opinions that arise, not from justifications, but from the unconscious beliefs that give rise to them, reinforced by tradition and consensus. When the moral is adduced from social theory, few of these problems are resolved, whether the allegiance of the individual to the self, the state or family, relations of power or influence, a disparity between drive and duty, self—and other-centered behaviors, or the option of a temperate life that avoids extremes in spite of constant pressure to take sides and abandon different perspectives. What is excluded is a relation to brain process (see below), which is presumed to be morally neutral or hardwired for self-preservation.

Often decisions formed in terms of what is best for the individual, for others and for the community, set in conflict the liberal attitude favoring personal freedom against a broader canvas of social responsibility and the collective will, or majority rule and the rights of minorities, or individuality and community. A variety of thought experiments probe these conflicts, such as a sacrifice of the one to save the many. The questions are often insoluble, precisely because they involve a fundamental attribute of mentality that has not been a point of interest for moral theory: namely, the tension of the whole/part, context/item or category/member relation.

VALUE

Values, concepts and judgments constitute a store of knowledge instilled by exposure to a given environment, including the effects of nurture and life experience. They serve to suppress or ameliorate egocentric drive, in order to radiate into the variety of needs and desires that constitute the fabric of individual and social life. The nature of character, or intent and choice, is related to the concept of value, which not only generates and constrains options but, as a mode of feeling, empowers and carries them outward. Value is central to morality, but what is its nature and origin? And how, as Köhler asked, does it arise in a world that is conceived as a vast machine, or from a brain that is interpreted as a computational system? The resolution of this problem, namely "value in a world of fact," lies in Dewey's claim that facts are irreducible values. The natural world is animated and enchanted by value. How, then, are we to account for value in a world that is, as Tennyson put it, red in tooth and claw?

I would argue that the place to begin is with the core of all matter as energy, non-directional or isotropic. The root of value lies in a transition from energy in inanimate entities to feeling in organism, which becomes the animating principle of life. Energy is time-reversible; feeling seeks closure and recurs in a direction toward the future. This direction is the seed of purpose and the subjective aim. The recurrence of feeling in a surge to the future establishes the inner dynamic of the entity, the urge to survive (recur) and the aim to reproduce (replicate), which is recurrence by proxy. In primitive organisms, feeling is not necessarily felt; it is the energy of life and the forward trend of growth. Gradually, feeling evolves to instinctual drive and takes on affective qualities. Feeling is the dynamic of mentation that accompanies and inhabits the development of concepts out of categories or the process of object-formation. Feeling is the becoming of an entity; the concept is the being it becomes. The becoming-into-being is the transition of drive-categories to conceptual-feeling to object-worth, with feeling or value as a shifting affective tonality over serial phases in object-development. At one moment, value is desire for an object, at another it is affection for a pet, and at still another moment it is fear or apprehension. Some objectless states, such as anxiety, will resolve into intentional states of fear. An emotion with an object or concept is also a (positive or negative) value. Every emotion has a conceptual frame; every concept has an affective tonality. Concepts without feeling are abstract non-existents. Non-conceptual and undifferentiated feeling in primitive organism not distributed into distinct affects or emotions is, minimally, the basis of existence and the directional life force.

Persistence is an illusion created by recurrence. Change is not across actualities but within the object—or self-replacement; the object or organism "causes itself" to recur each moment (causal persistence). The initial drive of hunger satisfies the urge to self-replication, assuring survival through the outgoing vectors of aggression and defense or approach and avoidance. Through the drive-satisfaction or consummation of hunger (thirst), energy is renewed and the organism grows and ages. Psychoanalysis gives primacy to the sexual drive in well-fed individuals, but starvation brings hunger and survival to the fore. The derivation of hunger to sexual drive continues the pattern of self-recurrence, in that, after final perishing, the organism "recurs" through progeny. Reproduction of like-others by sexual drive is the renewal of feeling in offspring. Survival of individuals through recurrence, and species through reproduction, is a prolongation of the iteration in all objects and entities. The repetition of a single organism each moment gives way to its replacement by like-others through copulation. One could say, in mating as in fertilization, 1 + 1 is not 2 but a novel One, a synthesis to unity.

It is evident that sexuality expresses the same active-passive or subject-object vectors as hunger, though these are usually mitigated in the partition to sexual drive. Avoiding predators and devouring prey are the aggressive and defensive vectors of hunger that transform to sexual drive in capture and submission, selection and pursuit, resistance and acquiescence. Along with the vectors of hunger and sexual drive, there are shared features in both categories: orality, olfaction, pleasure, appetite, consummation, periodicity, etc. Hunger and sexual drive individuate to a variety of needs. Those that derive from hunger include ambition, acquisitiveness and greed. Those that derive from sexuality include fetish, sadomasochism and other perversions, domination and submission, compassion and love. With the advent of conscious mind, the individuation of drive to desire allows an absent object to become the subjective aim of the source drive.

This evolutionary and maturational pattern is foundational to value, which is manifest early in the targets of drive-implementation, such as what to eat, what to avoid, possible mates, and so on. Drive categories are a unity of feeling and category that partitions to conceptual feeling. That is, feeling as drive energy accompanies the individuation of categorical primitives that fractionate to concepts and the objects of drive satisfaction. Such objects have a value for the organism that is not intrinsic to the object itself. A prey is a meal and as such satisfies a drive. The object, the prey, has no value other than as food. It exists to be devoured.

Valuation takes on an emotional quality as a residue of feeling with a direction towards completion. In the conscious mind, feeling is felt partly in the organism and partly in an idea or object. In such organisms, value is the rationale, the impetus and the goal of desire. It determines the intensity of an emotion, while its content (fear, affection, loathing etc.) and the nature of the affect (such as envy, pride, shame) are given by the concept or idea. That is, the specific nature of an emotion comes from the concept or category, while the intensity of the emotion comes from a concentration of undifferentiated feeling in the concept. Feeling assumes the specific nature of a particular emotion by virtue of its investment in a category or concept.

However, the intensity of feeling alone that is invested in a concept can alter its emotional quality, as when interest or curiosity shifts to absorption, or becomes affection, or turns to obsession or love. These emotions acquire different labels, as feeling concentrates in an object or idea and alters the emotion ascribed to it. When feeling spills into a concept, an emotion is created. When feeling withdraws from a concept, or object, the idea becomes abstract. The idea may be focal or narrow, e.g. technical, or more general, as in a universal, but in either case the concept seems affect-free, though even the most abstract ideas have some quota of feeling, if no more than interest or value. Value is implicit (internal) in all emotions as the aim and force of their content or quality; it is explicit (external) in other emotions, such as love, fear, or objects of need or want, in which value is perceived as something resident in the object.

Like the sense of beauty, feeling can be felt in the subject, in the object, or in both. The affective tonalities of concepts realize value in the subjective aim. As concepts partition to objects, value in the affective tonality externalizes with the forming object to become, or to be felt as, its intrinsic worth, that is, the value of the object itself. Value is bound up with valuing and experienced as something that arises partly if not wholly in the mind. Value arises in the observer, but actualizes in an external object as its worth, such as a home, a diamond, a pet or a lover. The progressive analysis of the pre-object and the conjoint specification of value into the final object occur together as the perception actualizes. Ordinarily, value is dispersed over the object field—as existence or realness—but can concentrate in one object in the form of interest. With increasing intensity, interest can develop to affection and to love, or to fear and hate. Put differently, the first act of value is to confer existence or realness on objects, that is, to diffuse feeling into the formation of the world which that feeling accompanies and in which it inheres. Conversely, objects become unreal in pathological states of derealization, when feeling is withdrawn. The object becomes thought-like—that is, it does not fully detach from the mind—and the value that follows it outward recedes to conceptual feeling in the retreat from world to mind. Normally, existence or realness transforms to interest when one object or event is the focus of attention. This grows in strength of feeling (value) when attention sequesters in a single object or property. Conceptual feeling will change according to the dominant idea at successive segments in mind/brain, but the endpoint of affect development is the outward reach of value that, in the form of worth, pervades an otherwise indifferent nature.

The value of a person from the standpoint of others is a result of the concentration of feeling in that person in the perceptual or social field. For most, family, friends, a beloved, one's child, have greater value than others, but for some a person has no greater value than any other object or organism. The negative side to this is disinterest or lack of perceived worth in others. The psychopath, the misanthrope or the monk concerned with his own salvation are examples of this attitude. The positive side of feeling weakly generalized over the field is the view, more idea than feeling, that all life is sacred, or that no one life is worth more than another. For those who might sweep aside microbes or practice internal ejaculation, this includes life beneath invertebrates, down to the lowliest forms. This distillation of value shifts feeling from a focus on the one to a category of the many.

In one instance, value dissipates over the perceptual field, such that organisms are not unlike inanimate objects, with slight distinction among living things. In the other, value has a locus in one object at the expense of the field as a whole. Each outcome is an expression of individual need that flows into the object field: a shallow distribution of value or its sequestration in one object of surpassing interest. One cannot predict how the process will eventuate, since locality and dispersion depend on what arises from drive categories, conceptual feeling and experiential memory in the progression to the realization of self and object. The process of isolating one object of value, the extent to which feeling grows or dissolves, the negative or positive valence, are determined by core beliefs and early acquired values, but the pattern in each is the same.

TOWARDS A THEORY OF MORALITY

The growth of mind/brain is directed to increasing individuation. The epigenesis of connectivity in the fetal and infant brain entails the elimination of excess or redundancy to achieve greater specification. The process of morphogenetic growth—specification by elimination—continues to the inhibition of an established connectivity. In each instance—elimination, inhibition, the sculpting of irrelevance—some content or figure (configuration) emerges from the background by the suppression of alternative routes of development. The pattern of early growth continues into cognition as the specification of wholes or categories into parts or members. It has been said that morphogenesis establishes "force lines" that develop into cognitive process (Pribram), which implies that mental process is a continuation of the process of growth. In the moment-to-moment unfolding of thought and its accompanying brain process, there is a progressive analysis of generality to precision or of context to specificity. Finding the right word or idea involves forgetting—failing to specify—competing possibilities. The elicitation of

objects or part-objects from a wider field of possibility is a striving to definiteness, as each moment recurs to finality.

The process can also show enhancement (retardation) at a phase of
incompleteness embedded in an otherwise complete perception. In such
instances—inner speech, thought, introspection—there is an accentuation
(neoteny) at a pre-terminal phase when potential is not foreclosed. The pre-
terminal accentuation makes it possible to distinguish a (subjective) image
from an (objective) act. The subjective phase is that of feeling and deliberation; the objective phase is behavior, while the correspondence of one to
the other is conceived as the regulation of action by thought. The pattern of
successive whole/part shifts and the outward direction of partition, the ebb
and flow of arisings and relaxations, the transmission of gestalts to particulars, or grounds to figures, and the lapse of particulars into prior categories,
create a tension in act and object of the antecedent and the consequent, of
category and particular, of mind and world, in which the categorical is felt
in psyche and the particular in the world. This tension appears in the transition of thought to act, of subjective value to objective worth, of desire to the
desired object, of possibility to fact and, importantly, with respect to moral
theory, in the relation of self to others or individual (part) to community
(whole).

Let us consider some features of moral thought and action that bear
on brain and mental process. In the past, this process has generally been
framed in the context of an evolutionary struggle that favors survival and
the satisfaction of the needs of the organism. The "eat or be eaten" of nature
is presumed to have persisted in human instinctual drive and self-preservation. On this basis, morality is the imposition on the animal inheritance of
learned values or rules of conduct that accentuate other-centered behaviors
and mitigate selfish ones, with a fundamental tension of mental categories
that enclose multiple possibilities and the selection of acts that implement irrevocable choices. The relation of intra-psychic experience to extra-psychic
behavior is the tension between what one might or should or could have
done—the choices one considers—and what one actually does, that is, the
relation of the potential of mental categories with the facts of comportment.
This relation is not only of potential to actual in the sphere of behavior, but
of self-realization in the context of social needs and responsibilities. The
relation of self to others or individual to communities is a relation of part
and whole centered in the world that corresponds to that of character and
conduct centered in the mind.

Evolution entails a population dynamic in which the aim is speciation. In higher organisms, especially those with an inner life, the extrinsic
process of speciation is internalized in the realization of the mental state.

Thought is an intra-psychic dynamic with a subjective aim. When action is inconclusive, it constitutes a search for the optimal mode of self-realization, as character adapts to necessity. The self is not realized into a community; rather, the community is, or has been, assimilated to the core that individuates the self. The self is not an autonomous entity, but a collage of family and society. The relation to community (family, tribe, cult, nation) on this view is not an external attachment; rather, the beliefs and values of the individual are assimilated from a wider surround. This assimilation entails a continuous parsing that begins with instinctual drive-categories. Innate categories specify sub-categories or concepts that expand through progressive individuation—from the inside out, so to speak—to create the belief and value systems of the individual. Value arises, not by addition, but by partition or splitting of innate categories to build up the repertoire of behavior.

When we see the young strive for independence from family values—the shoulds and the should nots that have been instilled in maturation—these values have grown through parcellation of the instinctual. Thus, the rebellion against a parent or a community is an internal battle of competing values, of what remains as authentic after the inculcation of the core. The adult who seeks to break with conformity and reject social norms exhibits a defiance of nurture to realize what he believes to be his genuine self, in conflict with a community that seems to hold him back at every stage. But the oppressiveness of the other(s) is for the most part a projection onto the collective of internal constraints on the individuation of the self. That is, the self is a composite of those very others who, as a virtual aggregate, are apprehended as a hindrance to self-realization. In fact, however, it is precisely the pressure to resist and remain part of the whole, to follow one's core beliefs and the dictates of thought to implement, for better or worse, the conceptual derivatives of the categorical primes, that give rise to the self-concept. In the struggle to analysis from bedrock categories, the community of others serves as an intrinsic set of constraints on the individuation of a singular personality. That is to say, choices conditioned by external events are driven by presuppositions and recurrent constraints that externalize in the other.

Earlier, the discussion took up various instances of indecision in a moral context. This can be interpreted along the same lines as an elicitation of choice within a category of what is possible, a process that recurs in bouts of partition until conflict is resolved. Each option is a sub-category for successive parsing—a decision tree—until final choice is implemented. The "tree" is not a node that bifurcates, but a resolution among possibilities. The category is imbued with feeling, as are all possible choices. Indeed, feeling is more efficacious than ideas as to which choice will prevail. Behind the category of possible choices are beliefs, values, experiential memories and world knowledge, which deliver into consciousness a limited menu of possibilities. Options in thought are consistent with character, which is a construct that forms in the recurrence of dominant themes in the self-concept.

Ordinarily, this complex narrows the range of possibilities to a conscious choice among a few alternatives in accordance with needs arising from the drives and the affective tonality of their derivations. Categories form spontaneously: how to rescue a drowning child, what to do about a dangerous enemy, a villain, a kidney transplant or a commitment. The decisions that arise from such categories—self-realizations that resolve uncertainty—feel volitional, even if they are conditioned by antecedents. Generally, the spontaneous feels less volitional, while agency requires choice, even if the options are to act or not to act.

The categories that are in play in conscious decision-making do not give rise to acts; rather, the specification of a choice provides a channel to constrain the act, which arises not from conscious thought, but from unconscious will or instinctual drive. That is, the final selection in thought, biased by feeling and forced into relief by the subordination of alternatives, delimits the category for the passage of the upcoming act. More precisely, in each recurrence of the mental state, the thought-category narrows down like a river that carves out an embankment. Repeated volleys of ideational content erode the choices that character rejects, leaving final decision as a conscious track for an action development that passes from tendency to performance. Decision, which is felt as initiated in consciousness, is in fact guided by antecedents, as the final act follows the path of least resistance arbitrated in conscious thought.

11

Mental process and
the psychology of groups

SUMMARY

IN SPITE OF THE variety in type, belief and value, emotionality and goals, whether peaceful or violent, all groups share certain attributes. In this essay, the main features of the group mind are discussed, first from a descriptive point of view, and then in relation to a process theory of the mind/brain state. The suspension of individuality by members in favor of the mentality of the group, or by the group in favor of the individuality of the leader, are extensions to social psychology of a theory of mind that entails a whole/part or category/item transition that is uniform in every act of cognition. The idealization of the leader and the ideals of the group reflect the specification of sub-categories of conceptual feeling. These object-specific categories account for sameness or identity, as well as idealization, or a belief in the exceptionality of the group and the authority of its leader.

The role of identification is attributed to shared belief systems, rather than a decision to assume the properties of others. The presumption of a regression to primitive cognition applies primarily to a retreat from objectivity and a return to an intra-psychic focus, with greater intensity of affect relating to the quality of love for the leader. The absence or suppression of competing options in the group mind and the restricted template for action by a dominant belief system is associated with the problem of free will. There is incessant opposition between group mind and individuality in all aspects of life. Moreover, to the extent the group functions as an individual, it displays the same tensions with other groups as that of the solitary person with other individuals.

INTRODUCTION

In this essay I propose to explore the relation of group mind to the struggle for individuality, the nature of members in group mind, the individuation of leaders and idealization, the tension between groups that, in their uniformity of belief, themselves function as organisms or individuals, and the pressures to submit to group mind that would seem to be the opposite of free will or, at least, call into question the freedom of choice and the responsibility that such freedom entails. Here I refer to the herd or crowd mentality, in which individual choices are subordinate to the will of a group or its leader. Generally, surrender, suppression or displacement of self-authorship occurs in intense religious belief, cults, military and social life, political movements, gangs and so on, at times by coercion and/or indoctrination, at other times (and of more interest) by willing submission combined with a personal need for sacrifice to a higher cause, purpose or greater good, or merely a need to be part of a community. This leads to shared ideology, fealty or allegiance, goals, and obedience to or dependence on members and a leader. The individual believes the decision to join the group is a free act, perhaps a greater freedom, to be found in the rejection of an alternative or conventional life path. In sacrificing oneself to what one perceives as a preferable choice or greater good (whether it is an angry mob or a spiritual commune), once the individual is a participant, every act and decision, even if accompanied by conscious deliberation, is made on behalf of the group or as an obligation owed to the leader. But true freedom, if it exists, is generally assumed to rest in having a multiplicity of options and making an individual choice among them.

The various writers who have addressed this phenomenon, particularly Le Bon[1] and Freud,[2] note the dissolution of conscious reason and the emergence of unconscious commonalty in thought. Whether by suggestibility or mass hypnosis, the contagion of the crowd produces a collective mind that, in servility, irrationality and lack of critical judgment, differs from the actions taken by an autonomous individual. Most are in agreement with this formulation, though the fact that crowd or group behavior can range from violence in social protest to acquiescence and passivity in an

1. Le Bon, G. (1895/1896) *La psychologie ds foules*. English translation. Fisher Unwin, London.

2. Freud, S. (1921) *Group Psychology and the Analysis of the Ego*. SE, 18:65–143.

ashram indicates that instinctual aggression is not a uniform consequence, and makes it less likely that the release of unconscious tendencies, simply put, is a critical or defining factor of this phenomenon. Ethical behavior in a group may increase, even if intellect or rational judgment declines. This is how H. G. Wells described the transition from the self-interest, greed, ambition and competitiveness of the everyday world to the courage, duty, self-sacrifice and nobility in a military encampment.

Freud's account consists largely of external descriptors that recycle past explanatory constructs: the lifting of repression on the unconscious, identification, oedipal conflicts, and a libidinal relation likened to love that approaches hypnotic trance. Underlying these relations is the instinct of the primal horde (Freud is following Darwin here). Groups can range from very small, such as family and friendships, or very large, such as churches or military services. They can arise informally or spontaneously, or by membership in an institution. In fact, a person who falls under the spell of a single individual may undergo a transformation much like a member of a group, confirming the importance Freud placed on a form of (desexualized) love. Regardless of the number of members or quality of the group, the critical questions are these:

- What happens to the ego or self-concept as autonomy merges with subordination to others?
- What process underlies the negation of free choice?
- In what sense is there liberation of a primitive cognition?

A further question is whether the dissolution of free will in group mind is an argument for the existence of free will. If free choice is given up, what is given up if there is no free choice? Does the individual who enters into a group mind make an implicit choice, a kind of decision making without opposing options? This raises the problem of how we make decisions, the relation of decision to reason, to emotion and action, and in what sense joining a group is a decision, if the only conscious option is not joining, or if the decision is implicit and unquestioned.

Actions are outcomes of beliefs channeled through concepts. The concepts—delimited categories—are the choices to be decided. In reflection, one option may overcome others, but does the option or idea cause an action, or is an action somehow guided by the idea? The lack of opposing values or options implies that one concept or category of thought serves as a template for action. Since beliefs lay down concepts, the more powerful the belief, the less likely there will be doubt or uncertainty. Strong beliefs resist contradiction or replacement, especially by those outside the perimeter of the dominant belief system. In contrast, individuals without strong beliefs, particularly if they are striving for meaning in life, perhaps with weak family or social ties, will be open to the influence of others, who seem to offer a future that coincides with what may be a mere tendency in one direction. Such individuals will be unguarded, vulnerable to the will of others and primed to absorb a belief system, especially when the tendency seeks affirmation or reinforcement. This being said, however, apartness is no doubt a stronger foundation for freedom than identification or belongingness. A strong individuality can lead to alienation, an extreme of which is captured in the cynical remark by Sartre that hell is other people.

Belief is the core of an intentional arc from instinctual drive, character and personality to actions and thoughts. The realization of an act in conformance with a belief is the satisfaction of a subjective aim. The final outcome of an act is an endpoint in the trajectory from belief to act, constrained by choice and adaptation, and initiated by feelings and presuppositions, some innate, others learned. Beliefs do not interact with thoughts, they impel them. A thought, even a simple or random idea, trickles out of a complex web of belief. To move one's finger requires an underlying belief in the body schema and an implicit conviction of the power of will, the ability to decide and the capacity to move. There are patients with brain damage who cannot locate their finger, or do not believe it is a part of their own body (autotopagnosia).

An individual inclined to a spiritual path but lacking conviction will not pursue goals in life. He will persist in uncertainty, without commitment, without a target and without a means of implementation. This leads him to seek resolution by exchanging individual struggle for the faith and certainty of others. In taking the path of least resistance, belief gradually hardens to compliance with the group mentality. Whether such an individual joins a convent, is an ardent member of a mosque or church, is fully engaged in tribal life or community affairs, succumbs to a gang, sect or cult, or is a disciple or follower of a dominant personality, there is collusion of belief with culture, need and temperament. Such factors influence the search for a leader: priest, guru, decision-maker or charismatic personality. Membership in a group is not a release of a primitive cognition or an aggressive impulse. A spiritual tendency can lead to devout quietism or passionate rebellion; an adventurous or rebellious attitude can lead to devotion to the military or police, or loyalty to a radical dogma, allegiance to the mafia and so on. Political beliefs can lead to a club-like atmosphere in a traditional party, to activism in undisciplined protest, or the fervor of a revolutionary crusade. The same process is involved in the distillation of will in a peaceful demonstration as in a violent protest, in devotion to a just cause or a rapacious gang. The distinction is not simple, since members will declare that free choice is involved regardless of the group or its ideals, or whether decision is spontaneous or with deliberation. This implies that conscious choice may not be essential to free will, though impediments bring choice to the fore, nor is the worthiness of the aim a factor, so long as members are not coerced. The central act is ceding personal choice to the mentality of others, or aligning personal belief with a group mind.

The authority and certainty of a leader feeds off the indecision and unanimity of members. The subjective aim of a group replaces choice; belief resolves to action without an intermediate phase of doubt. The individual becomes an anonymous entity, whose will and life can be sacrificed for the whole. We see this phenomenon in the increasingly vitriolic discourse among and between conservative and progressive groups in the United States today. Each group is not only unable to entertain doubt or competing views, but the group mind-set tends to idealize its values (see below) and demonize adversaries. Freedom of speech is attacked if it is used to shield an opposing belief, or suppressed, if it is inconsistent with group mind. The certainty of belief on one side resists contradiction, argument and fact coming from the other. As love idealizes the beloved, so its surrogate inflames group mind. Groups may begin with one or more leaders who actively recruit and organize the movement, or the leadership may derive from or seek the support of writers in social theory. It is not surprising that Hitler was familiar with the writings of Le Bon. There seems to be no reason for caution or moderation in justifying a movement of which we approve, or in condemning one that we deplore.

How do leaders infiltrate a psyche to replace individual will? A dedication to the leadership of the group can feel as if it has been freely decided upon, to the point where there is submission and totality of allegiance; it can be the very reciprocal of the individuality on which freedom depends. Identification is an important element. In some sense we all seek models for the self in parents, care-givers, teachers and leaders. The self is both a mirror of character and a composite of those we admire or wish to emulate. Perhaps, in identification and the transfer of will to others, there is a functional relation to command hallucination, in which an (imagined) voice replaces the verbal imagery (inner speech) that is essential to informed decision: that is, the psychotic, rather than thinking to himself, "I think I should eat a sandwich," hears a voice that seems to come from outside, commanding him to eat the sandwich. The person accepts the imaginary voice as not his own, belonging to an external authority, at times god or the devil. The cult leader has god-like qualities, is infallible and all-knowing. In both instances, a regressed self is passive towards a voice perceived as external, and follows its instructions implicitly. The hypnotic aspect of group mind would facilitate this effect. Is it possible that the gift of the leader is to implant and/or realize the inclinations of group members?

Certainly, the hegemony of a group stifles original thought. Indeed, studies of creative thought show that a single individual may generate more ideas than a group that is brain-storming. Of course, in an assemblage of genius, such as the Manhattan Project, such rules may not apply, yet it is also true that great thinkers and creative artists rarely collaborate. Individuality seems essential to genius. In this spirit, Schopenhauer, a paragon of individual genius, wrote that "reading is thinking with someone else's head."

There are degrees of independence in thought between spontaneity and deliberation. If deliberation prior to action implies choice, what can we say of its absence in spontaneity? A mob or riot can occur spontaneously and without a leader if members of the group mind share a common motive. Conversely, a spontaneous act of altruism results from values molded into character. Would we say that the soldier who falls on a grenade or the fireman who rushes into a burning building demonstrates less free will than one who contemplates an action until it is too late? Does implicit choice qualify as free, or does freedom apply only with consciousness of options? This leads one to ask whether free will is episodic and infrequent, is it a potential or an implementation, and is it continuous in conscious life, though to a varying degree? Are we the sum of our choices or the sum of our acts? Is freedom on display in rejecting a group or in joining it? Does freedom require conscious choice, or can a person freely follow a path without a consideration of alternatives?

In sum, to this point we have considered some attributes of the group mind, the relation to idealization and love, the weakening of reason and free will, the usurpation of individuality by the group and/or leader, the possible reversion to a primitive cognition, the lack of critical judgment, the certainty of belief, the inability to entertain competing ideas and the denigration of those with opposing views. The size of the group is less important than the bond among its members. A shared belief system can occur in any group from a radical terror cell to a dispersed group of scientists following the Zeitgeist to make the same discoveries in different places at the same time. The focus of belief differs, but it is so widespread a social phenomenon, even if its intensity wavers, that it approaches a universal of human behavior, though it is not, in my opinion, closely related to pack or herd instincts, or swarming. These largely extrinsic features of groups are clues to the underlying process out of which they arise, which is the topic of the following sections. The primary issue concerns the mental process that accounts for the phenomenon, and its implications for free will and decision.

THE ROLE OF BELIEF

Regardless of their size, aim or quality, participation in groups is an outcome of the individual belief system that is engaged by the group. In some instances, the belief system will be weakly formed or not opposed to that of the group. In other instances, it will correspond to the group mind, such that participation supports or reinforces individual belief, or distributes responsibility for action on the belief to the group members. Beliefs and values instilled in the core early in life lay down unconscious moral tendencies that are derived to conscious judgments, opinions and decisions.

Due to timidity, gullibility or indecision, individual belief and opinion engage or dissolve in group mind. Value guides the implementation of a belief in an action, but it is the beliefs, or their conscious derivations, that spill into action. This can range from docile spirituality, to passive resistance, to an angry mob or a violent riot, to a revolution. The belief may entail inaction and withdrawal into the life of a commune, or fervor and aggression that implement the goals of the crowd. The individual sinks into group mind, either in gradual transformation from independence to membership, or as a spontaneous participation that vents impulses seething beneath the surface. The individual will is relinquished and justified in the actions of the group. The outcome is conditioned by a belief that can destroy or heal, inspire or condemn, dictate or inform. Group mind can be compassionate or intolerant, or it can be driven by delusion and paranoid tendencies, but in most instances the person shares the absolute certainty of group mind and an indifference or opposition to others.

We can begin with the core beliefs. Refined by experience, they appear in childhood in the context of the animal inheritance—hunger, sexual and self-preservation drives and their accessories—which modulate acquired or instilled parental or social values. Drives as needs or tools for survival are foundational to the deepest-held beliefs, such that mental phenomena, including the self and the reality of the world, are real or true, that we are alive, that the past existed and the future is to come, that personal affairs matter in an indifferent universe and that life has meaning and is worth living. Such beliefs are implicit in action, yet not to be taken for granted. Persons with severe post-encephalitic amnesia may live in a transient present without a past or future, as in dream. Patients have been described who do not know if they are awake or dreaming. There are pathological cases in which the patient believes that they are dead (the Cotard delusion). Core beliefs are the soul of meaning in a search for validation. In this sense, meaning is what belief corresponds to. Such beliefs arborize to sub-sets that generate the activities through which the belief is articulated or justified. Given the source of acts, ideas and opinions from a set of core beliefs and values, the lack of critical analysis, the pressures on action and the lack of objective judgment, it is usually the case that we can predict a person's attitudes to a range of different positions on the basis of a single opinion.

Core beliefs are ingrained; the opinions to which they partition solidify as unquestioned facts. Ideas tend to be mutable and more readily altered. An opinion is a sub-set of belief that is driven by unconscious regularities that become habitual as verbal acts. Conviction does not require a belief to be true; false beliefs often carry greater conviction than true ones. Indeed, unshakeable beliefs instilled in learning thrive on a dearth of knowledge. There is a thin line between false belief and delusion; generally, a false belief that is shared by a large group—church, society—is seen as misguided, but it becomes delusional if outré and limited to individuals or small groups, even if the belief is true but not in accord with known facts. On his deathbed, Kant believed that insects were crawling on his skin (vermification). Is this false belief, delusion or hallucination? Is belief in fate, a virgin paradise, an after-life or a personal and loving god, a delusion or merely irrational, a belief without factual support? A mass delusion is often the operative factor in crowds.

Beliefs are inter-twined with values. Belief is the conceptual aspect; value is the affective aspect. Beliefs give object concepts that become the subjective aims of desire; interest or desire is value given to object concepts. *The dual aspect of belief and value—category and feeling—corresponds to "substance" or being (category) and process or becoming (feeling). Concepts individuate from categories to grow into objects; feeling propels the conceptual transition from instinctual drive through desire to object worth. Feeling is the process that transforms concepts to objects; concepts are the frames that feeling transforms. Without feeling, concepts are inert. Without concepts, feeling is blind.*

Simply put, the meaning of belief in an objective world corresponds to an instantiation of belief in action. The meaning of life and the search for purpose depend on a belief in the reality of existence. The generalized form of meaning and belief individuates to concepts—lexical, perceptual— or other categories of ideation. Connotation is the contextual ground from which belief partitions to instrumentalities; inner generality is parsed to precision. Reference is the individuation of context—the potential of the category—in the direction of a subjective aim. Stages in the derivation of belief to action correspond to phases in language and object realization. But in everyday life, belief is bound up with a pervasive search for the meaning that condenses its potential to a specific aim or purpose, similar to the passage from connotation to reference.

Many of us expect to find meaning in the world. Purpose and meaning seem to be outside of ourselves, something we search for, not something the mind creates. However, meaning is not the discovery of an external purpose; it is an uncovering of that which justifies the striving. The meaning we find in the world is the meaning we are looking for. The challenge to find meaning in the world points to an absence of definiteness, which gives us the feeling that life is without meaning. This is not the malaise, indifference or skepticism of an introspective personality, but the indirection of those drifting aimlessly until conditions allow submerged tendencies to be aroused. The mission and primacy of the group then replace the autonomy of the self, as self-realization transfers to the group aim.

CATEGORY/MEMBER

The fundamental phenomenon of group mind is the retreat of individuality into a shared belief system. The usurpation of individual decision by a shared category of belief is a relapse of the transition from whole to part or category to member that underlies all phenomena in the mind/brain state. The reverse of this process, the retreat of part to whole—the immersion of individuality in group mind or of a particular in its potential—occurs not only in pathology, but also in many aspects of cognition, for example in trance, reverie, love, creativity and imagination, where a return to the antecedents of a specific thought or object renews the potential of the category, increasing the value of the particular by suppressing alternatives or reviving novel data. General categories individuate to sub-sets that become specific frames of thought, such as scientific paradigms, fields of professional knowledge, dietary or physical regimens, cultural pursuits. These sub-sets correspond to isolated belief-systems; in each, individuals can be caught up in the dominant view of a group of like-minded individuals. The generality of the class of a belief tends to subdue independent thought to conform to group mind. Clearly, a return to precursor categories can renew individuality and creative advance, or conversely, the de-individuation assimilates to the dominant belief-system and the categorical nature of group mind.

Given the centrality of the whole/part or category/member relation in the mental state, the inference that members in a group exhibit the ubiquity of this relation in social affairs is surely warranted. Individuality demands recurrent specification, such that group properties are subsumed in those of the individual. There are constant pressures to exhibit compatibility, to "get along," conform to dominant trends and social attitudes, adapt one's thought for advancement, compromise at work, home or elsewhere to avoid conflict, strain and rejection, as well as to participate in an endeavor more meaningful than is possible for one person. There are also incentives to remain in the group for approval, fellowship, to avoid decision and criticism, and for the safety in numbers a group provides. Sustained recurrence of individuality is essential if the tug of the background is to be overcome by a confident apartness.

Individuality is achieved by those who reject group mind, or by those who are the leaders of the group. For them, apartness is eccentricity, in the sense of a deviation from the paradigmatic features of group mind. For one, this means to remain an outlier on the categorical periphery. For the other, it means control or manipulation to recruit followers to a personal belief system. In all areas of life, group mind is the salve of social adhesion and the antagonist of free thought and individuality. Nor does high intellect have immunity. Suffice it to recall the hegemony in linguistics and cognitive science of the (now disputed) theories of modularity and transformational grammar, which placed a stranglehold on academic circles and journal publications. An assertion of apartness often comes at the price of exclusion and ridicule, designed to restrain individuality to the group norm. Group mind enjoys a steady diet of its own ideas. Conversely, the certainty of group mind tends to proselytize resistant outsiders. In this respect, the uniformity of group mind behaves as an organism, a collective mind that resists the pressure to adapt to others. As organisms, group minds often face conflict with alternative belief-systems. For example, a spiritual cult is opposed by traditional religious institutions, the military by conscientious objectors, the rabid fans of one soccer team by those of another.

The group, in its certainty, can exhibit a confidence of belief that attempts to destroy or belittle those with contrary views. Until a group mind consolidates as a sustainable presence, by size and intensity of belief, or by secrecy and concealment, there is a danger of dissolution. Often, rites and ceremonies are necessary to reinforce cohesion. The group is also subject to the pressures of society as a whole. For a non-member, until independence is habitual and indelible, until apartness and unfettered choice are constants in personality, and until there is assuredness that one's ideas are valid or those of a group unacceptable, individuality entails recurrent specification out of an ambient field of uniformity. We see the tension of the self with the communal ground and the transcendence of the individual in myths of the hero and one-against-many themes in history, legends and tales. In the conflict of personal character with group mind, alienation, exclusion, opposition and/or neglect are near-inevitable consequences of authentic and unhindered thought, as of all creative or intellectual pursuits.

IDEALIZATION

The category/item relation is central to the idealization that motivates certain group behaviors. We see this in the bond of love or devotion among members, the feeling of significance of the group, the certainty and exclusivity of belief and especially the authority of the leader. Idealization is the attribution to a person or object of unique and elevated qualities. Given the emphasis on love in the interpretation of group behavior, especially by Freud, we can take as an example the process of falling in love, which is not unlike the assimilation to a group mind or the respect and admiration for a leader.

Initially, the other person is perceived as just another man or woman in a category of like members. At this point, value as existence is equally distributed over the object field. When that person becomes a focus of interest or attention, the field recedes to the background and the person becomes the dominant figure. As value increases, the intensity of feeling, which is felt in the mind, not the object, accompanies a recession to a dominant focus at the intra-psychic phase out of which the person individuated. The increase in value intensifies the emotional investment and brings mind-internal to the fore. This process occurs for the leader of a group as one individual among many, and for group mind as an organism opposed by other beliefs.

The result is that the individual is no longer solely a member of a generic category, such as men or women, but has become a sub-set within the category, actually a new category occupied by the individual. Instead of being a member of a conventional set of similar types, the person is a sub-category restricted to just that individual. That is to say, *Jane*, who was a non-descript member of the category of women, retains the attributes of the category, but is now the sole exemplar of the category *Jane*. The category of Jane has its own attributes that are not universally shared with members of the category *woman*, and assumes qualities that, from the observer's standpoint, are unique. This occurs to some extent for most people who have been a focus of attention, but the shift is pronounced when feeling penetrates the category as love or value. Jane continues to have the general attributes of the original category, but with the addition of unique attributes that distinguish her from other members.

This process, which occurs continuously with many objects, is the source of identity or sameness. Particulars give the ideal; categories give identity. A tree can be one of many trees barely noticed by an observer, but once the tree is a focus of attention, value concentrates in the tree and it takes on the sub-categorical status of an individual object. To whatever degree the tree, or any object, takes on value, it is recognizable and identifiable as the same on different occasions and under different conditions. The sub-category of a tree can also undergo idealization as the most beautiful tree in a garden. Unique features of shape, size, color or location distinguish the tree from other trees, preserving its identity over time. Features judged to be exceptional create an ideal of tree-ness. The formation of individuated categories accompanies the attribution of unique properties that distinguish them from similar others. These properties can be conventional or radically different. In love or feelings of respect or admiration, qualities such as beauty, intelligence or kindness are prominent. When attributes are conceptualized as extreme, unique or perfect and are infused with feeling, the self-identical nature of the object and its degree of idealization are established according to the approximation to perfection of the relevant qualities.

In this way, the leader (beloved) takes on attributes such as beauty, intelligence, superiority, additional to those of the general class of similar members. The affect-driven regression is a de-objectification that revives submerged emotional tonalities that range from affection to love and adoration. Since the category is antecedent to the particular, itself a category, the regression of group mind cited by many authors, which refers to uncritical judgment, violence or false belief, also explains idealization, which does not involve rational judgment, is not asserted in relation to objective reality and has the quality of an intra-psychic phenomenon, not an external fact.

Regression is less a resurgence of instinctual or animalistic tendencies—though this occurs in a riot or a mob—than it is a withdrawal from the fully external to an intra-psychic locus. This appears in a retreat from the particular to the categorical, from individual mind to group mind, from the impersonal to the personal, from feeling that is distributed over a field to an affective charge that is internal and concentrated, and from the real to the ideal. The idealization of a leader also has the effect of reducing the individuality of members. The ideal is adored, worshipped, loved, though members do not identify with such a leader, who is a paragon beyond their aspirations. This retreat from individuality replaces the independence of the convert with the ideals of the group and the authority of the leader. Individuality is distilled to belongingness. The subordination of a love-struck admirer to irrational desire, awe and wonderment is not dissimilar to submission to a leader.

WILL AND DECISION IN INDIVIDUAL AND GROUP MIND

If self-identity and volitional feeling occur with ordinary activities, what is lost in submission to a leader or assimilation to group mind? An accrued family of beliefs decants to a surrogate personality and the acquisition of shared aims and values, which compress uncertainties to fill absences, solidify goals and resolve the possibilities for alternative modes of thought.

The presence of choice and the voluntary feeling of decision depend on an incomplete resolution of mental content, so that a single option does not specify with the requisite clarity to guide an action. In effect, antecedent categories of potential do not individuate to a distinct particular. An occasion of choice brings into consciousness pre-terminal phases in the mental state. Indecision occurs to the extent that belief is not dispositive, or competing options are balanced and symmetrical. The most complex decision may require a yes or no, "to be or not to be", to act or not to act. The complexity can be in the choice or the act, which involves multiple choices as it unfolds. For such instances, there is retardation at a pre-object focus in the actualization of the mental state. In submission to the beliefs and will of the group, this phase is rapidly traversed. Belief is unconditional and opposing choices do not arise. Ends are agreed, and only the means of employment are in doubt. In effect, there is no choice; rather, the sole choice is to satisfy the group aim. Can this be termed volitional?

The process of decision involves a reinforcement of the micro-temporal path through which one option develops. As the strength of opposing options diminishes, the dominant idea provides a template for the development of action and for self-realization in decision-making. We assume that an independent thinker will show deliberation, and gradual but decisive strengthening in the actualization of an idea. The unequal weight of one option gathers force by recurrence and the withering of other choices. This creates a track over which action is derived in conformity with the prevailing idea. The specification of action through a path laid down by the idea ratifies the decision in repeated volleys.

We tend to think of free choice in terms of options. If there is only one choice it is not a real choice, and freedom is constrained by the lack of alternatives. But if the sole choice is what the individual desires, and if multiple choices would only impede or encumber decision, in what sense—apart from coercion—does an unopposed option limit freedom of choice? It has rightly been said, "Keep an open mind until it is made up, and then close it." Is this a recipe for freedom or its lack? Certainly, free will declines in relation to the multiplicity of choices and fades in decision without deliberation, but it seems most emphatic when choice is binary. If choices are conscious outcomes of belief and value, then the emotional push that transforms a truth judgment to action is the feeling that carries concepts to actuality. Does this mean that a decision is never completely rational, in that action requires emotion, or that affective intensity plays a role in the selection of action? Feeling may not be aligned with the right thing to do; for example, who would calmly argue that a loving brother should be tried for murder, or allow one's child to drown in favor of saving many others? But overcoming this reluctance, that is, hesitation based on feeling rather than rational judgment, is the true mark of free choice, or it is as free as any act can be.

In group mind, the dominant belief and its corollaries form an ideational pathway for implementation. The lack of freedom in group mind is not merely the unimpeded flow of action out of belief, which is deeply implanted and replaces individual priorities, but it also refers to the replacement of individual thought with that of the group. An absence of strong belief prior to joining the group, or as a result of indoctrination, or in cases where there is a reinforcement of a pre-existing belief or tendency concordant with group mind—often the basis for participation in mobs—allows the group or its leader to introduce a belief system or a restricted set of ideas that serves as a surrogate template for action.

In sum, to the extent that choices are free and actions are implemented in relation to the weight of a decision, we can say there is free will within the limits of human fallibility and the degree to which emotional biases can be resolved with rational judgment. None of us are free from the group minds in which we developed, to which we were and are exposed and to which we must respond, for they guide from behind our conscious choices. Overcoming the biases that condition our choices and insulating rational judgment from affective loyalties is the first step to true freedom of thought.

A final word is necessary on the assimilation of group mind into the beliefs and self-concepts of others. The primary challenge is to unify diversity in a common belief system and generate the emotional intensities that actualize beliefs, so they are not tacit acknowledgements but, in submission and self-surrender, and for better or worse, are potentially life-changing. It is not necessary to change the self, which will be resistant to transformation, but to locate the malleable core of the ongoing belief system. If this is altered, the self, as the agent of implementation, will follow a course proscribed by the guiding beliefs. A sudden change in a person's belief system, whether a rousing speech, a deathbed conversion, mob impulse or philosophical renunciation, such as Wittgenstein's rejection of the *Tractatus*, occurs when pre-existing modes of belief intersect with ones that cast doubt on the former and provide a deeper, more coherent explanation. What happens in the individual is not unlike a Kuhnian paradigm shift in science. Surely prior doubt or disaffection with current belief creates an opening to such a metamorphosis, which, like a visionary re-awakening—I was blind and now I see—is not unlike a creative storm.

12

Essay on Agency and the Will

"I want my own will, and I want

Simply to be with my will,

As it goes toward action."

RILKE

SUMMARY

THIS PAPER ASKS, DOES physical will or energic feeling as expressed in animal mind and instinctual drive become a power of the self to choose, to decide and to initiate action? It is argued that will has no causal role; rather, it distributes, as conceptual-feeling, into all objects and mental contents. The paper also explores the relation of decision to action and the process through which choices are implemented. While the roots of feeling in instinctual drive appear as a bias of voluntary action by unconscious disposition, the presence of conscious choice implies the possibility of unfettered choosing, and the mitigation of will to feeling allows the allocation of irresistible impulse to measured implementation. Evolutionary and maturational trends individuate will as impulse to a feeling of activity, with action the measure of will in relation to a decisional self.

Agency is consciousness of purposefulness but is not a mark of free-dom. Free acts occur within the limits of the possible occasioned by the parcellation of core categories to concepts. The muting of impulse to desire, the emergence of a self in a subjective field, and the appearance—illusory or not—of a duration that unites past and present in conscious temporal order, are the bases of the belief in free choice. The evolution of feeling from energy, the primitiveness and animal ancestry of drive, the transitive nature of action as process, the ineffability of will and the presumed non-conceptuality of action, account for the sense that will is the closest we come to the *in-itself* of experience. That is, a felt but objectless experience of will is a contact with energic process in nature and the ground of becoming.

INTRODUCTION

Will is primitive feeling centered in the body. The embodiment of will is the objectification of action. Feeling pervades purposefulness initially in the axis of the body, then in limb movements directed to the world. The micro-temporal sequence that lays down an action is buried in the final movement. Bodily action has, so to say, one foot in the mind and another in the world. The relation to the body and its incomplete detachment give the feeling that action belongs to the self. This is also true for images that feel volitional, but not for external objects in which loss of ownership is the price of detach-ment. Ordinarily, there is a sharp break in the passage from mind to world, but the continuum from image to appearance is exposed in the uncertainty whether phenomena such as love, pity or disgust, or beauty, owe to personal feeling or are intrinsic to the object. Does the individual love, pity or feel disgust or is the object (other) lovable, pitiful or disgusting?

Objects appear independent and impact the observer; actions belong to the self and carry intentions to the world. Actions (including speech) ob-jectify to interact with object-representations. When the hand grasps a cup, the objectification of an action reacts to a representation of an external ob-ject. The intuition of a causal relation of act on object, or the causal impact of one object on another, begins in the mind of the child when it reaches for an object. Infantile grasping is the basis of the intuition of agent-causation. This extends to the intuition of object-causation and passage in a causal series. We feel responsible for acts that are ours but not objects that belong to the world, even if act and object are co-temporal outcomes of a common process of self-realization.

Following Schopenhauer and, as intimated by Rilke, will has a dual aspect: as feeling in object-representations and as a companion to bodily acts. The question is whether the actual body is required for will or its image in the brain. Individuals who are paralyzed and without sensation below the neck due to spinal cord injury still have the feeling of will in the sense of wanting, striving, persevering, as well as a multitude of feelings, drive-based needs and impulsivities. What is the distinction between the body and its neural organization in the brain? Probably, an action must develop over an infrastructure of levels for the feeling of activity and volition since limb movements on stimulation of motor cortex are felt as passive or involuntary. This is also the case with the uncertain agency of tics, choreic movements and "restless legs". When a body part is severed, as in a phantom limb, there is a feeling of willed motion in the amputation. The abolishment of the phantom with a stroke on the opposite side of the brain implies that at least the feeling of activity can be generated by neural correlates independent of the limbs. The will to move may also occur in hemiplegic limbs if sensation is not cut off. Similarly, the inability to see a hand does not alter feeling, but loss of limb sensation divides the hand from the observer, who is unaware of its position or motion, or even if it belongs to him. Rats with denervated limbs will chew off their paws.

WILL IN RELATION TO ACTION

Will does not stand behind an act—or object-realization but is ingredient in object-formation and the essence of bodily motion. This recalls the debate by James and Wundt over *Innervatsionsgefühl*, the feeling of activity that distinguishes active and passive movements. Without this feeling, which probably relates to recurrent collaterals, that is, to perceptions of the action discharge, we might, like some psychotics who are closer to the real nature of mind than ordinary people, feel like puppets manipulated by invisible strings. Feeling gives motion to aim and a surge to the future; concepts give the choices into which feeling distributes. At every phase and in every content in the actualization of the mental state they are ingredient, one as the potential of a category, the other as the momentum and direction of process.

Feeling arrested when an object externalizes imbues action as a driving force. Consciousness of action develops on the objectification of motion. We are conscious of will as activity and as object-representation. A hypothetical consciousness of undifferentiated feeling, that is, feeling deprived of category, would be comparable to a physical entity conscious of its own energy. This would be consciousness of becoming without being. "Pure drive" is insufficient for consciousness, which depends on objectification. The unity of will contrasts with the multiplicity of feelings, but feelings are tributaries of will in relation to the objectifications of images. Metaphorically speaking, will is the root, feeling the branches. In this process, the becoming of objects is through the energetics of feeling. In becoming-into-being, will is feeling as potential or the processual aspect of concepts.

ACTION

An action is a qualitative category/item transform that proceeds from instinctual drive in bodily space to a proximal space about the body, to effectuation in a space beyond the body confines, with each plane enfolding its successor in the transition from inception to actuality. If we think of categories as wholes or frames that enclose potential contents, which themselves are categories for further partition, and if we think of actions not as mere outputs but as vibratory structures (Bernstein) that unfold over evolutionary planes, we get a glimpse of action as a traversal of mental phases comparable to that of objects, a process that also begins in a deep midline source, specifically, in brain formations for animal motility and posture in relation sensory and vestibular impulse. This primitive motility, centered in bodily space, passes to proximal, then distal asymmetric movement. A drive-based action of the body specifies partial implementations—oral, digital—in an extra-personal yet still bodily space. Vocalization also begins in an axial core with low frequency respiratory timing (breath or tonal group) that individuates to the speech melody or prosodic contour of an utterance, then to the fine temporal program of speech sounds, a parsing of oscillatory rhythms or kinetic frames that suggests a fundamental frequency passing to successive harmonics. Indeed, the analogy to music is apt since one could argue that music—non-semantic and relatively non-conceptual—is as close as "pure" action to the *in-itself* of reality. In sum, action entails a nested series of oscillators or rhythmic configurations devolving through categories from axial to distal, or from melodic contour to vocalization.

WILL IN ENTITY AND ORGANISM

Primal will extends to ideas as receptacles for feeling and is the basis for emotion, the intensity of which accrues from the feeling that is allocated. One path extends from drive as category to object-representation; another from drive as urge to its implementation in acts. The appearance of the world as a model of physical reality, the occurrence of will in action, its derivation from energy, the processual nature of act-development and the absence of content in action imply that the feeling of will is an intimation of the physically real not fully screened from consciousness.

Will in organism is the becoming from potential to actual, likened to causal effects in physical nature. The invisible process that is the engine of causal progression in the physical world can be construed as the energetic ground of actualization in organism. The forward direction of causal passage from one state to the next evolves, in organism, to growth and purposefulness. In human mind, feeling infiltrates categories and accompanies them to an intentional aim. However, the will is never a cause; it is ingredient in the becoming process. The elicitation of items from categories and their partition over successive phases—the becoming to final actuality—is the forward thrust of will as unconscious feeling.

The transmission from state to state in a causal series—the before/after of physical passage—shifts to the graded replication of mental states from proximal to distal, past to present. In causal theory, physical entities are conceived as atomic units, not epochs or momentary derivations. The cause is not assumed to affect the onset of the ensuing state prior to its distal segments. The effect, like the cause, is a development over duration. States are epochs, not stabilities. If all things are in a process of becoming, how does one process of change impact the next? The transition from one entity to the next might be saltatory, simultaneous or, in most accounts, continuous, in which case entities are not clearly demarcated. What then explains how isolates appear in continuous transition? In the microgenetic account, an entity does not exist at an instant but is a cascade of fractal-like specifications over an epoch of existence. Actualization creates a moment of change, with novelty in re-actualization constituting the effect.

If causal progression is the forerunner of actualization, the latter is a model for causation. Consider the minimal duration of an entity as its period of auto-replication, with change in the effect—an entity, the world—a changed reinstatement of one cycle of existence. We think of causation as a linear series from cause to effect, but on a processual view, the cause is replicated in relation to intrinsic instabilities and ambient conditions. In other words, the cause—more generally, the momentary state of the world—replicates itself with novelty in the replication. The novelty is the effect, which is a re-instatement of the cause with change in recurrence; that is, an effect is a recurrence of a cause replaced by an endogenous actualization with novel constraints at successive phases in the epoch of that state.

WILL AND AGENCY

Will as primal force is the motive of existence and, in organism, the forward direction of purposeful action. Will infiltrates action but does not stand behind it. Is agency then the consciousness of directionality, like the stone of Spinoza that, conscious of its motion, thinks itself free?[1] This would imply that agency occurs when the self is conscious of a subjective aim, and that agency does not arise without a conscious focus, or in the absence of aim even with consciousness though consciousness implies, indeed requires, a subjective aim, except for non–intentional or objectless states such as anxiety or panic.

In some respects, will and feeling are the reciprocal of agency, in the necessity for conscious representation and the processual, thus unconscious, nature of feeling. If "pure", that is, non-conceptual, feeling could occur it would be no more to consciousness than a sense of activity. For consciousness, feeling must objectify in an image: in drive as a category; in action as the body-image; in emotion or thought as a concept or idea. In the absence of an idea, consciousness of feeling would not arise. Love and fear have objects, as do all affect-ideas such as pity, envy, pride and humiliation. Feeling is uniform but the quality is determined by the idea or category. That is, we are conscious of category (idea, concept, object) as an embodiment of feeling but not the process of feeling through which categories partition or objects are realized. Agency occurs for images as well as actions; we feel agents to certain images, thoughts and memories. There are no "free-standing" images. They relate to a self as agent or observer in association with active or passive feeling. The sense of agency requires a self that is conscious of mental content or conscious of action as objectified appearance.

Essential to agency or voluntary feeling is the presence of a self as an agent in relation to an internal or extra-personal (but still, as in action, partly internal) outcome. The relation of self to outcome corresponds to that of proximal to distal content in a conscious mental state. This implies that the feeling of agency is less a feeling than a consciousness of direction from self to image. Put differently, unconscious feeling provides the direction that underlies consciousness of agency. The forward progression of thought and action owe to the directionality of feeling, but consciousness of feeling and consciousness of the direction of feeling (aim, intentionality) require an image—or object-appearance that enfolds the energic quality of feeling and carries the act to completion. In sum, feeling is essential to agency but

---

1. Letter LXII, p. 390, 1674–6.

agency is consciousness of the becoming of the self—self-concept, body-image—into acts and images. These mental contents arise as momentary objectifications (neotenies) in the mental state when a self becomes conscious of, and is an agent to, the transient appearances, inner and outer, that are its own derivations.

WILL AND SELF

Feeling concentrates the subjectivity of will in the self-concept, infusing motive in drive-based categories at a liminal plane in the mental state. The impetus of feeling fractionates categories, which arborize to a multitude of appearances—inner and outer—that take on valuation as they become what they are. Because the unity of will binds the self to a diversity of images, images are not floating in inner or outer space but are linked together by a common impulse. In this respect, the so-called binding mechanism of cognitivism is the process of feeling that binds the diversity of mental contents in diachronic relation.

The self, as a dominant locus in a sea of subjectivity, is a bottle-neck that distils drive-categories to personal identity. Drive is a manifestation of will invested in instinctual categories that condense to the self as an agent of implementation. The body-image combines the representation of feeling in the body with feeling as the thread—the becoming—from self to aim, with consciousness the relation of self to what actualizes. Without feeling, nothing happens. Without categories, feeling is unbound energy. The coalescence of feeling in the self provides a center for the individuality of will and a source for its propagation to the world. In other words, will begins in drive energy that becomes personal feeling in the self, impelling the mental state to acts and objects that, as appearances, recover the origins of will in world entities. In the outward flow will, as a locus of individuality, returns to its home in the energic process of physical nature.

The purposefulness of subjective aim in the relation to actuality begins in drive, concentrates in self and disperses in objects. In human mind, the categorical primes of drive individuate the subjective field to a focus of feeling. The tributaries of will in the actualization process give coherence to the multitude of images and objectified feelings that populate mind and world. The subjugation of emotion and imagery to the directionality of becoming and the commonalty of feeling that runs from drive to actuality provide a thematic to what otherwise would be a jumble of random images and affects. Becoming is the link from self to objects, perceived in the progression of world order and the causal relatedness of entities in nature.

Consciousness of the trajectory from self to image accounts for the elevation of purposefulness to agency. This can be examined in alternate mental states, especially in dream, where the passive quality of self and the absence of agency give the sense that we are victims of our own imagery. In the dream, the self has the quality of an image that participates in the flow of events, not as an agent of their direction or control. How can we explain the absence of agency for dream events that follow a narrative to a definite outcome? Feeling, at times intense, is bound up with imagery as in wakefulness. There is also dream-consciousness with the self an observer of events. Perhaps the lack of motility in dream accounts for the attenuation of will, the loss of purposefulness and the randomness of much imagery. The absence of perceptual objects foreshortens the distance from self to actuality, bringing the self into a proximate relation to dream phenomena. In wakefulness, the antecedence of self in relation to outcome, the actualization of the agent prior to the outcome, or the transition from self to subjective aim, contributes to the sense of agency. In dream, the relation of self to object is replaced by a relation of self to pre-object or image, with contraction of the trajectory from onset to finality. Moreover, dream-content and the unconscious are simultaneous until serialized on waking. The lack of temporal order during the dream and the tenuous relation of self to subjective aim due to the proximity of self and image, obviates the sense of a self in an active relation to its own derivations.

UNCONSCIOUS ORIGIN OF ACTS

This leads to the problem of how conscious choice is instigated if acts are decided prior to awareness? Studies on the voluntary movement of a finger show brain activity prior to the consciousness of reaching a decision. These studies, which record the moment of decision before conscious action, apply to the neural basis of decision and the consciousness of choice, even though the choice is merely *when* to lift a finger. We also know that purposeful finger movements arise at the peaks of the oscillation of unconscious resting tremor, implying a non-conscious origin in preliminary kinetic rhythms. Similar findings apply to speech in respiratory timing, melodic contour and so on.

Given that acts of cognition develop out of unconscious strata, and taking into account the observations described above, it would seem that decisions and actions, including the set of options to be decided, are forecast in advance of conscious deliberation, that is to say, the options being deliberated or the conscious presentations to be decided are biased from below. If the progression in an act of cognition is from instinctual categories through conceptual feeling to conscious thought, and the contents of consciousness are outcomes of this process, surely those contents will have been determined before they appear as conscious choices. This conclusion follows even we disregard the influence on thought and behavior of unconscious need, repressed traumas, egocentric motives, presupposition, etc.

However, an actualization over phases does not predestine a specific outcome, act or set of options. Freud, a determinist, thought there was an automatic transfer from memory or unconscious thought to consciousness, that is, an unchanging passage from the perceptual image to the memory image to the conscious idea. I would argue there is a series of qualitative transforms in which developing configurations undergo successive whole/part or category/member transitions. On this view, the conscious content is not a copy of its unconscious precursors but the outcome of a wave of qualitative fractals. What issues into consciousness specifies out of a multi-tiered system of antecedent potential, with the possibility at any phase of deviation, novelty or unexpected branching. Conscious contents are not retrieved unaltered from an unconscious source but emerge over a sequence of category/item shifts, the endpoint of which depends on sensory and other shaping factors that guide the individuation. The outcome is not predetermined at its origination. The potential for any one of a multiplicity of items in each partition is obviously tempered by sensory constraints and limitations on diversity imposed by present conditions, expectations, experiential and affective bias, but not conditioned by an ancestral straight-jacket or billiard-ball sequence to reproduce configural predecessors in the actualization process.

AGENCY AND THE VIRTUAL PRESENT

Consciousness and the duration of the present are essential to the possibility of voluntary action The present allows a suspension of passage so that a cause does not perish in an effect. Otherwise, a decision to act would no longer exist in the mind when an action occurs. The self and the act of decision must be co-present in the now for voluntary feeling. One can say volition "lingers" in an arc that encloses self and thought or action, a trajectory that is the basis of consciousness and intentionality. That is, consciousness is a knowing relation of self to world, with imagery at segments close to objectification. Implicit imagery is necessary for consciousness-of content, for example the verbal imagery of inner speech. This relation of self to world or mental content, which is ingredient in decision, is the difference between automatic speech or action and deliberative thought. In dream, the relation is compressed, the present is instantaneous and the self, as in animal awareness, is a victim or spectator but not an agent.

If this account is correct, that is, if the self stands behind decision in the actualization process, and is so ordered when simultaneous contents are serialized in present duration, even with duration as an illusory span across passage, the illusion is necessary for serial order in consciousness, without which there is mere succession. That is, the priority of the self in volition requires duration for the consciousness of sequence, which is otherwise lost in causal progression. There are other illusions that foster actual behaviors, such as the idealization of the beloved that promotes bonding and family, or an illusion of perspective that gives depth to a two-dimensional painting and consequent pleasure to the observer. The illusion of duration allows a sequence of events to be held in the mind, so the succession of before and after can shift to that of past and present, thus "retaining" the past in the present. In the feeling of free will, the self is the momentary past, the image is the near-present, and action, like object perception, is the forward edge of the now, all simultaneous in the mental state but so ordered that the self is an agent of thought and action.

Some have postulated mental states without a self to whom they belong, but every state of consciousness in human mind has a self that is conscious. Moreover, in the mental state it is the self, not consciousness, that loves, hates, remembers, and shudders at the thought of death. Fear can occur without a self, but not the fear of events in the future or outside the immediate surround. Without a self, and without the consciousness of temporal precedence, the idea of free will evaporates, since freedom loses much of its meaning in an organism that has no self or subjective center to which free will can appeal.

FEELING OF AGENCY

Agency is less a state than a feeling. It is strong when we contemplate and then act, or attend to an action or mental content with decisional possibilities, that is, the explicit decision to effectuate a psychic or external event. The feeling of agency differs with the content of the mental state. As discussed, thought images have a volitional quality, some memory and eidetic images as well, but not hallucinations, after-images or auto-symbolic images. Conceivably, images that refer to earlier planes in the mental state have a less volitional character than those that refer to more superficial layers. This might point to the need for some psychological distance between self and image. The creative image that develops spontaneously lacks the voluntary feeling in the verbal imagery of thought.

The feeling of agency arises in the passage of will through the self into acts or mental contents. The bias to action or perception determines whether the feeling is of an active or passive nature. For example, inner speech can feel voluntary when it develops toward speech, even without vocalization, and it can feel receptive when it is "heard" in the mind even without passing into perception or hallucination. The aim of drive is action in the world. The aim of perception is an independent world in which action occurs. Affective tonality accompanies act and object development; in one, the becoming is emphatic, in the other it is what becomes. Though we create the world, we do not feel agents to its creation. The receptiveness of the perceptual gives way to the dynamic of the motoric.

Agency is essential to free will but not decisive in whether or not the will is free. Is the occurrence of voluntary feeling an indication an act is freely decided and, if not, why do we feel it as such? One can say that agency is most intense in consciousness of action, and especially of decision, which is retardation (neoteny) at phases implicit in behavior. The accentuation of the preliminary in conscious choice heightens agency by impeding it. The fact that action recedes a bit from externalization to precursors in the mind, or moves from partial externality to an interior locus by a delay in implementation, exposes an infrastructure of potential in the possibility that precedes what actualizes. This intercession of possibility is equivalent to the freedom to decide.

Ironically, most actions of daily life are not accompanied by consciousness of decision or agency yet we look back on them as freely chosen, while the deliberation that goes into choice is the hallmark of free will but may hamper the agent's capacity to decide. Agency is ordinarily for what is possible, not for what is automatic or determined. The question is whether possibility is revealed or chosen and if revealed, whether what is given can then be freely chosen? That is if choices arise spontaneously, is there free choice among them? It is implausible to think a person searches the unconscious for options, even for a memory or word, but rather on the item that comes up, or on a fragment that calls up the remainder. To dip into the unconscious is to create conditions that allow unconscious material to actualize. Still the quality of revival reveals the knowledge and character of the person, and in that sense the contents that develop to consciousness arise from the genuine core.

FROM CHOICE TO ACTION

If agency is consciousness of purposefulness, and will is not causal but achieves awareness as activity and forward urge when it objectifies, how can we explain the sense of a self that is unhindered in action and free to decide what to do? The feeling of free will is essential to responsibility and the belief that the control of action is not determined by antecedent history and is independent of—though most evident in—the presence of options that arise from needs, goals and personal reflection.

Having discussed the process of decision and the reinforcement by knowledge and value of the recurrence of an established sequence of partitions in the revival of a thought, it remains to consider the implementation of a decision in action or behavior. We know that purposeful movement initiated by a decision to act arouses deep midline structures in the brain, perhaps as much as 8/10ths of a second prior to consciousness of the decision. If a mental state recurs in about a tenth of a second, this is sufficient for a brief sequence of states prior to the consciousness of decision and action. The succession of states is necessary to prime consciousness and the feeling of volition. Consciousness and agency require a series of states for a prior state to be incompletely revived in a current one. The present depends on forgetting to establish a posterior limit to the knife-edge of perception, while voluntary feeling requires an opposition of self to an intentional aim, which depends on duration for unconscious simultaneity to pass to serial order. This might account for the delay prior to consciousness of decision and the ensuing action, but not the process from decision to action. The question then is, if ideas or rational decisions do not initiate actions, how does choice influence behavior or how does the feeling of agency translate to action.

Every choice is a category with an affective tonality—"conceptual-feeling"—that precipitates briefly in subjective space as an embodiment of feeling in idea. The affective quality may appear to be minor but there is always a quota of feeling in the most abstract or rational ideas, binding them in spatiotemporal context and urging them to completion. The greater weight of one choice over others is determined by concordance with core beliefs and intensity of feeling. The implementation of choice is not a passage from idea to action but an action that begins in drive and the self, and develops in relation to the dominant option. That is, the dominant option acts like a gravitational field that bends or constrains the developing action in a certain direction.

When two or three options arise in consciousness, the eliminative trend usually favors one course of action over another. The bias is not fixed but can be adjusted by increased knowledge or alteration in conceptual feeling. This is

how a person is convinced, or convinces himself, to change his mind or adopt a
different point of view. When an alternative is buttressed over successive states
by further knowledge or increased affective pressure, there is a reinforcement
of the track of the option that provides a channel of derivation, such that the
category/member shift leading to that option is supported by the repetition
of revived partitions to advance a novel subjective aim. Since each mental
state develops over its predecessors, the pattern of derivation can be selectively
re-excited, or damped by neglect. Coincident with the reinforcement of one
option is the weakening of others or their inhibition, either by contradictory
knowledge or diminished recurrence that reduces selective pressures that guide
the re-instantiation. That is, the path of whole/part shifts through which con-
tent develops can be strengthened or weakened over subsequent traversals,
though in most instances core beliefs and values tend to dominate the phase-
transition and the final commitment to act.

If the dominance of one option over others follows on the relation to
belief and value, it is not the option that expresses free will, or even which
option is decided, but rather, as it is often depicted, the ability to do otherwise in spite of the necessity of one path of decision. Yet to do otherwise
might just as well reflect subliminal options—rebellion, self-destruction,
irrational impulse—that are not apparent to the self or others. The belief in
free will requires that one's will follows one's beliefs, with the becoming of
feeling to actuality the path from will to action. The continuum from self
to action in the implementation of belief gives the supervenient belief that
we decide and control our acts. Ultimately, one's actions are the outcome
of one's beliefs in relation to expectation and perceptual immediacy. This
continuum recurs in every act of cognition, with the becoming of the self to
a final representation, the consciousness and compliance of will and subjective aim, and the purposefulness of behavior owing to the directionality of
feeling, interpreted as freedom of action. The final object in the world, or
idea in the mind, is not a causal transfer but a becoming-into-being with
continuously novel content. *The central point is that outcomes are not fixed*
or determined but actualize a process of becoming as tendencies or proclivities
that survive elimination at successive segments in the unfolding of the state.

Deliberation and decision can recur and change over time but action
is all-at-once and irreversible. Decision arises in a context of deliberation;
action arises from, or through, the decisional category. Ordinarily, decision
is continuous over time through recurrence of the idea. The idea results
from a segmental retardation of object-formation; a similar retardation in
action accentuates the feeling of volition. Inner speech might be conceived
as a pre-action equivalent to the pre-perceptual origin of thought. However,
though inner speech precedes vocalization, it is not a motor antecedent but

the vocal equivalent of an idea. The transition in speech from inner to outer is comparable to that from choice to action. In both, a pre-object representation develops to motility.

To return to pre-activation, the argument is that a series of mental states is necessary for forgetting, for consciousness and serial order and for the duration in which a self is distinct from act and idea. The subjective duration of the present has been estimated at a few seconds of clock time. If so, a duration of 800 milliseconds, which is a liberal estimate of the duration prior to consciousness of decision, could enfold a sequence of forgetting (incomplete revivals) sufficient for a disparity with the current state, and so to create a conscious duration for a self-directed action. This seems a fair approximation to what might occur in the passage from decision to action. Otherwise, it is unclear how an idea could initiate an action without the agent intervening, whether an intent to move a finger, a decision to join the military or a commitment to oppose a government, however different in complexity, personal risk and moral value.

Action and perception arise from a common source and develop in parallel through divergent but inter-connected systems. This is essential to the temporal lag in conscious perception and action. In order for the act to be purposeful and conscious with a decisional aim, it must be derived in relation to ideational content and the body image. An action develops out of midline, axial motor systems, then passes to a proximal, and then distal, innervation. There is a dynamic structure of kinetic rhythms that is the backdrop for asymmetric limb movement specified out of antecedents that retrace stages in forebrain evolution. In this way, the core self, which is bound up with bodily feeling, and revived in every act in concert with consciousness and duration, takes on a volitional quality. Since reason does not channel action but replaces it, it can precede or follow as explanation or justification, but decision zeroes in on a target to provide a psychic corridor through which the act can develop.

ACTION IN THE WORLD

One unusual feature of action alluded to above is the feeling of belongingness in bodily or vocal action. The act is not fully interior; it retains a thread to the self even as an event in the world. In this respect, it is transitional from mind-internal to mind-external, from the subjective to the objective, evidence against a sharp divide induced by object-perception, and supplementing other phenomena such as eidetic imagery that are also transitional and point to a continuity from mind to world. From a causal perspective, action is felt as a directed outcome of will, that is, the self as cause of a movement (agent-causation). The core self, bound up with drive and the axial musculature, is early in the realization of action with distal and asymmetric movement an endpoint of category/member transition through intermediate segments. Does the agent cause an action, or does the action develop out of the potential of the self? Is a whole/part specification or qualitative partition of fractals a causal series or one that is derived by constraints from generality to precision?

This feature of action as a bridge to the world makes us agents of change, not passive onlookers. Ironically, the mental phenomena that control volition are objects experienced as independent that, once uncovered, reveal the agency buried in the image. Agency as a manifestation of will applies to many forms of imagery in addition to action. We are given a world that in actuality we create with action as the mental representation of motion. Motion alone gives only a feeling of innervation or activity. Action cannot even be initiated without "sensory feedback", nor are we conscious of the action without an image of the action in perception. Action, like an object, is a perceptual representation. The terms "body image" or "body schema" refer to perceptual knowledge of the body which, together with will, drive or feeling, empowers the image to act in the world. One series of object appearances gives a picture of a world in which change is inferred by replacement; in another series a temporal sequence of movements is stabilized in perception as an effectuation of body in the world. The dynamic of continuous change in motility is imperceptible without being objectified. The illusion of object replacement combines with the frozen kinetics of action as a linked sequence of motions in space. This is the paradox of Zeno; action as an incremental series of perceptual segments, and movement as a continuous physical transition.

Reflect on:

The Lord: How many *Tathāgatas* have you honored, *Mañjuśrī*

Mañjuśrī: As many as there are the mental actions which have been stopped in an illusory man.

The stoppage of a mental action, to my mind, refers to an illusory stability in the objectification of an action, without which the action would unfold in a rhythmic continuity that would otherwise be imperceptible. The body is the center of action. Bodily action is continuous but realized like a moving object or event. The body itself—the bodily image of the person—is no less illusory than the conscious representation of action that articulates, spatializes (stops) and transforms a temporal series into discrete moments of activity. This raises an additional challenge to free will in that actions, even if freely decided, are monitored secondarily as appearances. Perception is a step away from physical reality; action, a step away from the physiologically real.

If the action-development provides the distinction of active and passive movement, and actions are realized in consciousness as a connected sequence of object-like segments, does this imply that conscious action, for the reason of its dependency on perception, is an illusory phenomenon and, if so, what effect would this have on free will? One still has the physical act, including the physical (brain) correlates of choice. The mental correlates permit access to, or knowledge of, the physical events underlying them and can be interpreted as instruments to test the reality of experience, which otherwise would be unknowable. On these grounds, the stoppage of a mental action is the break imposed on the continuity of physical action by conscious perception and the duration of the now; the illusory man refers to the phenomenal nature of mind combined with the perceptual image of the body.

The spatial world moves slowly forward punctuated by occasional bursts of excitement. It is only in doing that we are truly alive, and only by freely deciding that doing has import. While the reality of free will is of particular significance to the agent, it matters little to others if acts are caused and inevitable or free and unpredictable, yet the more predictable an action, to an individual, a group or society, the more comfortable, harmonious and orderly the society. Every individual has to navigate the actions and reactions of others. Rules of conduct imposed on behavior are comparable to adaptive constraints on actualization. Rules impose extrinsic limits on action to which an individual can acquiesce or resist. In most instances, rules are internalized as values that regulate behavior or choice, as in mitigating drive-based acts to social norms. Without such regulation—general rules or adaptive constraints—there is no standard or convention to judge whether freedom is a response to psychic valuation and social regulation or is random behavior. Deviation from the norm is one measure of freedom; conscious decision to act in accordance with social norms or moral laws is also a free choice, even if behavior conforms to a proscribed course of action. The choice to do otherwise is essential but is it a real choice if never exercised?

ILLUSION AND WILL

If by illusion we mean not real, and if by real we mean physical reality, all mental phenomena are illusions. Perception mirrors, thus approximates, reality, but reality in physical motion is also mirrored in perception. The gift of perception has a cost: the duration over passage that segregates change and increments transition. Apart from the inferred proximity of reality to the perceptual, the now is a human perspective on the before/after continuum. One can ask if an illusory duration is layered on the present-less behavior of animal awareness, that is, the illusion of duration on top of the illusion of the perceptual world, or does the realness of illusory phenomena, once recognized, allow a deeper insight to mind and world?

Even if all mental phenomena are illusory (Vaihinger, 1924/1965), there is one that is not, the will, which traces back through drive to feeling and energy. The will as the source and direction of feeling out of instinctual drive, is a physiological impulse with feeling an immediate manifestation of brain activity. In the course of its development, instinctual will arborizes into tributaries, such as idea and object-value, but *ab origine* it is a physical impulse sustaining life and mind that is identical to brain activity. The expression of will through categories of instinctual drive begins the conceptual partitions through which feeling specifies into the affective tonalities of ideas and objects.

The reality of will contrasts with the psychic entanglements of its development, yet feeling remains a derivative of energy as a foundational ingredient of the mind/brain state. There is no direct control of one mental entity by another, though irresolution appears as intra-psychic opposition. A self that is co-present with decision is a dominant locus in a brief series of mental states, followed by or alternating with a parallel series in which decision (choice, action) dominates. The transition of choice through the self, its reinforcement through recurrence and constraints of decision on action, are empowered by the passage of instinctual will into occasions of conceptual feeling.

The question is, how does physical will or energic feeling, as expressed in animal mind and instinctual drive, become a power of the self to freely choose, decide and initiate action? The roots of feeling in instinctual drive appear as a bias of unconscious disposition, yet the presence of choice implies the possibility of unfettered choosing, while the mitigation of will to voluntary feeling allows the allocation of irresistible impulse to measured implementation. These evolutionary and maturational trends import will to volition, and transfer action directed by drive through a decisional self. Agency occurs within the limits of the possible, occasioned by the parcellation of core categories to competing concepts, the muting of impulse to desire, the emergence of a self and the appearance—illusory or not—of conscious duration that unites past and present in temporal order. The changing present is positioned between the before, as past, and the after as an oncoming future.

Consistent with the concept of parcellation of thought and perception, action also is not selected out of an array of possibilities but results from the elimination of alternatives, even when the act feels directed, it is difficult to support a deterministic account of action as a resultant of a causal chain. Since knowledge can influence choice through recurrence and strengthening of tendency, and since the act arises in the transition of the self to ideation, it is unlikely that decisions are forecast by causal bias. A series of mental states necessary for duration coupled with the temporal lag in perception underlie the pre-activation of decision and action. If the arousal of neural events prior to conscious decision generates a state in which a final decision is not pre-determined, given that "unconscious thought" is creative as well as habitual, free will remains a possibility in spite of indications to the contrary. Naturally, the self is not free of personal experience, values and emotions, and the options to be considered tend to be limited, usually binary, yet within the constraints of outer conditions and inner disposition, the self can still decide and decision can influence action. Freedom is not unlimited but it does hold within a certain range. Yet it must be added that the impact of personal decision, however free and real it may be, shrinks to a trifle in contrast to the much to which we are shackled.

Bibliography

Atmanspacher, H., Filk, T. & beim Graben, P. (2011). "Can classical epistemic states be entangled?" In: D. Song et al., edd. *Quantum interaction – QI* (105–115). Berlin: Springer.

Bachmann, T. (2000). *Microgenetic approach to the conscious mind. Advances in Consciousness Research,* 25. Amsterdam: John Benjamins.

Bar, M. (2004). "Visual objects in context." *Nature Reviews Neuroscience,* 5(8), 617–629.

Bergson, H. (1923). *Durée et simultanéité, à propos de la théorie d'Einstein.* Paris: F. Alcan.

Breitmeyer, B. & Öğmen, H. (2006). *Visual masking: time slices through conscious and unconscious vision.* Oxford: Oxford University Press.

Brown, J. (1977). *Mind, brain, and consciousness: the neuropsychology of cognition.* New York: Academic Press.

Brown, J., Leader, B. & Blum, C. (1983). "Hemiplegic writing in severe aphasia." *Brain & Language,* 19(2), 204–215.

Brown, J. (1984) "Hallucinations, imagery and the microstructure of perception." In: Vinken, P., Bruyn, G. and Klawans, H. (eds.), *Handbook of Clinical Neurology,* Volume 45 (351–372). Amsterdam: Elsevier.

Brown, J. (1989). "The nature of voluntary action." *Brain & Cognition,* 10(1), 105–120.

Brown, J. (1998). "Psychoanalysis and process theory." In: Bilder, R. & LeFever, F. (eds.), *Neuroscience of the mind: Centennial of Freud's project.* Annals of the New York Academy of Science, 4, 91–106.

Brown, J. (1999). "Neuropsychology of the self-concept." *Journal of Nervous and Mental Disease,* 187, 131–141.

Brown, J. (2005). *Process and the authentic life.* Heusenstamm: Ontos-Verlag.

Brown, J (2010). *Neuropsychological foundations of conscious experience.* Leuven, Belgium: Chromatika.

Brown, J. (2012). *Love and other emotions.* London: Karnac.

Brown, J. (2014). "Mind and brain: a contribution from microgenetic theory." *Journal of Consciousness Studies,* 21:54–73

Brown, J. (2017). *Metapsychology of the creative process: continuous novelty as the ground for creative advance.* Exeter, UK: Imprint Academic.

Brown, J. & Pachalska, M. (2003) "The nature of the symptom and its relevance for neuropsychology." *Acta Neuropsychologica,* 1(1), 1–11.

Cytowic, R. E. (1989). *Synesthesia: a union of the senses.* New York: Springer Verlag.

Doyen, S., Klein, O., Simons, D. & Cleeremans, A. (2014). "On the other side of the mirror: Priming in cognitive and social psychology." *Social Cognition,* 32, 12–32.

Ey, H. (1973) *Traité de hallucinations* (2 vols). Paris: Masson.

Freedman, D.J. & Assad, J.A. (2016). "Neuronal mechanisms of visual categorization: an abstract view on decision making." *Annual Review of Neuroscience,* 39, 129–147.

Freud, S. (1922) *Group psychology and the analysis of the ego* (tr. J. Strachey). London & Vienna: International Psycho-Analytical Press.

Freud, S. (1924). *Collected papers, vol. 1: On the history of the psycho-analytic movement.* London: Hogarth.

Gur, M. (2015). "Space reconstruction by primary visual cortex activity: a parallel, non-computational mechanism of object representation." *Trends in Neuroscience,* 38(4), 207–216

Heeger, D. J. (2017). "Theory of cortical function." *Proceedings of the National Academy of Science* U S A., 114(8), 1773–1782.

Held, R. & Hein, A. (1963). "Movement-produced stimulation in the development of visually guided behaviour." *Journal of Comparative and Physiological Psychology,* 56(5), 872–876.

Hoel, E.P., Albantakis, L., Cirelli, C. & Tononi, G. (2016). "Synaptic refinement during development and its effect on slow-wave activity: a computational study." *Journal of Neurophysiology,* 115(4), 2199–2213.

Hubel, D. H. & Wiesel, T. N. (1959). "Receptive fields of single neurones in the cat's striate cortex." *Journal of Physiology,* 124(3), 574–591.

Hubel, D. H. & Wiesel, T. N. (2004). *Brain and visual perception: The story of a 25-year collaboration.* Oxford: Oxford University Press.

Le Bon, G. (1895/1896). *La psychologie ds foules.* English translation. London: Fisher Unwin.

Marcel, A.J. (1983). "Conscious and unconscious perception: an approach to the relations between phenomenal experience and perceptual processes." *Cognitive Psychology,* 15(2), 238–230.

McTaggart, J. (1934/1968). *Philosophical studies.* New York: Books for Libraries

Nauta, W.J.H. & Feirtag, M. (1986). *Fundamental neuroanatomy.* New York: W.H. Freeman & Co.

O'Callaghan, C., Hall, J.M., Tomassini, A. et al. (2017). "Visual hallucinations are characterized by impaired sensory evidence accumulation: Insights from hierarchical drift diffusion modeling in Parkinson's Disease." *Biological Psychiatry, Cognitive Neuroscience & Neuroimaging,* 2(8), 680–688.

O'Callaghan, C. & Lewis, S.J.G. (2017). "Cognition in Parkinson's Disease." *International Review of Neurobiology,* 133, 557–583.

Ohman, A., Carlsson, K., Lundqvist, D. & Ingvar, M. (2007). "On the unconscious subcortical origin of human fear." *Physiology of Behavior,* 92(1–2), 180–185.

Pachalska, M., MacQueen, B. & Cielebak, K. (2018) "The creative potential of microgenetic theory." *Acta Neuropsychologica,* 16, 125–155.

Pribram, Karl H. (1991). *Brain and perception: holonomy and structure in figural processing.* Hillsdale, N.J.: Lawrence Erlbaum Associates.

Rumelhart, D.E. & McClelland, J.L. (1986). *Parallel distributed processing: Exploration in the microstructure of cognition.* Vol. 1. Cambridge, MA: MIT Press.

Sanides, F. (1969). "Comparative architectonics of the neocortex of mammals and their evolutionary interpretation." *Annals of the New York Academy of Sciences*, 167(1), 404–423.

Schelling, F. (1800/1993). *System of transcendental idealism* (tr. Peter Heath). Charlottesville, VA: University of Virginia Press.

Schilder, P. (1935). *Image and appearance of the human body*. London: Kegan

Schindler, A. & Bartels, A. (2016a). "Motion parallax links visual motion areas and scene regions." *Neuroimage*, 125, 803–812.

Schindler, A. & Bartels, A. (2016b). "Visual high-level regions respond to high-level stimulus content in the absence of low-level confounds." *Neuroimage*, 132, 520–525.

Schneirla, T. C. (1959). "An evolutionary and developmental theory of biphasic processes underlying approach and withdrawal." In: M. R. Jones (ed.), *Nebraska symposium on motivation* (pp. 1–42). Oxford, England: University of Nebraska Press.

Smith, J.D. & Minda, J.P. (2001). "Journey to the center of the category: The dissociation in amnesia between categorization and recognition." *Journal of Experimental Psychology: Learning, Memory, and Cognition*, 27(4), 984–1002.

Spinoza, Benjamin de. (1690/1966). *The correspondence of Spinoza*, edited and translated by A. Wolf. London: Frank Cass.

Turvey, M.T. (1990). "Coordination." *American Psychologist*, 45, 938–953.

Vaihinger, H. (1924/1968). *The philosophy of 'As if': A system of the theoretical, practical and religious fictions of mankind* (tr. C. K. Ogden). London: Routledge and Kegan Paul; reprinted 1968, New York: Barnes and Noble.

Van den Bussche, E., Van den Noortgate, W. & Reynvoet, B. (2009). "Mechanisms of masked priming: A meta-analysis." *Psychological Bulletin*, 135, 452–477.

McCulloch, W.S. (1965). *Embodiments of mind*. Cambridge, Massachusetts: M.I.T. Press.

Whalen, P.J., Kagan, J., Cook, R.G. et al. (2004). "Human amygdala responsivity to masked fearful eye whites." *Science*, 306(5704), 2061.

Whitehead, A. N. (1934). *Nature and life*. Cambridge, UK: Cambridge University Press.

www.ingramcontent.com/pod-product-compliance
Lightning Source LLC
Chambersburg PA
CBHW070411270326
41926CB00014B/2779